Flags of the World

FLAGS
of the
WORLD

Edited by
E. M. C. Barraclough C.B.E., R.N.
and W. G. Crampton M.ED.

FREDERICK WARNE

Published by
Frederick Warne (Publishers) Ltd, London
Frederick Warne & Co. Inc., New York
1978

LIBRARY OF CONGRESS CATALOG CARD NO. 68-22445

ISBN 0 7232 2015 8

Printed and bound in Great Britain by
William Clowes & Sons Ltd., London, Beccles and Colchester

0014.678

Contents

Preface

This is the third revision of *Flags of the World* that I have had the privilege to edit. Now it is time for me to give way to someone younger, I therefore hope that the reader will forgive me if, in this Preface, I strike a personal note.

Flags and the way that they have been used had always held a fascination for me, but until I became editor of this book I had little idea how great a part they have played in the history of the world. Somebody once wrote—I quote from memory—'a flag is such a simple thing, no more than a piece of coloured cloth, and yet, for it men will die'.

There is scarcely a turning point in the history of any country that does not have a special flag; for our own land, the Raven Banner of the Vikings, the Union Jack that celebrated the joining together of the four countries of the islands, the Stars and Stripes of America and all the flags that have blossomed forth in the newly independent countries of the Commonwealth. In this book, I have tried not only to describe the many flags of the world but also to tell just a little of the history and romance that is attached to them.

Writing this book has at times been a frustrating task, but it has also been very pleasurable; it has brought me many friends of many nations; Klaes Sierksma of the Netherlands, Dr Gunther Mattern of Switzerland, Georges Pasch—it is impossible to mention all of them but I am indeed grateful for their friendly help. I would like to make special mention of Dr Whitney Smith of the Flag Research Center (*see* p. 21), whose assistance in gathering information has been invaluable, and to give my thanks to the Protocol Department of the Foreign and Commonwealth Office, in particular to Mr Dennis Quinn.

I must thank all those members of the staff of Frederick Warne who have helped me so kindly and patiently, and especially Mr Stuart, the Art Editor, who retired last year—I take this opportunity of thanking him for all that he has done to make my work so easy and I wish him many happy years of retirement.

Mr I. O. Evans, the editor of the sister volume to this work, the *Observer's Book of Flags*, sadly died earlier this year. He was one who contributed to the growing interest in flags and banners in the world and we co-operated in the preparation of these two books.

Lastly I come to William Crampton, who helped me with the 1969 edition. He is the co-editor of this one and my successor in future editions. I take this opportunity of wishing him success.

E.M.C.B.

Flags of the World has been described as a national institution, and the editor of it bears a heavy responsibility to a wide and attentive readership at home and abroad. Captain

Barraclough, who has supervised the development of this integral feature of Britain's contribution to flag studies since 1965 has also himself become something of an institution. Among the more volatile spirits who have made flag study an international avocation he has lent a weight of dignity and maturity. I feel that he has always exemplified the motto: 'Be not the first by whom the new is tried, Nor yet the last to cast the old aside.' During his period of Editorship, as he is characteristically too modest to mention, he has developed contacts between flag students in Britain and those abroad. He attended the first international gathering in Muiderberg in 1965, from which grew the International Federation of Vexillological Associations, which now numbers sixteen national groups. He aided and abetted the formation of the Heraldry Society's Flag Section, and was its first chairman. He later gave his name and support to the Flag Institute in its formative days. In 1975 at the sixth international congress he was awarded a medal of honour to mark his long period of service to vexillology. These twelve years have seen this new science grow from the hobby of a few individuals to an international network of scholars and associates, who are coming to have some influence on the development of flags and flag-usage themselves.

It is therefore a great pity that Captain Barraclough should feel impelled to play a less active role in the world of flags and flag-study. The accumulation of knowledge and expertise in this field is a long process, since its documentation is so scanty that it is only after many years that one comes to have a thorough grasp of the subject. These long years of accumulated lore are something I shall lack when taking up the baton from Captain Barraclough, and so I trust I shall be able to call on his advice and guidance for a long time to come. I trust too that he will continue his good work in developing flag study as a reputable science, and in developing flag-usage and flag-design in the dignified and ship-shape fashion we have come to expect.

W.C.

[1] Introductory

THE ORIGINS OF FLAGS

Since time immemorial man has felt the need of some sign or symbol as a mark to distinguish himself, his family or country, and such symbols have taken many differing forms, of which one is the flag.

The word 'flag' seems to have come into use in the sixteenth century and soon became the general name for the many types of flag that existed under a multiplicity of titles, such as banners, ensigns, gonfanons, and so on. Although the majority of these names still exist they are used very loosely and mean different things to different writers. It is generally agreed that the word flag derived from the old Saxon or Germanic word *fflaken* or *ffleogan*, meaning to fly or float in the wind. Thus a flag is something that must be free to be agitated by the wind and can be defined as a device on a piece of pliable material which is fastened to a staff or mast along one of its edges, leaving the rest to fly or flap in the breeze. The name flag is now generally confined to the pattern which flies from a vertical staff, whilst the type that hangs from a horizontal bar is called a banner (but *see also* p. 17).

One of the earliest references to flags or banners is that in the year 1122 B.C. It was recorded that the Emperor Chou, founder of the Chou Dynasty in China, had a white flag or banner carried before him. We have no record as to what this flag was like; however, a very early representation of a Chinese flag is on the tomb of Wou Leang T'Seu of the Han Dynasty (200 B.C. to A.D. 200). A low relief on this tomb shows horsemen, although one is riding a somewhat peculiar steed, the first bearing a flag and the other what appears to be a banner.

Early Chinese flags

There is also mention about the end of the fifth century B.C. of a primitive form of flag known as a *phoinikis*, or 'purple garment', in use in the Athenian Navy. This may have inspired the legend that at the battle of Salamis (480 B.C.) Themistocles, the Greek Commander, ordered a red cloak to be affixed to an oar and hoisted aloft. At this signal the Greek fleet, although outnumbered four to one, bore down and routed the Persians under Xerxes. Apart from these isolated scraps of what might be called folk-lore there is no record of flags having been used in the western world until shortly before the time of Christ. We know that the ancient Egyptians marched to war beneath the sacred emblems of their gods and the fans of feathers of the Pharaohs, and that the insignia of the Assyrians were discs bearing devices which almost invariably included bulls in some form or other. As well as the *phoinikis*, the Greeks also used symbols of their deities, for example the owl of Athens, or legendary animals such as the pegasus of Corinth, the minotaur of Crete, the bull of Boeotia and, strangest of all, the tortoise of the Peloponnesus.

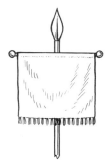  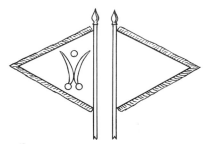

Roman vexillum   *Flag from wall painting at Paestum*   *Early Moslem flags*

The first 'flag' in the western world of which there is historical evidence and of which illustrations exist was the Roman *vexillum*. Although the exact date is unknown this appears to have come into use about the year 100 B.C.

It is perhaps not unreasonable to assume that flags, originating in China, travelled westwards until they arrived in the Middle East, and the Romans, finding them there, adopted them for their own use.

The view that Europe and the rest of the world owes the idea of the flag to China may now require second thoughts however. Fifty miles to the south of Pompeii lies the impressive site of the ancient Greek city of Paestum, which was founded by Greek colonists in the seventh century B.C., but which by the end of the fifth century B.C. had fallen under the domination of the Lucanians, a southern Italian tribe. Recent excavations have revealed some remarkable tomb paintings. Two of these show bodies of warriors parading round the walls of the tomb, led by a standard bearer. The two paintings are much alike, although one portrays the standard bearer on horseback, whilst the other (in a better state of preservation) depicts him on foot. One explanation is that the warriors are returning from a successful war and the leader is carrying the spoils of that war. A more probable account, however, suggests that the scene shows the funeral of an officer with the troops parading behind the standard. The plausibility of the second

The Raven Flag

A flag from the Bayeux Tapestry

explanation is increased by the fact that the rich cloth object borne on a special short staff by the soldier, with its golden streamer behind, does indeed look very much like a banner or flag. Evidence points to their having been executed by a Greek hand, yet in all the vast legacy of Greek art that we have received there is no other trace of anything resembling a flag. The paintings date from the fifth century B.C., and although they are, so far, the only evidence available to us, we must recognize that whether the flags were Lucanian in origin or merely captured by them, such objects were not unknown in Italy in the years 480–400 B.C. On the other hand it must be noted that after their brief appearance at Paestum, flags seem to have disappeared entirely until the introduction of the Roman *vexillum* around about the first century.

The Romans appear to have used the *vexillum* as a tactical distinguishing mark to enable one detachment of a legion to be recognized from another. This was a simple piece of material, usually purple or red, generally quite plain, occasionally carrying some device, and often richly fringed. It was hung by its upper edge or two top corners from a cross-bar on a lance and carried in addition to the eagle, which was the 'standard' of the legion. Other simple flags were used in classical times, but these were of minor importance and so far as the western world was concerned the *vexillum* remained the only 'flag' until the ninth century A.D. In fact the Venerable Bede, writing of the conversion of King Edwin of Northumbria in 622, and of King Ethelbert's meeting with St Augustine a few years earlier, speaks of *vexilla* being borne before them. Henry of Huntingdon mentions that in the Battle of Burford in 752 the Wessex standard was a golden dragon.

In the ninth century flags were used in western Asia, and there exists evidence of standards of the grandsons of the Prophet Mohammed; these were triangular fringed flags flown from a vertical flagstaff, one plain green and the other with the traditional double sword (or dagger of Ali) of the Moslems.

In the year 878 the famous Raven Flag of the Vikings appeared on the scene. This flag was surrounded by stories of magical properties and mystery. It is reputed to have been the first flag to be flown in the continent of North America, taken there by Leif Ericsson on his famous voyage in about the year 1000. We do not have any actual illustrations or accurate descriptions of this flag; however there are in existence Northumbrian coins of the early part of the ninth century which show a heavily fringed triangular flag flying from a vertical staff with the upper edge horizontal. This flag had a cross as a device, but other Northumbrian coins of this period show a stylized raven, and taking these fragments of evidence together with what is shown on the Bayeux Tapestry it seems probable that the flag was something like that illustrated here. It has the distinction of probably being the first flag in Britain to fly from a vertical staff.

The Bayeux Tapestry, an embroidery made between 1070 and 1080, tells in pictorial form, rather like a modern strip cartoon, the story of William, Duke of Normandy's invasion, the Battle of Hastings and his conquest of England in the year 1066. To the student of flags it is of great interest, for it shows first and foremost that by the year 1066 flags were well established. The principal flags shown on the tapestry are gonfanons or war flags. These were square in shape with a number of tails, mostly three but in some cases four or five; the number of tails seems to have had no particular significance. One of the most ornate is that presumed to have been blessed by the Pope and given to Duke William. This is decorated with a cross and has three tails, the majority of the others have simple designs of roundels and stripes.

Depicted in the tapestry are three more flags which are of peculiar interest: the first, the dragon standard of the English King Harold; this is shown twice, once held by the standard bearer and again in the scene of Harold's death where it is lying on the ground. How the dragon came to be used as a battle standard is one of those intriguing stories of which the answer will always be somewhat wrapped in mystery, but it is fascinating to speculate how the dragon came to be a symbol in the far west and also in China.

In the scene depicting the deaths of the brothers of Harold a flag is shown lying on the ground. This is triangular in shape and fringed, very similar to flags shown on the old Northumbrian coins of the ninth century which have been mentioned. Harold is reputed to have fought between two banners, one the 'dragon' and the other his personal banner which was said to be richly embroidered with precious stones. It is presumed that it is this latter which is shown lying on the ground, but this can only be speculation as there is no decoration or device shown on the flag.

Finally, there is shown a Norman flag, semi-circular in shape, fringed and charged with a bird. It has been suggested that this flag represents the mythical Raven Flag of the Vikings, the ancestors of the Normans; others reject this view, saying that the Raven of the Norsemen was never depicted in the tame position shown on the flag in the tapestry, and that this flag was that of the Celts of Brittany whose leader Alan commanded the third division of the Duke's army. Although the exact role of this flag must always be open to speculation, the opinion that it is the legendary Raven Flag is supported by the position that it occupies in the tapestry. For it is, together with a gonfanon, placed directly behind Duke William in the scene showing the Duke leading his knights into battle. It seems unlikely that the flag of one of the divisional commanders would have been shown in such a prominent place.

HERALDIC FLAGS

The next stage in the development of flags was the advent of heraldry. It is not easy to define heraldry as it is an art that has grown and developed over the centuries. Primarily it is a method of identification by means of devices placed on shields, and while the practice of decorating the shields of warriors was in vogue many years earlier, the art of heraldry dates from about the second quarter of the twelfth century. The need for some form of identification arose when the heavily-armoured combatants took to wearing helmets with visors which covered their faces and thus rendered them unrecognizable; and so the devices on their shields became the means by which they were identified. This practice reached its peak in the popular pastime of jousting, or the 'knightly tournament'. These events were organized by heralds who controlled the assumption of the various devices

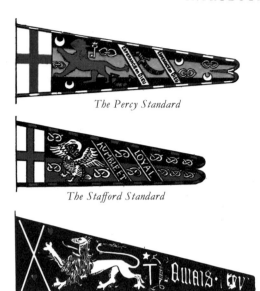

The Percy Standard

The Stafford Standard

The Douglas Standard

Armorial Banner of the
late Sir Winston Churchill

by the contestants, and thus the art of designing and regulating armorial devices became heraldry, and an alternative name for heraldry is armory.

In the course of time the first simple designs on shields grew into complicated designs called Achievements of Arms. It soon became the custom to pass these insignia down from father to son, and so the Arms became the badge of the family, and thus heraldry became closely linked with genealogy.

The College of Arms in London, the Court of the Lord Lyon in Edinburgh and the Office of the Chief Herald of Ireland are the authorities who, in these days, control heraldry in England and Wales, Scotland and Ireland respectively.

Although the art of heraldry is principally European, and has grown and developed in Europe, it is not the prerogative of any one country, and Japan has a very similar system of insignia known as 'Mon'. This has developed quite independently of European heraldry, its roots reaching back to about A.D. 900.

It was not long before the heraldic emblems came to be emblazoned on flags. The first such flags were simple extensions of the gonfanon, which has already been mentioned, and consisted of a flag on the lance, but the gonfanon soon became a banner, the flag of a king, lord or knight, on which his arms were displayed. The early banners were generally longer in their vertical dimensions (width) than the horizontal (length), but very soon the great majority became more or less square in shape. Some of the banners were, and still are, extremely beautiful. Examples can be seen in St George's Chapel, Windsor, where the richly decorated banners of the Knights of the Garter are hung above their stalls. A recent example of such a banner is that of the late Sir Winston Churchill, which depicts the quarterings of the noble families from which he was descended.

About 1350, during the reign of Edward III of England, the term 'standard' came to be used to describe the banner of an important noble, or member of a royal house. The origin of the word standard is obscure: originally a standard was an emblem that 'stood by itself', i.e. it was not carried by a bearer, although strangely enough the flag-bearer came to be called a standard-bearer.

The earliest standards consisted of a device, often religious, and sometimes accompanied by a flag or flags, carried at the top of a tall pole or the mast of a ship, mounted on a waggon or some form of cart. A standard of this type, with a 'pyx' and three banners, was present at the battle of Northallerton in 1138, which in consequence has been called the Battle of the Standard.

The use of the title standard to describe this form of device was not confined to England but was general throughout Europe. In the course of time the standard came to be the name given to the personal banner of a king, or important nobles such as dukes, and in the twelfth century the standard of a noble became a long slender flag—what we would now call a pennant. On the Continent the designs varied, but in England the term came to be applied to any flag of noble size that had the Cross of St George or St Andrew next to the staff, with the rest of the field divided horizontally into two or more stripes, either the livery or the prevailing colours in the arms of the bearers, and it was decorated with the motto and badges of the owner. The flag was richly fringed or bordered. There is at the College of Arms a drawing of the Standard of Sir Henry de Stafford, as shown here, and one of the oldest flags in existence is the very Standard of the Douglas carried at the Battle of Otterburn (Chevy Chase) 1388. This is still in the possession of Douglas of Cavers at the family seat in Roxburghshire. The Douglas Standard is known as the Douglas Banner, which is not strictly according to English usage, but the titles banner, ensign and standard were often confused; generally the banner or ensign was the personal flag, and the standard the official flag.

Heraldic standards and ensigns are still in use in Scotland where at Highland gatherings the standard of the chief is set up before his tent as a rallying point for his clansmen, and the standard is often displayed on the pipes of the pipe major of the chieftain.

FLAGS FOR ALL PURPOSES

Thus it can be seen that originally the flags were the banners or insignia of individuals. A nation or tribe or regiment used the flag of its king or leader. Gradually, however, the use of the personal flag of the king as the national flag of the country was abandoned and in its place the nations adopted flags of a design which had some national significance— often the flag of the patron saint. The first of such national flags appeared in the Mediterranean when the city state of Genoa adopted the banner of the Cross of St George as the flag of their state; this was in the twelfth century. With the introduction of national flags the personal flag of the head of state became his standard, flown only when he was present.

In the course of time some, but by no means all, countries adopted the practice of having more than a single national flag. A few countries have a special ceremonial or state flag in addition to the 'everyday' national flag. The majority, although there are notable exceptions such as France and the United States of America, have special variations of their national flags as the flags or ensigns for their ships.

Not only are there national flags, but practically every province or county of a country and also each city or town of any importance has its own flag. Many of these provincial

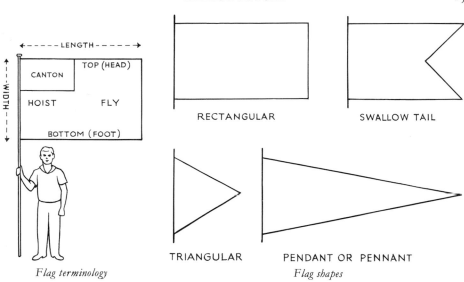

Flag terminology

RECTANGULAR   SWALLOW TAIL

TRIANGULAR   PENDANT OR PENNANT

Flag shapes

flags, especially the European ones, are of great interest and ancient design, for Europe was once divided into many small principalities which in the course of time have combined to make the nations we know today. In modern times the use of flags as a 'sign of distinction', to use an old English expression, has grown so that there is scarcely a corporate body, be it a large commercial undertaking, a sports club, or an international organization such as the United Nations, which does not have its own flag.

Finally, one of the most important functions of flags is that they provide a means of sending messages over a distance, i.e. for signalling, and for this role special flags and codes have been devised (*see* Chapter Twelve).

DESCRIBING FLAGS

In heraldry certain rules and conventions have been adopted which greatly facilitate the description (or 'blazon') of a Coat of Arms and certain rules and conventions have also been adopted to assist in the description of flags. Both for flags and heraldry the description can be greatly assisted by a simple drawing.

When describing the details of a flag it is assumed that the flag is flying from a staff held by the right hand of a bearer who is facing the observer, with the flag flying over the head of the bearer towards his left. That side of the flag which faces the observer is called the 'obverse' and the other side is called the 'reverse'. Generally these two sides are the same, but sometimes they differ; this usually occurs in complicated and intricate heraldic flags, or flags with inscriptions. When dealing with the flags of those Arabic nations and others who write from right to left and whose flags carry inscriptions, the flag staff must be held in the left hand of the bearer and fly from his left to his right. In describing a flag where the obverse and reverse differ, it is obvious that separate descriptions must be given for each side.

The description of flags is simplified if the various characteristics are described in the same sequence. Firstly the shape of the flag is given, i.e. square, rectangle, triangle, pennant-shaped (*see* p. 15), with more than one tail or swallow-tailed etc. Then come the proportions or dimensions: the vertical dimension is known as the 'width' although some now call this the 'hoist', and the horizontal dimension is known as the 'length'. As flags come in varying sizes it is usual to describe their proportions as the ratio of the width to the length, i.e. a flag in which the length is twice the width is described as proportions one by two. Next is given a description of the field, the basic or background of the flag; to assist in doing this the field is roughly divided into two parts, the 'hoist' and the 'fly', the hoist being that portion next to the staff, and the remainder the fly; generally the hoist is taken to be one-third of the total area of the flag and the fly two-thirds, but these fractions are not rigid and can be varied to suit individual cases. Then the description should continue to give the salient features of the flag. A very common device is to have a special emblem or badge in the top corner of the flag next to the hoist; this is known as a 'canton'. To be more specific a canton is a rectangle placed in the corner of the flag next to the staff. Usually it is not larger than a quarter of the area of the field, although this is not vital. In describing the flag one can say that it has a plain field, or a vertically or horizontally striped field, or that the field is divided vertically or horizontally. If the flag consists of three stripes of three different colours it can be called a vertical or horizontal tricolour. There are some who say that the term 'tricolour' can be only used when the three stripes are of equal width, but this is not considered to be essential.

A simple flag like that of Malta would be described thus: 'A rectangular flag, proportions two by three, divided vertically into two equal parts, white to the hoist and red to the fly, with a white George Cross fimbriated in red in the top corner of the hoist.' It will be noted that the heraldic term 'fimbriated', meaning a narrow border, has been used; although as a general rule the heraldic method of describing the blazons is not generally used for flags, the occasional use of the simple heraldic terms can sometimes be helpful. Fimbriated, as has been stated, is a narrow border; 'a saltire', a diagonal cross similar to that of St Andrew. 'Charged with' means that a device or badge has been placed on the flag. Also there are many flags which are charged with a Coat of Arms or similar heraldic devices; in such cases it is easier to use the heraldic conventions to describe such a charge. Thus a student of flags should have a working knowledge of heraldry and the conventions used by heralds to describe heraldic devices. However, with flags it is usual to use the ordinary names for the colours instead of the heraldic rules where there are metals, tinctures, furs etc. The colours used for flags will be discussed more fully below in the section dealing with flag design.

In modern times the flags currently in use are in general confined to the following: banner, standard, ensign, jack, pennant, guidon and colours. The many old names such as pennons, pennoncelles, streamers and so on are not now employed and are only used in the historical sense. In order to clarify this matter the following are brief historical notes about each, together with the modern meaning of the title.

As explained in the section dealing with heraldry the 'banner' is a flag of a distinguished person, or it may be used to describe the flag of a body of persons. Thus a banner can be described as an ornate flag with a heraldic type of design used for ceremonial purposes. The term banner is also often applied to the form of flag which is suspended from a horizontal bar similar to the old Roman *vexillum*, principally in use for ecclesiastical purposes. The device often seen in processions, consisting of a large piece of material supported by two poles and carried by two persons, is not in the strict sense of the word a banner; a banner is a form of flag and a flag must be free to flap in the wind (*see* p. 9).

The history of the 'standard' has also been outlined on page 13, and although the title standard is used to describe the banners of certain notables and regimental flags, it is in general now given only to the banner of a head of state, e.g. the Royal Standard of Great Britain, or the Standard of the President of the United States of America.

The word 'ensign' is derived from the Latin *insigne* and *signum*. Originally a rather abstract word meaning a sign, or signal, it came to be the name given to a flag or banner used as a distinguishing flag. It is not clear whether the Army or the Navy first used the term; probably it was the Navy for the first record of the word is dated 1574 and refers to ship ensigns. There was a short period of time when the regimental flags of the Army were called ensigns, but this did not last long, and while the term ensign is still occasionally used in heraldry, for all practical purposes it can now be taken that it is the name given to the national flag of a ship. In most countries, but not all, the ensign discharges a dual function: it not only shows the nationality of the ship wearing it (for ships 'wear' their ensigns), but also the function of the ship, whether it is for instance a warship, a merchant ship, a ship in government service such as customs, or a yacht. Thus most countries have two or more, very often three different ensigns—one for their warships, one for their merchant ships and one used by the ships in government service. These ensigns are often further differentiated by carrying or, as it is called, being 'defaced' by the badge of the particular government office to which the ship belongs, or, in the case of a yacht, the yacht club. As has been said, the practice is not the same in all nations, for instance the United Kingdom has a great variety of ship ensigns, whereas France and the United States of America have very few.

The name 'Jack' when applied to flags is described in the Oxford Dictionary as a 'diminutive of the National Flag flown from the bows of a ship'. The term 'Jack' was first used in the British Navy to describe the Union Flag that was at that time flown at the main masthead. Although this flag was not quite as large as the ensigns worn by ships at that time it was, nevertheless, a flag of fairly generous proportions. As diminutives are often used as terms of affection and familiarity, it seems possible that the sailors of that time used the diminutive 'Jack' in that sense, i.e. as a nickname or affectionate way of speaking of this flag. Whatever the origin, the term 'Jack' was firmly established towards the latter part of the seventeenth century. A vote of the Houses of Parliament on 1 May 1660 referred to 'such standards, fflags and Jacke Colours of the ffleete', and in 1666 a Warrant was issued by the Lord High Admiral 'for taking into custody such Masters of merchant ships as shall presume to wear the Kings Jack'. These are only two of many examples, and they make it clear that a Jack was a special distinguishing flag. This is further confirmed by the fact that the special flag (very similar to the Red Ensign) introduced as the distinguishing flag for privateers, and similar flags 'defaced' with a badge as the distinguishing flags for Government vessels which were not ships of war, were also called Jacks.

Although at first Jacks were flown from the masthead it soon became the practice to fly them from the sprit topmast which was fixed to the bowsprit. This seems to have been quite unofficial and how this practice came about is obscure. The reason was probably twofold. Firstly it was much easier to hoist the Jack there, and also the mastheads came to be needed for the distinguishing flags of admirals. When the square sails set on the sprit topmast were replaced by fore and aft sails these obscured the Jack and so the Jack ceased to be used whilst the ship was sailing and was only flown in harbour. The practice of only flying the Jack *whilst* in harbour has been universally adopted and has persisted to this day. But on exceptional occasions it is still flown whilst the ship is under way. The staff from which the Jack flies is called the jackstaff because the Jack flies from it. It is incorrect that the Jack is called the Jack because it flies from the jackstaff. The Jack can be of any design so long as it has some traditional connection with its country.

The 'pennant' or as it was formerly spelt the 'pendant', is a long narrow flag which has apparently developed from the 'streamer'. These long flags, often of immense length, can be seen in many pictures of old ships from medieval days to well on in the seventeenth century. When describing a pennant it is necessary to differentiate between that and a triangular flag. The proportions of the latter are generally in the nature of one by one and a half: which means that the horizontal dimension is one and a half times as long as the vertical dimension, whereas in the case of a pennant, the proportions are at least one by four. A pennant is an important part of the array of flags (or colours, *see* below) that are worn by warships; they also form an important part of the International Code of Signals.

'Guidon' is derived from the French *guide-homme* and is a military flag. The Regimental Colours of certain British cavalry regiments are called guidons; these are forty-one inches long and twenty-seven inches in depth, with a slit in the fly and the corners rounded off. The name guidon is also given in other armies, for instance that of the United States of America, to a 'marker flag'. This is a small flag which is used in parades to mark the place at which the different companies etc. are to form up.

The term 'colours' was originally applied to ships' ensigns. Captain Boteler in his *Six Dialogues*, dated 1633, has his Admiral say: 'Colours and Ensignes I take to be all one.' And in the British Merchant Shipping Act of 1894 it is laid down that 'the proper colours for any ship or boat owned by a British subject is the Red Ensign'. In the course of time, however, the term colours has come to be given to the whole array or suite of flags, e.g. the proper colours for a warship are the ensign, jack and pennant; for a regiment, in most countries, the national or sovereign's banner and the regimental banner; for a merchant ship its ensign and house flag.

Although the arts of the heraldic artist and the designer of flags are very akin, they differ in certain important aspects. A heraldic flag of complicated design is a beautiful thing and very suitable for ceremonial occasions, processions and the like, but the normal flag has to stand up to very strenuous conditions of wind and rain and all that the elements can bring. Ideally the different colours should consist of different pieces of cloth, or bunting as the flag cloth is called, sewn together to make the correct design. A painted design would last but a short time at the masthead of a ship. Furthermore the flag should be the same, or very nearly the same, on both sides so that it consists of but one thickness of material. A flag flying in an exposed position is more or less transparent, especially when the sun shines upon it, so unless the two sides 'match up' the flag will have to be made of two thicknesses, increasing its cost, and such a flag never flies as well as one of a single thickness. Then the designer must think of what colours to use, and if he is aiming at designing a flag that can be made as a 'sewn flag', he will be limited by the colours in which bunting is manufactured and will not be able to choose fancy or exotic colours. The British Admiralty, or as it now should be called, the Ministry of Defence, Navy Department, has certain standard colours of bunting, and most flags in Britain have their colours adapted to fit in with these. The standard colours with the British Colour Council numbers are given below:

Black	B.C.C.220	Crimson	B.C.C.36
Azure (light blue)	B.C.C.131	Green	B.C.C.100
Intermediate Blue	B.C.C.196	Red	B.C.C.210
Royal Blue	B.C.C.218	White	B.C.C.1
Blue (Navy Blue)	B.C.C.219	Yellow	B.C.C.113

The flag designer would be well advised to have regard to one of the basic rules of heraldry that 'metal should not be laid on metal, and colour should not be laid on colour'. In other words, white (silver) should never be placed next to yellow (gold), and white or yellow should always be interposed between any of the other colours. The object of this simple rule is to make the various colours stand out distinctly from each other. It does not make the rule any less desirable because many well-known flags contravene it.

It has been mentioned that the material which flags are usually made from is called 'bunting'; silk is also used, but it is confined to special ceremonial flags. Bunting is a hard and durable woollen fabric specially made for flags, and used to come in cloth nine inches wide. The modern bunting is now almost invariably made of a mixture of wool and synthetic fibres, generally nylon or terylene in the United Kingdom. This cloth is even harder and more durable than the old woollen bunting.

FLAG EMBLEMS

The majority of flags which exist follow well-established patterns. For instance, there are many flags which are striped, either vertical or horizontal, sometimes with only one, two or three stripes, sometimes with many more stripes. Then again it is very common to have a simple flag with the more complicated national flag or some other device in the canton. Again, although many authorities charge their flags with heraldic devices, there are a great number of flags which are decorated with a cross: the Cross of St George, with its horizontal and vertical arms; a diagonal cross or saltire, such as the Cross of St Andrew; or one of the many forms of heraldic crosses which exist, such as the Maltese Cross.

The cross in all its forms is, of course, the emblem of Christianity and has undoubtedly found its way into the European flags because so many of the national flags were in the beginning the emblem of the patron saint. There are many legends about these crosses, perhaps one of the best known being the story of the *Dannebrog*, the flag of Denmark (*see* p. 111).

The star and crescent is the emblem of many Mohammedan countries, but it was not always so. The crescent is more a symbol of Constantinople than of Mohammed and dates from the days of Philip of Macedon, the father of Alexander the Great. When, so the legend runs, that enterprising monarch besieged Byzantium in 339 B.C. he met with repulse after repulse, and tried as a last resource to undermine the walls, but the crescent moon shone out so gloriously that the attempt was discovered and the city saved.

Thereupon the Byzantines adopted the crescent as their badge, and Artemis or Diana, whose emblem it was, as their patroness. It is further possible that the crescent was adopted by the Ottoman Turks to celebrate their eventual capture of what was then Constantinople (later Istanbul) in 1453. More probable, however, is the general use of the crescent, which is in fact one of the oldest devices in human history, by Moslems from at least the fourteenth century onwards. A book published in 1350 shows several examples of Moslem flags with crescents.

Stars did not appear on Moslem flags until comparatively recently, and there is little evidence for their use in conjunction with crescents until the eighteenth century. The crescent-and-star was in fact more of a heraldic badge in the West, being used, for example, by King Richard the Lion Heart in the late twelfth century (and hence today by the city of Portsmouth). It seems to have become the badge for general use through-out the extensive Ottoman Empire, and to have spread to other Moslem countries over a long period until it became the universal badge of Islam that it is today.

FLAG CODES AND ETIQUETTE

Some nations have a carefully laid down code of flag etiquette which gives precise instructions as to how the flags can be used under all conditions. Such a country is the United States of America. The United Kingdom at the other extreme has no code at all and there are some people of other countries who are horrified at the familiar way with which the British treat their flags. The above generalization does not apply to ships, because at sea there has grown up an etiquette of how the flags should be used and where they should be hoisted and the occasions when they are used. Throughout the world when the ship is in harbour the ensign is invariably hoisted at 8.00 a.m. local time and lowered at sunset (in arctic waters where the days are unusually long these times are sometimes modified). A ship salutes another ship by dipping its flag.

Half-masting a flag to indicate mourning is a curious custom, the origin of which has yet to be ascertained, but its observance appears to go back to the sixteenth century as another of the customs of the sea which has spread to the land. Then there is the custom of dressing the ship overall, called by those who are not sailors 'rainbow fashion', which is used to decorate ships on special occasions. Theoretically a ship should only be dressed overall when at anchor or moored up in harbour. It would have been impractical for an old sailing-ship to get under way when dressed overall, but this custom is now more honoured in the breach than in the observance by most merchant ships, which can often be seen under way with their dressing flags still hoisted.

It is often puzzling to know whether one should say a ship is wearing a flag, or bearing a flag, or flying a flag. However, it is generally agreed that a ship is wearing its national ensign or national colours and that the other flags are flown. The only exception to this is that when a ship has a Royal Standard aloft it is said to be wearing the standard.

When a ship is in a foreign port it is the custom to fly in a prominent position the maritime ensign of the country in whose port the ship is lying. This is known as a Courtesy Ensign and it should be noted that where there is any choice, it should be the ordinary merchant ship ensign of the country being visited which is flown.

The red flag is now a flag which is associated with revolution, but it was originally called the flag of defiance and is so described by Bowles in *Naval Flags of All the Nations in the World*, published in May 1783.

The black flag with skull and cross bones is always supposed to be the pirate flag; however, there does not appear to be any historical evidence for this.

One often reads of the term 'flags of convenience'. This is a device whereby ships are registered (for convenience or economy) in, and wear the merchant flag of, Panama, Liberia, Honduras or Costa Rica. They are sometimes called the 'panlibhonco fleet'.

VEXILLOLOGY

In subsequent chapters the many flags of different nations and other authorities will be described, but before proceeding it is gratifying for the student and lover of flags to note that there has been a great increase in the interest taken in flags; so much so that flag societies have been formed in many countries, and a name, vexillology, has been coined to describe the study of flags, their history and modern development, and all to do with flags. Although there are some reservations, the term vexillology has been adopted by many, and no doubt will in the course of time become universal. The inventor of the expression is Dr Whitney Smith, the Director and one of the founders of The Flag Reasearch Center of 3 Edgehill Road, Winchester, Mass. 01890, USA. This organization publishes six times a year a journal called *The Flag Bulletin*. This bulletin is of great value to all who are interested in flags and wish to keep abreast of all the many changes that are continually taking place. In addition to the American organization, there are flag research societies in a number of other countries, e.g. the Netherlands, Switzerland and France, and new ones are springing up all the time. In England there exists The Flag Institute, of which William Crampton is the Director, and which is located at 8 Newton Lane, Chester. The Flag Institute, like its American counterpart, publishes a periodical, *The Flag Institute Bulletin*, which contains much of interest to the student of vexillology, whether he is concerned with historical or with modern flags.

An International Federation of Vexillological Associations has been formed, and holds international congresses every two years. The seventh of these took place at Washington, USA in June 1977, and was attended by over a hundred delegates from many different countries.

(2) The United Kingdom of Great Britain and Northern Ireland

The United Kingdom differs from most other countries in that she has no official national flag. The Union Flag is a royal flag used by the sovereign and the services and representatives of the sovereign. However, it has twice been stated in Parliament—once in the House of Lords by the Earl of Crewe in 1908, and once by the Home Secretary in 1933—that there is no objection to any British subject using the Union Flag ashore. The Merchant Shipping Act of 1894 forbids its use afloat. This Act states that the Red Ensign is the proper colour for any ship or boat owned by a British subject.

Although evidence is somewhat sketchy it appears probable that St George became the Patron Saint of **England** in the year 1277, and his cross was first used as the emblem of England during the Welsh wars of Edward I, when it was displayed on the bracers of the archers (that is to say, the protectors on their arms) and on the pennoncelles (small pennons) on the spears of the foot soldiers. In the Scottish wars of Richard II (in 1385) the Cross of St George was placed on the surcoats of the soldiers and about the same time the Scottish soldiers started wearing the Cross of St Andrew.

Of all the saints, probably less is known about St George than many others. He was a soldier who was martyred in the reign of Diocletian in A.D. 303. Why he became England's Patron Saint is one of the mysteries. Probably it was because as a soldier he was popular with the crusaders and so came to be chosen in place of Edward the Confessor who was a native British saint. Nevertheless, it cannot be denied that his red cross on a white field makes a fine and distinctive flag for England.

The reason for the choice of St Andrew for **Scotland** is also somewhat obscure—he was the apostle who in A.D. 69 was crucified on a diagonal cross (known as a saltire in heraldry), and was buried in Patras in Greece. In the year A.D. 370 a monk called Regulus, hearing that the saint's remains were to be removed to Constantinople, took an arm bone and other portions of the body of the saint and escaped with these to sea. After a stormy voyage he was wrecked on a rocky coast which turned out to be Scotland. Where Regulus is reputed to have landed, a church was founded to house the relics of the saint, either at the time or, as some legends have it, in A.D. 736 when Angus, son of Fergus, King of the Picts, adopted St Andrew as his Patron Saint. The church and the little hamlet that grew up around it has now become the university town of St Andrews and is the seat of an ancient bishopric. The first record of the saltire of St Andrew being used as the national emblem of Scotland is not until the end of the thirteenth century but there is, nevertheless, reason to believe that St Andrew was venerated in Scotland from a very early date. The choice of St Andrew as Scotland's patron saint rather than Columba or

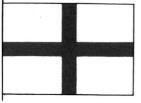

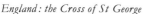

England: the Cross of St George   *Scotland: the Cross of St Andrew*   *First Union Flag 1606*

Commonwealth Flag 1649   *Present Union Flag 1801*   *Ireland: Cross of St Patrick*

another of the saints of the old Church of Scotland probably reflects its replacement by the Church of Rome in the eighth century, making the choice of one of the latter's saints (albeit one with strong Scottish connections) a natural one.

And thus the Cross of St George became the flag of England and the white saltire cross on a blue ground the flag of Scotland. It is worth remembering that these are still the flags of England and Scotland. When the thrones of England and Scotland were united under James I of England (James VI of Scotland) in 1603 it was necessary to have a flag representing the two countries, now Great Britain, and in the year 1606 a Royal Proclamation announced the introduction of the first Union Flag, which was described as 'the red cross, commonly called St George's Cross, and a white cross commonly called St Andrew's Cross, joined together'. This flag remained in force until the execution of Charles I and the establishment of the Commonwealth, which led to the introduction of the special Commonwealth Jack, which consisted of St George's Cross in the hoist and the gold harp of Ireland in the fly; but with the Restoration and return from abroad of Charles II in 1660, the Union Flag of James I was reintroduced and remained as the flag of Great Britain until 1800 when Ireland was incorporated in the Union of Great Britain and it became necessary to have a new Union Flag. This was brought into force by a Proclamation issued on 1 January 1801, and the flag which was established combines the three crosses of St George, St Andrew and St Patrick—the flag of the United Kingdom until this day.

The choice of St George for England and St Andrew for Scotland has already been remarked upon; the choice of the so-called 'Cross of St Patrick' was also curious. St Patrick was the Patron Saint of **Ireland**, but he was not a martyr and so was not entitled to a cross as his badge. The Irish have never used this cross as a national emblem. In reality it originated in the arms of the powerful family of the Geraldines, whose presence in Ireland as representatives of Henry II was due to the efforts of the English sovereign to subjugate the country. Ireland's traditional badge is either the shamrock or the golden harp. On becoming an independent country. Eire adopted quite a different flag (*see* p. 125).

The design of the first or 1606 Union Flag was comparatively simple as it only required the combination of the two crosses of St George and St Andrew. Nevertheless, when first introduced it did run into difficulties as the Scottish mariners objected and said that the Cross of St George was placed over and above that of St Andrew. The design of the Union Flag of 1801 was more difficult because in this the three crosses had to be accommodated.

The new Union Flag was described heraldically as follows: 'the crosses Saltire of St Andrew and St Patrick Quarterly, per Saltire countercharged Argent and Gules; the latter fimbriated of the second, surmounted by the Cross of St George of the third, fimbriated as the Saltire.' This description was accompanied by a drawing but the drawing and description could be interpreted differently, so much so that between 1801 and the present time there have been a dozen different versions of the Union Flag. The differences have only been in minor details. These varying patterns have now been reduced to two. The one which is adopted most universally is the pattern used by the Royal Navy which is also the pattern flown on the Houses of Parliament and on government offices. In this the Irish (red) saltire is reduced in width by having its fimbriations taken from itself instead of from the blue ground.

The other pattern, established in 1900 by the War Office, attempted to comply literally with the proclamation of 1 January 1801. In this pattern two saltires are of equal breadth and the fimbriation of St George's Cross has been reduced. It was, of course, in an endeavour to ensure that both the Cross of St Andrew and the Cross of St Patrick were of equal size that they were, as the heralds described, countercharged. This requirement has not been met in the Navy pattern flag but the differences are so small as scarcely to be noticed and it must be agreed that the Union Flag with its colours fresh and new, flying in the breeze, is an outstandingly beautiful flag.

The original Union Flag was introduced in 1606 as a maritime flag, and in 1634 a Royal Proclamation laid down that the Union Flag was reserved for His Majesty's Ships of War and forbade merchant ships to wear it. It has been explained (*see* p. 17) how this flag came to be called a 'Jack', and how the term Union Jack came into being. It is quite clear that the name Union Jack was the name given to the distinguishing flag of His Majesty's ships, and that it is proper to call this flag a Union Jack when flying in a ship, but this flag which was formerly purely maritime is now used as the National Flag of Britain and some consider that it is incorrect to call it a Union Jack when it is not flying in a ship and that when flying ashore it should be called the Union Flag. Strictly this view may be correct, and there would be no doubt as to its correctness if the flag used were the 1900 War Office pattern, but this is not so, and the flag that is seen in Britain flying from the Houses of Parliament and other public buildings is the pattern adopted by the Royal Navy.

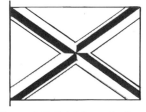

Cross of St Patrick countercharged

The Red Ensign

Furthermore it has been called the Union Jack in modern times in Parliament and so by common usage it is considered that it is correct to call this flag, which is to all intents the National Flag of the United Kingdom, the Union Jack. It would also appear that the 1900 War Office version should not be called the Union Jack; in fact it is generally known as the 'Great Union Flag'.

As mentioned above, the proper flag for a merchant ship registered in the United Kingdom is the Red Ensign. The original form of the Ensign (with the cross of St George in the canton) was specified as long ago as 18 September 1674 for this purpose, but for a long time the Red Ensign was the same as the squadron ensign of the Red Squadron, and this was only rectified by the abolition of squadron colours in 1864 (see Royal Navy, p. 32). The Red Ensign acquired its present form on 1 January 1801, at the same time as the Union Jack. The Ensign may not be defaced by any badge or mark except by special permission (see Flags Worn by Merchant Ships, pp. 227–8).

A flag which shares the position of 'National Flag' with the Union Flag is the Royal Standard of the United Kingdom. The first Royal Standard was that of King Richard I, which was flown in 1198, almost one hundred years before the Cross of St George. This consisted of the three lions 'passant guardant' in gold on a red field. There seems to be some possibility that before the banner with three lions came into being there were earlier ones with one or two lions. It is said that William the Conqueror bore two lions on his shield. This is possibly how the arms of Sark, which was originally part of the estates of the Dukes of Normandy, came to be two lions.

Although this flag is now universally known as a Royal Standard, properly it should be called the Royal Banner (see p. 13).

During the course of its life the Royal Standard has undergone many changes. In 1340 it was for the first time divided into four quarters, the *fleurs-de-lys* of France in the first and fourth quarters. However, this fairly simple design did not persist. With the ascension of James I to the throne of England the banners of Scotland and Ireland were introduced.

The first Royal Standard of the Sovereign of Great Britain consisted of the old Standard of England in the first and fourth quarters, the Standard of the King of Scotland in the second and the harp of Ireland in the third.

The Standard of Scotland is golden and bears the red 'lion rampant' within a tressure of the same colour, heraldically blazoned as 'Or [for gold], a lion rampant within a double tressure flory counterflory gules'. The exact date of the adoption of this banner is not definite, but it appeared on the great seal of King Alexander II, who married the daughter of King John in the early part of the thirteenth century. There are some who say that this banner is more properly the flag of Scotland than is the Cross of St Andrew, but the weight of evidence points to the latter being Scotland's National Flag. The symbol of a harp as a badge for Ireland is somewhere obscure. It is generally accepted that the early Standard of Ireland had three golden crowns on a blue background. It seems that Henry VII substituted the harp for the Irish crowns, but neither the crown nor harp nor any other device for Ireland appear in the standard borne by any sovereign until the reign of James I.

With the execution of Charles I and the establishment of the Commonwealth under Cromwell, standards of a completely new design were adopted. The first, known as the Commonwealth Standard, had a red field with the Cross of St George and the harp of

Banner of Kings of England 1198–1340

Royal Banner of Scotland 1222–

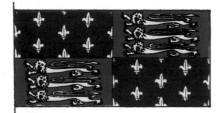

Royal Banner of England 1340–1405

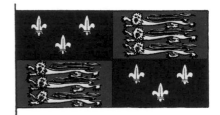

Royal Banner of England 1405–1603

Royal Banner of England 1603–89

*Banner of Oliver Cromwell
as Lord Protector*

*Royal Banner 1689–1702
(without inescutcheon 1702–7)*

Royal Banner 1707–14

Royal Banner 1714–1801

*Royal Banner 1801–37
(cap changed to crown 1815)*

Ireland on a blue field surrounded by a wreath of laurels. From 1653 to 1660, the period of the Protectorate, a standard known as Cromwell's Standard came into being. This consisted of quarters one and four, the Cross of St George; two the Cross of St Andrew; three the Irish harp; with an escutcheon of the arms of Cromwell, a white lion rampant. With the return of Charles II the Stuart Standard was reverted to.

In subsequent years the Royal Standard underwent many changes and became more and more complicated until in 1801 it changed to what was very nearly its present form—with the lions of England in the first and fourth quarters, the lion of Scotland in the second and the harp of Ireland in the third, with a little escutcheon in the centre, bearing the Arms of Hanover.

When Queen Victoria came to the throne in 1837 the Arms of Hanover were removed leaving the Royal Standard of Great Britain in its present form.

Note is very often made that Wales is not represented in the Royal Standard. The Welsh Standard dates from about 1240. It was first used by Llewelyn the 'Last', who was the last native Prince of Wales. The standard was a quartered coat, gold and red, with four lions passant countercharged. The question of incorporating the Arms of Wales into the Royal Arms has been considered but has never been confirmed; they are displayed in the Standard of the Prince of Wales.

In 1960 when arrangements for Her Majesty's forthcoming visit to India were being considered, it was felt that a new personal flag of distinctive design would be more appropriate for use in the nations of the Commonwealth. The Royal Standard had become associated in the public mind with the United Kingdom.

Accordingly a banner or square flag consisting of Her Majesty's initial 'E' in gold ensigned with the Royal Crown all within a chaplet of golden roses on a blue field was authorized. This flag was fringed with gold and was used during the Queen's visit to India in 1961; subsequently it was felt that for those Commonwealth countries of which she is Queen it would be appropriate if the new device described above were used by Her Majesty in conjunction with the arms of the country she was visiting. Flags have accordingly been designed for Sierra Leone, Canada, Australia, New Zealand, Jamaica, Trinidad and Tobago, and Malta. The details of these flags are given later when the flags of these countries are described. As Sierra Leone, Trinidad and Tobago, and Malta have now become republics and no longer recognize Her Majesty the Queen as their Head of State, the Queen's personal flags for these countries are now no longer used.

Royal Banner 1837—
('The Royal Standard')

The Queen's Personal Flag

The Duchy of Lancaster

Standard of the Prince of Wales

When Her Majesty visits a Commonwealth country for which a personal flag has been approved, the appropriate flag is used instead of the Royal Standard. It must be appreciated that these personal flags do not in any way replace the Royal Standard—this is the banner of the Sovereign of the United Kingdom of Great Britain and Northern Ireland, whereas the personal flags which have been described are the personal flags of Queen Elizabeth II with her cypher upon them.

The Queen is also hereditary Duke of Lancaster, and a flag for the office of the Duchy of Lancaster has long been in use. It is the old royal Arms of England with a label 'of France' first granted in the fourteenth century. The Duchy merged with the Crown on the death of John of Gaunt, 14 October 1399.

The standards used for the children and grandchildren of the Sovereign have a white label placed along the top of the Royal Standard. In the case of the children the label has three points and in the case of the grandchildren it has five points. When the eldest son of the Sovereign is created Prince of Wales he has an additional difference in the centre, namely a small shield bearing the Arms of Wales described above. This shield is ensigned with the Prince's coronet.

Prince Charles:
Personal Flag for Wales

Prince Charles:
Personal Flag for Scotland

HRH Prince Philip,
Duke of Edinburgh

Prince Charles has a personal flag for use in Wales, adopted at the time of his investiture in 1969. This flag consists of a square version of the Arms of Wales mentioned above, with a green shield in the centre charged with the coronet of the Prince of Wales. He also has a number of Scottish titles: Duke of Rothesay, Earl of Carrick, and Baron Renfrew, Lord of the Isles, and Great Steward of Scotland. A special banner for use in Scotland was created in 1974 using the Arms connected with these titles. The first and fourth quarters are for the Great Steward of Scotland, the second and third for the Lord

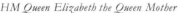

HM Queen Elizabeth the Queen Mother   *HRH Princess Anne*

of the Isles, and the inescutcheon of the Royal Arms of Scotland with a white cadency label for the Duke of Rothesay.

Prince Charles, as eldest son of the sovereign, is also Duke of Cornwall, a duchy created in 1337. Its Arms are derived from those of the former Earldom. A flag of the Arms is flown over offices of the Duchy and on its ships which ply to the Scilly Isles. The banner is black with fifteen gold discs, or 'bezants'.

Other members of the Royal Family also have their own personal standards or banners. That of HRH Prince Philip, the Duke of Edinburgh, consists of four quarters: the first is for Denmark, the second for Greece, the third for Mountbatten, and the fourth for Edinburgh. The first three quarterings represent the royal families from which the Prince is descended. In the standard of HM Queen Elizabeth the Queen Mother the Royal Arms are impaled with those of her own family of Bowes-Lyon. The latter are a good example of canting or punning arms, with the blue lion rampant for Lyon in the first and fourth quarters, and the three bows 'proper' for Bowes in the second and third. It is the usual practice for the consort of a reigning monarch to impale her Arms with his.

The standard of HRH Princess Anne has a label of the kind mentioned on p. 28. It lies over the Royal Arms, and consists of three points, the centre one with a red heart and the outer two with red crosses of St George. HRH Princess Margaret's standard has a label with a thistle between two roses.

HRH Princess Margaret   *The Royal Standard for Scotland*

Scotland has its own version of the Royal Standard in which the Red Lion rampant occupies the senior positions in the first and fourth quarters, whilst England's three lions are in the second, and the harp of Ireland in the third. In 1953 the then Secretary of State for Scotland raised the question why this form was not employed when Her Majesty was in residence in Scotland. In reply it was pointed out that the version of the Royal Standard officially adopted in 1801 was that which had England in the first and fourth quarters and Scotland in the second, and this had always been used both in Scotland and

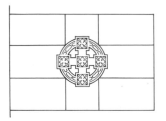

Wales: Y Ddraig Goch   *The Church of Wales*

in the Commonwealth. It was, however, agreed that there was a long-established practice that when there was a distinctive Scottish use the Scottish version of the Royal Arms might be displayed. With the express approval of the sovereign these Arms have come into use on official buildings and stationery. It is also to be noted that on such occasions as international football matches many Scottish supporters wave not only the flag of St Andrew but also the Royal Banner of Scotland, the red lion rampant. Many people think that this practice is incorrect, so it is worth quoting an extract from a reply to the Secretary of State mentioned above: 'The Red Lion rampant. With regard to the flying of the Lion Rampant flag, by virtue of the Royal Warrant issued in September 1934 there is no objection to the display of this banner by Her Majesty's subjects as a mark of loyalty to the throne.' But it is said by some that the validity of this warrant has yet to be tested in the courts.

The flag of **Wales** is known as *Y Ddraig Goch*, the Red Dragon. The dragon itself is a very ancient emblem, perhaps the oldest in continuous use in the British Isles, but its colouring and its use on a flag of white and green are of fairly recent date. Owain Glyndŵr is said to have used it in this form in 1401. White and green were the livery colours of the Princes of Gwynedd, and were adopted by the Tudors, and used extensively by them throughout the sixteenth century. At the beginning of this century the official flag of Wales was plain white with the heraldic badge of a red dragon on a green mound. This is the flag carried by hereditary right by the premier baronet in Wales at the Investiture of its Prince. On 11 March 1953 the Queen approved a further official version, consisting of the field of white over green charged in the centre with the new Royal Badge, which includes the royal crown and the national motto *Y Ddraig Goch Ddyry Cychwyn* on a ribbon around the shield. The latter is usually translated: 'The Red Dragon gives Impetus'. As a flag this did not prove popular, although the badge is widely used for official purposes, and on 23 February 1959 royal approval was given to the traditional flag, and this is now in very widespread use. The version illustrated here was introduced recently by the Welsh Tourist Board and the Red Dragon it bears can be seen at major road crossings into Wales.

The flag of the Church of Wales was introduced on 9 December 1954, and is a banner of the Arms. It is to some extent based on the former unofficial flag which was of black with a golden cross. The new flag has a golden cross of Celtic design (a 'wheel-cross') on a larger blue cross on a white field.

Northern Ireland was until recently the only part of the United Kingdom with its own internal self-government, having been established as such on the partition of Ireland in 1921. The semi-official flag which the former government approved for general use on land in 1953 was a banner of the Arms, i.e. white with a cross of St George, and a crowned white star of six points (one for each of the six counties) and in the centre of this the Red Hand of the O'Neills, which also features in the arms of the province of Ulster. The flag of the Governor had the shield of arms on an orange disc within a garland of laurel in the centre of the Union flag. There was also a flag for government vessels, the Blue Ensign with a white disc in the fly containing the initials GNI.

Flag of Northern Ireland

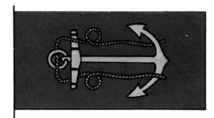

*Flag of the
Lord High Admiral*

THE ARMED FORCES OF THE UNITED KINGDOM MINISTRY OF DEFENCE

The Defence (Transfer of Functions) Act 1964 came into force on 1 April of that year. Until this date the Royal Navy, the Army and the Royal Air Force had been controlled by the Board of Admiralty and the Army and Air Councils. The new Act transferred the control of all three services to the Secretary of State for Defence under whom the Defence Council exercises command and administrative control; the government office is known as the Ministry of Defence. This new Act has resulted in the demise of the Board of Admiralty, and the Army and Air Councils. It is not the province of this work to go into the organization of government departments more than is necessary to explain their effect on the flags of the armed services. With few exceptions the flags and ensigns used by the Navy, Army and Air Force remain the same. The main changes are that the flags of the Army and Air Councils have disappeared and in future the flag formerly flown by the Board of Admiralty will be used only by the Sovereign who has now assumed the office of Lord High Admiral, and that the authority formerly vested in the Admiralty for issuing, on behalf of the Sovereign, warrants for ships to wear special privilege ensigns has been transferred by Royal Proclamation to the Secretary of State for Defence. (*See* Merchant Shipping Act 1894, p. 227.)

The historic flag of the Lord High Admiral was used by the Lords Commissioners of the Admiralty, known as the Board of Admiralty, the body constituted to carry out the functions of the Lord High Admiral. This flag, which flew from the Admiralty in Whitehall for 114 years, was hauled down at a ceremony on 31 March 1964. Exactly when this flag, which is known as 'the Anchor Flag', came into being is uncertain, but the anchor as the badge appeared on the Lord High Admiral's seals at a very early date. The Admiralty flag, or as it should more properly be called, the flag of the Lord High Admiral, is a yellow horizontal anchor on a red field, very similar to the original seventeenth century design, although the detailed arrangement of the rope cable has differed slightly from time to time.

In the past the Admiralty Flag was flown from any ship in which two or more of the Lords Commissioners of the Admiralty were embarked; but as the Sovereign has now assumed the office of Lord High Admiral, he, or she, will be the only person to use this historic flag. Thus it will, with one exception, only be seen flying from a ship which is carrying the Sovereign. The exception is that it will continue to be flown by ships of the Royal Navy at their launching.

The Union Flag is flown at one end of the building of the Ministry of Defence, and the 'Joint Services Flag' at the other. This represents the three services with vertical stripes of dark blue for the Royal Navy, red for the Army, and light blue for the RAF, and the joint emblem in the centre. This is known as the 'unified device' and consists of a white and blue eagle for the RAF, two red swords in saltire for the Army, and a blue foul anchor for the Navy surrounded by a garland and surmounted by the royal crown.

The flag of the Chief of Defence Staff is similar to this, except that the bands are horizontal, with the first quarter occupied by the Union Jack. The unified device for the Chief of Defence Staff has the Garter in place of the wreath. The Vice Chief of Defence Staff and the other 'joint' officers of 'three-star' rank have the plain unified device with a wreath of oak leaves in place of the Garter. 'Joint' officers of 'two-star' rank have the unified device but without any wreath. A flag for officers of 'one-star' rank has still be to designed.

The Minister of Defence has the 'joint' colours arranged horizontally with the Royal Crest over all in the centre.

Royal Navy The early history of ship ensigns has been described in Chapter One. The Red, White and Blue Ensigns of Great Britain came into being in the early part of the seventeenth century as tactical flags for use in the Royal Navy which was normally divided into three squadrons, the red, white and blue. A Royal Proclamation dated 18 September 1674 granted to merchant ships the right to wear the Red Ensign. The White and Blue remained solely for the use of HM ships until the year 1864 when they were abolished as they had become unnecessary and were puzzling to foreigners.

The Order in Council dated 9 July 1864 abolishing Squadronal Colours reads as follows:

> Under the Regulations established by Your Majesty's Order in Council of the 25th July, 1861, for the governance of the Royal Naval Service, the Flag Officers of the Fleet, whether Admirals, Vice-Admirals, or Rear-Admirals, are classed in Squadrons, of the Red, White and Blue, and are (with the exception of the Admiral of the Fleet) authorized to fly their flags of the colour of the Squadron to which they belong, this regulation necessitating the adoption of ensigns and pendants of a corresponding colour in every ship and vessel employed under their orders, each vessel is therefore supplied with three sets of colours, and the frequent alterations that have to be made when the Fleet is distributed as at present, under the Orders of many Flag Officers, is attended with much inconvenience from the uncertainty and expense which the system entails.
>
> The increased number and size of merchant steam-ships render it a matter of importance to distinguish on all occasions men-of-war from private ships by a distinctive flag; the latter vessels bearing at present the same red ensign as your Majesty's ships when employed under an Admiral of the Red Squadron. It also appears desirable to grant (under such conditions as we may from time to time impose) the use of a distinguishing flag to such ships of the merchant service as may be employed in the public service, or whose commanding officer (with a given proportion of the crew) may belong to the Royal Naval Reserve. We therefore most humbly submit that Your

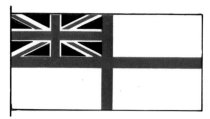

The White Ensign

Minister of Defence

Chief of Defence Staff

Majesty may be pleased by your Order in Council to prescribe the discontinuance of the division of Flag Officers into the Red, White, and Blue Squadrons, and to order and direct that the White Ensign with its broad and narrow pendants, be henceforth established and recognized as the colours of the Royal Naval Service, reserving the use of the Red and Blue colours for such special occasions as may appear to us or to officers in command of Fleets and Squadrons to require their adoption: the White flag with a Red St George's Cross to be borne by Admirals, Vice-Admirals, and Rear-Admirals on their respective masts: Commodores of the first class to carry a White broad pendant with the Red Cross at the main-top-gallant-mast-head, Commodores of the second class a similar pendant at the fore-top-gallant-mast-head, and senior officers when two or more vessels are present to bear the broad pennant [sic] at the mizzen-top-gallant-mast-head. The Blue Ensign and Union Jack, with a White border, to be carried by all vessels employed in the service of any public office; by vessels employed under the Transport Department and the Civil Departments of the Navy (with the Seal or Badge of office to which they belong as at present), and, under our permission, by ships commanded by Officers of the Royal Naval Reserve Force, and fulfilling in other respects the conditions required to entitle them to the privilege. The Red Ensign and the Union Jack, with a White border, continuing as at present the national colours for all British ships, with such exceptions in favour of Yachts and other vessels as we may from time to time authorize to bear distinguishing flags.

The White Ensign is charged with the red Cross of St George, with the Union Flag in the upper canton next to the mast.

It is laid down in *Queen's Regulations and Admiralty Instructions*, 1956, Article 1236, that 'Her Majesty's ships, when lying in home ports and roads, are to hoist their Colours at 0800 from 25th March to 20th September inclusive, and at 0900 from 21st September to 24th March inclusive; but when abroad, at 0800 or 0900 as the Commander-in-Chief shall direct; and they shall be worn if the weather permits or unless the Senior Officer present sees objection thereto, or directs otherwise, throughout the day until sunset when they are to be hauled down.' These instructions apply in like manner to the use of the Union Flag at the jackstaff.

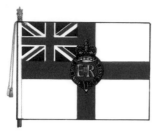
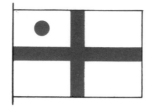
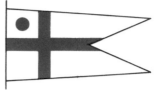

*Queen's Colour of
the Royal Navy*   *Vice-Admiral's Flag*   *Commodore's Broad Pennant*

In large ships the guard and band are paraded, and as the ensign is slowly hoisted the National Anthem of the United Kingdom is played. Should the ship be lying in a foreign port, then the anthem of that country is played, as are the anthems of any warships of other countries that are present.

In small ships the bugle sounds the 'General Salute', or 'Alert' is piped on the boatswain's pipe.

At sunset no guard or band is paraded, but the bugle sounds 'Sunset' (Retreat), or the pipe 'Alert', as the ensign is lowered.

When at sea Her Majesty's ships wear their ensigns continuously by day and night. Her Majesty's ships do not, on any account, lower their flags to any foreign ships whatsoever, unless the foreign ships shall first lower their flags to them.

The Jack is not worn when ships are: (1) under way (at sea), except when dressed with masthead flags; (2) in dock or when undergoing a dockyard refit.

There are certain Royal Naval establishments, e.g. civil and medical, at which the Union Flag is normally flown. However, when HM ships are dressed on ceremonial occasions, the White Ensign in addition is flown at the gaff or yardarm or from a separate mast.

During a period of hostilities the medical establishments continue to fly the Union Flag but in addition fly the flag of the Red Cross at the gaff or yardarm.

It is a serious offence for any vessel to wear improper colours, the authority being the 73rd Section of the Merchant Shipping Act, 1894 (*see* p. 227).

In action a warship always displays not less than two White Ensigns; if one should be shot away, then there is no danger of the ship being regarded as having surrendered.

One yacht club alone, the Royal Yacht Squadron, is authorized to use the White Ensign (*see* p. 236).

While on the subject of ensigns, a few words concerning their use ashore will not be out of place. The following is an extract from an Admiralty memorandum dated 18 February 1936:

> The White and Blue Ensigns of His Majesty's Fleet are purely maritime flags, and in general their use on shore is incorrect. There has, however, been a customary extension of the use of the White Ensign from the harbour ship used as a Fleet establishment to barracks and other buildings on shore serving the same purpose....
>
> It is common also for the White and Blue Ensigns to be used on cenotaphs and other memorials to naval personnel.

With these exceptions the use of these ensigns on shore is improper ... the White Ensign is nothing else but the national colours of a ship of war in commission and no past service in the Navy or other connection with the Navy make it correct to hoist it on private buildings on shore.

However, with the permission of the Admiralty, the White and Blue Ensigns may be used on shore for decoration purposes during periods of national rejoicing, provided they (1) are hung out, (2) are suspended on a line, or (3) form part of a set of small flags on a shield or the like on a wall, as part of a display of flags; they should not, however, be flown at the head of a flagstaff.

Although there is no mention of the use of the Red Ensign on shore in Section 73 of the Merchant Shipping Act of 1894, it would appear that no objection would be raised if it were used for decoration purposes in the manner described above.

The White Ensign used for ceremonial purposes known as the Queen's Colour, was an innovation of 1924. There are a certain number of them for use by Naval Guards of Honour. Each has a field three feet nine inches long and three feet at the hoist, and is made of silk. It has no fringe, and is secured to the staff by a gold-and-white cord with tassels in the usual way. The staff is topped by a gilt Royal Crown set upon a mace-shaped base which is charged with three silver foul anchors. In the centre of the flag is a crimson circle, bearing the Royal Cypher and surrounded by the Garter, which is ensigned with the Royal Crown. This is the only White Ensign which is charged with a badge.

The Admiralty Board which has been established to take the place of the old Board of Admiralty has now adopted as its flag the old flag of the former Navy Board which has been used as the flag of the National Maritime Museum (*see* page 47). This flag was flown at sea for the first time from HMS *Birmingham* in which members of the Admiralty Board were embarked at Her Majesty's Jubilee Review on 28 June 1977.

The highest ranking officer in the Royal Navy is the Admiral-of-the-Fleet who flies the Union as his proper flag. An Admiral flies the English National Flag of St George; a Vice-Admiral a similar flag but with a red disc, the diameter of which is half the depth of the white canton in which it is placed; and a Rear-Admiral has an additional red disc which is positioned in the lower canton next to the mast. Commodores 1st and 2nd Class have now been merged in the single rank of Commodore, whose Broad Pennant has one red ball in the canton and is the same as that of a former Commodore 2nd Class.

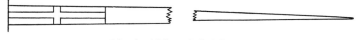

Masthead (Commission) Pennant

During the Second World War a special Broad Pennant was introduced and flown by the Royal Naval Reserve Commodore of Convoys. This pennant is white with a blue St George's Cross. On 2 November 1959 the privilege of flying this Broad Pennant was granted to Commodores on the active list of the Royal Naval Reserve; there are normally two such Commodores.

Space only permits a very brief account of the interesting history of the Masthead Pennant (pendant) now an integral part of the 'Colours' of a warship (*see also* Chapter One). This flag appears to have had its origin in the oft-times very long 'streamers' that dated from the thirteenth century and were used as a decoration. Pepys tells us in 1674

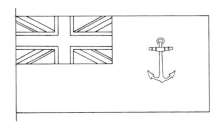

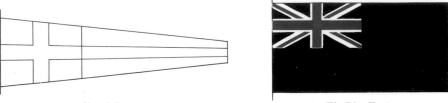

Church Pennant   *The Blue Ensign*

that it was customary for men-of-war of all nations to fly a masthead pendant so that they might not be mistaken for merchantmen. There seems to be no basis for the legend that during the Dutch wars of the seventeenth century the Dutch ships hoisted a broom. At least the many paintings and drawings by the Van der Veldes and other artists of the battles of these wars show both English and Dutch ships with pendants.

During the period that Squadronal Colours were used there were red, white and blue pendants, but now there is only the white, and according to *Queen's Regulations* all Her Majesty's ships and Establishments which are commanded by a Naval or Marine Officer (unless they are the ship of a flag officer) fly the pennant continuously, by day and night during the period that they are in commission. As has been stated flag ships fly the appropriate flag of the flag officer accommodated in the ship.

The Church Pennant has a field divided horizontally red over white over blue, bearing the red cross of St George on a white background in the hoist. It is hoisted to indicate that the ship's company is engaged in divine service. The earliest known use of the Church Pennant is to be found in Article 10 of the *Additional Instructions* of 1778, but there is a picturesque tradition that it dates back to the Anglo-Dutch wars and was used to indicate a truce whilst services were being held.

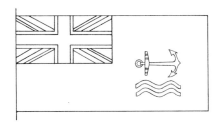

Royal Fleet Auxiliary Service   *Other Auxiliary vessels*

The plain Blue Ensign is worn by British merchant men commanded by an officer of the Royal Naval Reserve, having a certain number of RNR officers and ratings on board, and holding an Admiralty Warrant which is issued in accordance with the conditions laid down in *Queen's Regulations and Admiralty Instructions*.

During the early part of 1950 it was decided that Commodores RNR, whether on the active or retired list, may, when afloat, use the Blue Ensign in their own right, provided that Admiralty permission has been obtained.

The Blue Ensign, defaced with an appropriate charge or badge in the fly, is now distinctive of Public Offices, the Consular Service, the Colonial Governments and their ships, and a variety of other services.

Sea Cadet Corps badge

Regimental Colour of the
Royal Marine Commandos

In 1971 those civilian ships in the service of the Crown were reorganized into three groups. The Royal Fleet Auxiliary Service, which consists of highly specialized ships which operate in close support of the fleet at sea, together with certain vessels with quasi-military functions, wears the Blue Ensign defaced with a vertical yellow anchor.

The Royal Maritime Service which comprises ocean-going ships such as ocean tugs, Admiralty cable ships, and salvage vessels, wears the Blue Ensign with a horizontal yellow anchor. The third group, which embraces all other ships in the service of the Crown which do not fall into the first two categories, mostly harbour craft and certain depôt ships, etc., have a Blue Ensign with a horizontal yellow anchor, and below the anchor two wavy yellow lines.

Towards the end of 1942 the Sea Cadet Corps, the voluntary pre-entry training organization for the Royal and Merchant Navies, was granted permission by the Admiralty to use the Blue Ensign with the badge of the Corps in the centre of the fly. The badge has been described as follows: 'Within a circle, the words *Sea Cadet Corps* and a

Royal Marines:
Commandant-General

Royal Marines:
Lieutenant- or Major-General

Royal Marines: Brigadier

six-pointed star, and ensigned with a Naval Crown, a foul anchor; beneath the whole upon a scroll the motto *Ready Aye Ready*. The circle and scroll are light blue, edged with gold; the crown is also gold, but the anchor, star and lettering are white, and the dark blue field of the fly shows through behind the anchor.

A certain number of yacht clubs have an Admiralty Warrant to use the Blue Ensign, and a number have an Admiralty Warrant to use the Blue Ensign and Red Ensign defaced by the badge of the club. A list of such clubs is to be found in the 'Navy List' (*see also* Chapter Fourteen).

In the famous 'Sea Regiment', the Royal Marines, the Army principle of two Colours, Queen's and Regimental, is carried out. The Queen's Colour is the Union, and bears in

Queen's Colour of the 3rd Battalion Coldstream Guards

Regimental Colour of the 3rd Battalion Coldstream Guards

Guidon of the 11th Hussars

the centre the foul anchor with the Royal Cypher interlaced, ensigned with the Royal Crown and *Gibraltar* above; in base is the globe surrounded by a laurel wreath, and underneath the famous motto of the Corps, *Per Mare Per Terram* ('By Land by Sea').

The Regimental Colour is blue. In the centre is the foul anchor interlaced with the Royal Cypher, 'G.R.IV', ensigned with the Royal Crown and *Gibraltar* above; in base the globe is encircled with the laurel wreath and the motto is beneath it. In the dexter canton is the Union, and in each of the other three corners is the Royal Cypher of the reigning Sovereign ensigned with the Royal Crown. The Regimental Colours of the Royal Marine Commandos is illustrated. It will be noted that these not only bear the Royal Cypher of the new reign and the new design of Royal Crown but also the numerical designation of the Commandos to which they were presented.

The significance of the globe and motto is evident. The laurel wreath was won at the capture of Belle Isle on 7 June 1761, and the honour *Gibraltar* for the capture and defence of the Rock in 1705. When the Duke of Clarence (afterwards King William IV) presented Colours to all four Divisions in 1827, he said that the King, George IV, had 'directed that whatever King or Queen they might serve under hereafter, though the Cypher of the reigning sovereign must appear on their Standard, still in those of the Royal Marines, the Cypher G.R. IV was for ever to appear'.

Senior Royal Marine Officers have distinguishing flags for use in miniature on motor-cars; these all have a dark blue field, two by three.

The Commandant-General's is rectangular with, in the centre, a yellow foul anchor surmounted by the Royal Crest in proper colours.

That of Lieutenant- or Major-General is a burgee, i.e. it has a triangular piece cut out of the fly, and has a similar anchor, but ensigned with the Royal Crown, both in white.

A Brigadier displays a triangular flag charged with the white foul anchor.

Flags and Colours of the British Army   The story of the development of the flags, or as they are now termed the Colours, used in the Army is not clear-cut like the story of the flags and ensigns of the Royal Navy, and to this day there is no universal rule; each branch of the Army, infantry, cavalry, etc., has its own individual pattern of flag.

As has been explained, the Cross of St George was first used as the distinguishing emblem of the soldiers of Edward I, and it came to be the banner that marked the King or Commander and the rallying point of the whole army. But in feudal times the different

The Army Flag   *The Army Ensign*

'Companies' marched under the banner of the baron or knight who recruited them and whose retinue they formed.

The introduction of standing armies in the sixteenth century and their organization into regiments led to the introduction of 'Regimental Colours'. The infantry were the first to adopt these, and at first each company of a regiment had its own Colour, or ensign as it was then called. These early ensigns were very similar to those used in ships: the field was in the regimental colours with the Cross of St George in the canton, and a device that denoted the rank of the commander of the company. After the restoration of Charles II the pattern was changed and the basic ensign consisted of the Cross of St George (sometimes with a fimbriation) on a field of the colour of the regiment.

One of the earliest reports that we have of British Army flags is that which informs us that at the Battle of Edgehill (1642) the Royal Foot-Guards of Charles I lost eleven out of their thirteen Colours. There is also a Royal Warrant dated 13 February 1661 authorizing Colours for the Foot-Guards.

The junior officers in the British Army were called ensigns until 1871 when they became second lieutenants. The rank of 'ensign' was derived from their former title of ensign-bearers and to this day a second lieutenant of the Brigade of Guards is known colloquially as an ensign. Although this term is no longer official in Great Britain, the rank of ensign, equivalent to sub-lieutenant in the Royal Navy, is still retained in the navy of the United States of America.

There appear to have been no very definite regulations controlling the Colours of the Army until the year 1747, when the present pattern was evolved. And although up to now only the Colours of the infantry have been mentioned, the other arms of the Army, the cavalry, artillery etc., soon followed suit and adopted Colours of their own, although these were often of a different type from the rectangular banner of the infantry.

When ensigns came to be called 'Colours' is also not clear, but now there are three types that are in use in the British Army. They are: (1) the Standard, carried by the Household Cavalry and the Dragoon Guards, rectangular in shape, thirty inches in length by twenty-seven inches in width; (2) the Guidon (*see* p. 18), carried by the Royal Scots Dragoon Guards and the Inniskilling Dragoon Guards, and formerly by the 11th Hussars, immortalized in 'The Charge of the Light Brigade'; (3) the Queen's Colour and the Regimental Colour, carried by the Foot-Guards and the Infantry of the Line. There is an interesting point here: in the case of the Guards the Queen's Colour consists of an ensign-type flag with the Union in the Canton, and the Regimental Colour the Union, whereas in the case of the Line Regiments the reverse is the case, with the Queen's Colour the Union and the Regimental an 'ensign type'. Finally it should be noted that the 'Rifle Regiments' have no Colours.

All these flags are made of silk, beautifully embroidered with a golden fringe. The staff on which the Colour is carried is known as a 'Colour Pike'. The Colours bear in addition to the badges of the regiment the battle honours of the unit that they represent. The Colours of the British Army are all regarded with the greatest respect and veneration. Examples of these lovely flags shown are those of the 3rd Battalion of the Coldstream Guards.

The British Army also has a number of other flags. In 1938 King George VI approved a badge for the Army which consisted of the Royal Crest superimposed on two crossed swords, all in full colour. This badge displayed on a red field is the flag of the Army; unfortunately it appears to be very rarely used.

In October 1966 the Queen gave permission for sea-going vessels of the Army to be designated as 'HM Army Vessels'. These ships have permission to wear the Union Jack and the Army Ensign. The latter was introduced in June 1967 and consists of the Blue Ensign with the same badge as in the Army Flag placed centrally in the fly.

A number of ships and boats are operated by the Army. Those which are combat craft and manned by Army personnel wear the Army Ensign. This is a Blue Ensign defaced by the badge of the Army. The Royal Corps of Transport, successor to the Royal Army Service Corps, also operates a fleet of ships and boats. Some are manned by service personnel and some by civilian crews. All these fly the Ensign of the Royal Corps of Transport. This is also blue, is defaced by two crossed swords, and does not have the crown and lion which are in the badge of the Army.

Senior Army officers fly distinguishing flags on their motor cars.

Royal Air Force Ensign

*Queen's Colour of
the Royal Air Force*

Royal Air Force   As the Royal Air Force was only formed in recent times its flags have no long history and generally are similar in pattern to those of the Royal Navy. Thus the Royal Air Force's principal flag is its ensign; the field of this is blue, of a shade known as air force blue; in the canton is the Union and in the fly the distinguishing mark used on aircraft of the Royal Air Force—a target of red, white and blue, the blue being outside and the red in the centre.

The colours of the Royal Air Force are red, dark blue and air force blue. The red represents the Army (Royal Flying Corps) and dark blue the Royal Navy (Royal Naval Air Service), the two arms from which the Royal Air Force sprang; the lighter blue represents the Royal Air Force in the air.

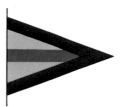

Unit Colour:
Royal Air Force College,
Cranwell

Marshal of the
Royal Air Force

Royal Air Force
Group Captain

As in the Royal Navy and the Army the Royal Air Force has 'Colours' for use on ceremonial occasions; these were approved in principle by the late King George VI in December 1947. They comprise: (1) The Queen's Colour for the Royal Air Force in the United Kingdom; (2) the Queen's Colour for individual units; and (3) the standard for individual operational squadrons. All three are made of silk and are similar to the Colours used by the Navy and the Army. The Queen's Colour for the Royal Air Force is in the form of the Royal Air Force Ensign, with the Royal Cypher in gold, ensigned with the Royal Crown in proper colours in the centre. Examples of the Colours are shown, the unit Colour being that of the RAF College, Cranwell.

Distinguishing flags are flown by senior officers of the Royal Air Force—these flags are also flown in the bows of the Royal Air Force marine craft on ceremonial occasions. The Marshal's flag is air force blue, in the centre a broad red horizontal band between two narrow ones, with a dark blue border top and bottom. That of the Air Chief Marshal has seven stripes of equal width, dark blue top and bottom, with, between, three air force blue and two red stripes. The Air Marshal and the Air Vice-Marshal's flags are similar with dark blue borders, the former having on the air force blue centre a red stripe the same width as the dark blue stripes, and the latter two thin red stripes half the width of the dark blue. The Air Commodore's flag has a swallow-tail or broad pennant having one very narrow red stripe in the centre of a light blue field, with dark blue edges top and bottom. Group Captains and Wing Commanders have triangular flags: the Group Captain has one red stripe in the centre, the same width as the dark blue edgings, and the Wing Commander two red stripes each half the width of that of the Group Captain. The field of all these flags is the air force blue.

It is of course impossible for an aircraft to display a flag whilst flying, but when Her

Royal Observer Corps badge

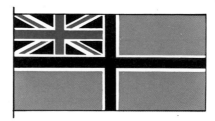

Civil Air Ensign

Majesty, or any other member of the Royal Family, is travelling by air their standard is hoisted on a small staff over the aircraft during the period when they are embarking or disembarking. In a similar way the Royal Air Force Ensign is flown when important personages are travelling by air.

Attached to the Royal Air Force is the Royal Observer Corps. This Corps has its own ensign which is similar to that of the Royal Air Force except that the red, white and blue target is replaced by a special badge. This badge was approved by the late King George VI in 1945. The badge consists of the figure of an Elizabethan coast-watcher holding aloft a torch, within a small wreath of laurel, surmounted by the Royal Crown and in the base a scroll containing the motto *Forewarned is Forearmed*.

As there is a special ensign for British merchant ships, so there is a British Civil Air Ensign. This ensign is of air force blue; it is charged with a dark blue cross edged with white with the Union in the canton. This ensign may be worn by any British aircraft registered in the United Kingdom when it is grounded and by air transport undertakings which own such aircraft on, or in proximity to, buildings used by them. There is also a special flag for airports, that of the British Airports Authority.

British Airports Authority   Flag for Ambassadors   Badge in centre of flag
                                               and Ministers

THE QUEEN'S REPRESENTATIVES, DEPARTMENTAL AND PROVINCIAL FLAGS AND FLAGS OF CIVIC DEPARTMENTS

Her Majesty's Ambassadors and Ministers (and in their absence, Chargés-d'Affaires) fly the Union Flag with the Royal Arms on a white circular background, surrounded by a garland, in the centre. This flag is flown over our Embassies and Legations on certain prescribed days in the year, and it is also used when the holders are afloat. Two flags are used by the Consular Service. When ashore, Consuls-General, Consuls, Vice-Consuls etc. are distinguished by the Union Flag with, in the centre, a Royal Crown on a plain white circular background. When on duty afloat, the Blue Ensign is flown, with the full Royal Arms in colour in the fly and without any white background. The Consular Blue Ensign, being a personal distinguishing flag, must be flown at the bow, and not at the stern, which is the accepted position for the National Colours. No further flag is necessary, but if for some special reason it is desired to wear a flag at the stern, then this should be the Red Ensign.

The flags of the representatives of the Queen in Commonwealth countries and colonies, and where applicable the Heads of State of those countries, which have elected to become republics within the framework of the Commonwealth, are dealt with later.

A Lord Lieutenant of a county flies the Union Flag, charged in the centre with a golden sword, placed horizontally, point towards the fly, and with the Royal Crown above.

Lord Lieutenant of a county

Coast Guard Ensign

There exist in Great Britain a large number of civic bodies. Some, such as Her Majesty's Customs and other ministries, are official government departments; then there are a number of semi-official departments, such as Trinity House, and the nationalized industries. An increasing number of counties and towns have adopted coats of arms from which they have evolved flags. Finally, there are the purely civilian organizations, the charitable and the sporting. It is only possible within the scope of this work to give a selected number of examples of all these varied flags.

Vessels employed by the Ministry of Agriculture and Fisheries in fishery research work wear the Blue Ensign with, in the fly, a weird-looking fish in white, surmounted by a Royal Crown, the whole enclosed in a yellow circlet.

The badge of HM Customs is a plain portcullis and chains surmounted by a royal crown; this is placed in the fly of the Blue Ensign which is worn by Customs vessels and is flown ashore at Custom-houses.

A new flag for the Coast Guard was introduced on 28 October 1974. It consists of the Blue Ensign with the Coast Guard badge in the fly all in yellow, ensigned with a royal crown in proper colours, and may be seen flying at look-out stations all around the coast.

In medieval times the banner of the Cinque Ports played an important part in the maritime history of England. Its banner was divided vertically red and blue, charged with three gold lions and three silver ships' hulls 'dimidiated', making up the weird 'ship-lion' whose fore part was a lion and whose after part was a ship. The personal flag of the Lord Warden is now the only flag of this ancient organization. This has a very complicated design including dimidiated ships and lions, and representations of Dover Castle and other devices.

The Corporation of Trinity House, London, is one of those peculiar bodies that are found in few places other than Great Britain. It is the authority responsible for the lighthouses, lightships, and buoyage, or as the old term has it, the 'sea-marks', of

Lord Warden of the
Cinque Ports

Commissioners of
Northern Lights: Ensign

Trinity House: Master

Trinity House:
Deputy Master

Trinity House: Ensign

Trinity House: Jack

England and Wales. It is the chief pilotage authority of the United Kingdom. Although it provides a public service, and some of the funds to do this are collected by the Commissioners of Customs (Light Dues), it is a private and not a government organization, although working very closely with the government departments concerned—the Ministry of Defence (Navy) and the Department of Trade.

The arms of the Corporation, which are used in differing dimensions and with different embellishments in all the five flags of Trinity House, consist of a white field charged with the red Cross of St George, in each quarter of which there is a representation of a sailing-ship of the period of Queen Elizabeth I, in black, sailing on a blue heraldic sea towards the hoist. The flag of the Master (in modern times an office held by a prince of royal blood—at present HRH Prince Philip, the Duke of Edinburgh) consists of this device, proportions one by two, on which are superimposed in the centre the complete display of the armorial bearings of the Trinity House Guild or Fraternity, granted in 1573. On 10 June 1952 a flag for the Deputy Master, who is the executive head of the Corporation, was approved. This is similar to that of the Master, except that its proportions are two by three instead of one by two, and it is charged with the crest only, and not the whole achievement of Arms. It is flown from all ships, depôts, etc., when the Deputy Master is present, unless the Master is also there, in which case his flag is flown.

On important occasions the Royal Yacht is escorted by the *Patricia* or one other of the Corporation's vessels—an ancient privilege of which it is justly proud. In an Admiralty letter dated 21 June 1894, permission was granted 'for the Elder Brethren of Trinity House to fly the White Ensign of HM Fleet on board their Steam and Sailing Vessels on all occasions upon which Ships are dressed, and while escorting Her Majesty in company with Royal Yachts and Ships of War'.

The Ensign of the Corporation is the Red Ensign defaced with the badge of the Corporation in the fly.

All Trinity House vessels, tenders and lightships wear this Ensign; it is also flown at (1) all the Corporation's lighthouses, (2) Trinity House throughout the year, except on those occasions when special distinguishing flags are flown, (3) district depôts in addition to the Burgee (*see* below), always providing the necessary facilities exist for so doing.

The Trinity House Jack consists of the banner of the Corporation in the proportions five by four. Strictly, this is the flag of Trinity House and should only be called 'Jack' when flown as a diminutive at the jackstaff of vessels belonging to the Corporation.

The Burgee (or Cornet) consists of a red triangular flag charged with a rectangular panel similar to that on the Ensign. It is flown at (1) the masthead in tenders when they are in port; also when they are under way with the District Superintendent on board; (2) all district depôts.

Another distinctive suite of flags is that of the General Lighthouse Authority for Scotland and the Isle of Man, namely the Commissioners of Northern Lights. The Commission is constituted in accordance with an Act of Parliament passed in 1786. Their flag has a white field, one by two, with the Union Flag (1606 pattern) in the first quarter, and a representation of a lighthouse, in blue, in the fly. There appears to be no record of the date of origin; however, in the absence of the St Patrick's Cross in the Union, it seems probable that it was adopted before 1801.

It is flown at the main masthead when the Commissioners are embarked; in addition, they fly their 'Pennant' at the fore masthead. The title of the last mentioned is rather misleading in that this flag functions much in the same way as a house flag or yacht burgee. It is blue and bears a white cross, charged with a very narrow red cross; in the first quarter, the lighthouse is white. The ensign is the Blue Ensign defaced with the lighthouse in white; this is worn in tenders and flown on lighthouses and depôts on shore. It was adopted in 1855.

The City of London has a white flag with the red Cross of St George bearing in the canton the red sword of St Paul. These are the arms of the City and date back at least to 1381 and perhaps 1359.

The Lord Mayor of London flies from his car a white flag with a narrow cross of St George whose arms do not meet at the centre, over which is placed the full achievement of the Arms of the City of London.

The Arms of the Greater London Council differ from those of the previous London

City of London

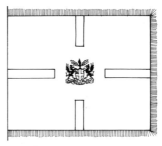

Lord Mayor of London

*New Forest District
Council: Civic Flag*

*Honourable Company
of Master Mariners*

National Maritime Museum

County Council in that the Cross of St George and the mural crown in the latter have
been replaced by a red chief bearing a Saxon crown in gold. The lower part of the shield
retains the wavy bars of blue and white representing the Thames. Many smaller towns
and districts have acquired new Coats of Arms, following the wholesale reorganization
of local government in recent years, and from these have developed a borough or council
flag. Some of these consist of plain field with the Coat of Arms in the centre, but others,
of which that of the New Forest District Council is typical, use their civic badges. This
particular flag is green with the civic badge, rather than the Arms, near the hoist, all in
yellow.

Banners of the Arms of the Livery Companies of London were once widely used, but
few are seen today. They formerly appeared in water pageants on the barges of the
various companies, and hence came to be known as 'Barge Flags'. A good example of a
banner that still is in use today is that of the Honourable Company of Master Mariners
which received the Royal Charter in 1930 and a grant of livery two years later. To
commemorate the occasion the Anglo-American Oil Company presented it with its first
flag.

A well-known flag to those who go to sea is that of the Royal National Lifeboat
Institution. The flag is primarily for use on shore. On lifeboats it is painted on the bows,
and these vessels use no other flags. Other vessels belonging to the RNLI fly a Red
Ensign with the flag as a rectangular badge in the fly, very similar to the Trinity House
Ensign.

The National Maritime Museum has been granted a new flag to replace that surrendered to the Admiralty Board (*see* p. 35). The new flag is very similar to that given
up, the only difference being that two of the anchors are now crowned by small ships.

'A1 at Lloyd's' is a phrase known to every merchant seaman, whether his ship is
registered with this famous marine insurance institution or not. Lloyd's is a source of

Royal National Lifeboat Institution

Port of London Authority: House Flag

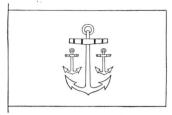

Admiralty Board Flag

*Archbishop of Canterbury
and Primate of All England*

information about ship movements, cargoes and everything to do with sea transport. It also keeps a register of yachts, and publishes the flags of yacht clubs and yacht owners as an appendix to this register. Its own flag is flown from its signal stations: this is the Blue Ensign with their badge in the fly (Lloyd's were once allowed to use the White Ensign). At sea boats carrying their agents fly their Burgee, which has a red cross fimbriated blue on a white field, with the badge in the canton.

Most of the Port Commissioners around the coasts of Britain have their own flags; many of them have warrants to wear the Blue Ensign on their harbour craft. The Port of London Authority has for its badge a sea-lion grasping a trident, all in yellow. The House Flag is the banner of St George bearing the Arms on a blue circular field within a red ring edged in yellow and inscribed with the name *Port of London Authority*. The Arms represent St Paul superimposed on the Tower of London, and holding his attribute, a sword. The ensign is the Blue Ensign with the badge in the fly in gold.

At the end of the First World War an Association open to all who had served in the armed forces was formed. After the Second World War the scope of the Association was extended to include personnel of the Merchant Navy, and a women's section was formed. This was the British Legion, now the Royal British Legion, and there is scarcely a town throughout the country without its 'Legion' branch. Each of these branches, and also each of the branches of the Women's Legion, has its standard, and there is also a national standard preserved at the headquarters.

This was introduced on 14 October 1973, after the addition of the word 'Royal' to the Legion's title. It is 3 ft 9 in long, and 3 ft wide and consists of three unequal horizontal stripes of blue, gold and blue. The Union Flag is in the canton, and in the centre of the fly is the badge in full colour. In the case of branch standards, the three stripes are equal, and have the branch title across the gold stripe. In their case the Union Flag occupies the full depth and half the length of the top blue stripe.

And last, but by no means least—the Church of England. For many years there was controversy as to the proper flag to hoist over a church. A common practice was to hoist the flag of St George. A pronouncement by the Earl Marshal on 11 February 1938 settled this by laying down that as far as any church within the Provinces of Canterbury and York is concerned, the Cross of St George may be flown with, in the first quarter, the arms of the See in which the particular church is ecclesiastically situated. Descriptions of these arms will be found in *Crockford's Clerical Directory*. The two Archbishops and all Bishops of the Dioceses of the Church of England are entitled to fly banners of the Arms of the diocese. These may appear on the cathedral or be used as car-flags, and are usually squarish. The example shown is that of the Archbishop of Canterbury. Cathedrals may also have flags which are not those of the See, but of the Cathedral itself.

[3] The Commonwealth and Dependencies of the United Kingdom

The British Commonwealth, which grew out of the British Empire, and which is now simply called the Commonwealth, is composed of a number of independent countries and a number of 'Dependencies', as the former colonies are now known.

Of the thirty-six independent countries, seventeen recognize the Queen as Head of State and the other nineteen are republics. Both groups, however, recognize Her Majesty as Head of the Commonwealth. The representatives of the Commonwealth nations in the United Kingdom are known as High Commissioners, distinguishing them from the Ambassadors of other nations. Those states that recognize the Queen as their head have a special standard for her use in that country; her representatives in those countries, the Governor Generals, also have a special flag, the design of which is common to all of them. The flag is blue with the Royal Crest of the lion and crown in full colour in the centre, and the name of the country on a scroll beneath it. The Presidents of those countries that are republics have standards of varying design.

The National Flags of the independent countries display great diversity of design and only three of them resemble in any way the flags of the United Kingdom. Because of this and because in all but the minor points mentioned above they are completely independent, being responsible for the conduct of their own affairs, both internal and external, the description of their flags will be given in the chapter that deals with the continent in which they are situated.

Although the independent countries of the Commonwealth have no formal ties with the United Kingdom and the Dependencies they do have close and special relations, and this factor is best illustrated by the Commonwealth Games. These are athletic contests between all the members of the Commonwealth which take place every four years, alternating with the international Olympic Games which they resemble in miniature; and like the Olympics the Commonwealth Games have their own special flag which is flown at the arena of the contests. This flag has a white field with red, white and blue border with, in the centre, the badge of the Games.

As stated above there remain a number of dependencies for whose administration the United Kingdom is in some measure responsible. They differ considerably—some are associated states, some protected states and some colonies, but broadly speaking it can be said that all are responsible for their own internal government, while the United Kingdom is responsible for their external relations and foreign policy.

Strictly speaking the Union Flag of the United Kingdom is the flag of a colony, but nearly all have and use as their National Flag a Blue (and in one case a Red) Ensign,

Commonwealth Games

defaced with the badge of the colony which is generally placed on a plain white disc. The Governor, or Lieutenant-Governor, flies the Union Flag, with the distinctive badge of the colony or dependency on a disc surrounded by a garland of laurel, complete with berries, superimposed on the centre of the St George's Cross.

Although some retain their old 'colonial flag' most of the associated states and protectorates have flags of an individual design. All these flags, and those of the colonies, will be described, but before doing this there are two special 'states', part of the British Isles and closely linked to Great Britain, and yet with a large degree of independence, namely the Channel Islands, and the Isle of Man, which should be dealt with.

The flag of the **Isle of Man** is red with the 'three legs of Man' in the centre in white with gold embellishments. How this device came to the Isle of Man is something of a mystery, but it is also found in a slightly different form in Sicily and may have been brought to both places by the Vikings. In the past some versions have shown the legs running in an anti-clockwise direction. However, since 1968 the more ancient clockwise position has been restored. Moreover the Union Jack has been replaced by the Manx flag on public buildings, and on all official occasions. On 18 September 1971 the Manx Red Ensign was restored for use by all ships registered in the Isle of Man. This is the British Red Ensign with the Legs of Man in the fly. The flag of the Lieutenant-Governor is the Union Flag with the Arms of the island in the centre within a laurel garland. This is flown from Government House when he is in residence.

Isle of Man: National Flag

Isle of Man: Merchant Flag

The Channel Islands consist of two principal authorities, Jersey and Guernsey. Guernsey has a number of dependent islands, including Alderney and Sark which each have flags of their own for use on land. The flag of **Jersey** is white with a red diagonal cross. The flag has been in use for a considerable period, and some claim it to be one

Arms of Jersey   *Flag of Jersey*

represented on eighteenth-century flag-charts. It is flown on all official occasions on
public buildings as well as on business establishments, and the Bailiff flies a diminutive
version from his car. During the German occupation the then Bailiff suggested the use of
the flag for ships sent from the island to France for civilian purposes, and this and the flag
of Guernsey were used in these circumstances, and thus kept flying. The Lieutenant-
Governor flies the Union flag with the shield of Arms in the centre within the usual
garland. The Arms of Jersey are the same as those of England, i.e. red with three lions
passant guardant in gold. The use of these, which dates back to Edward I, was confirmed
by Edward VII in 1907.

Arms of Guernsey   *Flag of Guernsey*

The flag of **Guernsey** is the same as that of England, a red cross on white, and
its use in the island is attested as far back as 1406. The flag was sanctioned by Edward VII,
and later by George V in December 1935. Like that of Jersey it was used by local
shipping during the German occupation in the Second World War. The flag of the
Lieutenant-Governor follows the same pattern as that of Jersey, except that the shield
has a sprig of leaves over it. This feature is derived from the seal granted by Edward I in
1297. Like Jersey, Guernsey and its dependencies have no distinctive flag for use at sea
other than the Red Ensign.

The island of **Alderney,** which is one of these dependencies, has a local flag which is
the same as that of Guernsey and of England, but with a green disc charged with a gold
lion holding a sprig of leaves, and with gold curlicues around the disc. All these features

were taken from the seal adopted in 1745. The flag was approved by Edward VII in 1906, for use on land only.

The flag of **Sark,** or rather of its Seigneur, is also derived from its seal, which bears two lions passant guardant only, the Arms of Normandy and reputedly the original Arms of William the Conqueror. The first quarter of the flag is red, merging into the red of the Cross of St George. The lions are spread out over the whole of this enlarged quarter. A letter from the late Dame of Sark, Sybil Hathaway, DBE, confirms that a flag of this pattern has been in use on the island for the last two hundred years.

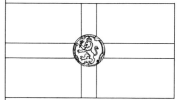

Flag of Alderney

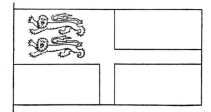

Flag of Sark

In recent years there have been considerable changes in the form of government amongst the islands of the West Indies. Jamaica, Trinidad and Tobago, the Bahamas, Barbados and Grenada have become independent, the other islands have become 'States in Association' with the United Kingdom, whilst others have retained their former status. The 'Associate States' are Antigua, Dominica, St Kitts, St Lucia, and St Vincent. These all have full internal self-government, the right to determine their own date for independence, and their own Arms and flags. All except St Vincent and Dominica adopted quite new flags on achieving Associate Statehood.

The new flag of **Antigua** was adopted on 27 February 1967, and was designed by a local art teacher, Reginald Samuel, who entered the winning design in a special competition. The design represents the dawn of a new era for the inhabitants, rising over a sea of blue and white, within the red field symbolizing the dynamism of the people. The Governor uses the Union Jack with the Arms in the centre, according to the usual pattern. The new Arms of Antigua are related to the flag, and show the sun on a black field over blue and white wavy lines. At the base of the shield is a green mound with a stone tower, standing for the sugar-mills of former times. The supporters are two deer representing the island game reserve of Barbuda, holding plants of sugar cane and sea-island cotton. The crest is a pineapple, and the motto is *Each Endeavouring, All Achieving.*

Flag of Antigua

Flag of St Kitts

The flag of **Dominica** has remained unchanged following Associate Statehood on 1 March 1967. This flag came into use on 9 November 1965, and consists of the Blue Ensign with the whole Arms in the fly. The Arms were adopted on 21 July 1961, and consist of a shield divided quarterly by a cross countercharged in yellow and blue. In the first quarter is a coconut tree on yellow; in the second a toad (a Dominican *crapaud*); in the third a Carib canoe, and in the fourth a banana tree. The supporters are two Siserou parrots and the crest is a British lion on a rocky mount. The motto is in the local dialect and may be translated 'After the Good Lord we love the Soil'. The Arms also appear in the centre of the Governor's flag. Like Antigua Dominica has no special flag for use at sea.

St Kitts, or St Christopher-Nevis-Anguilla as it is officially known, was established as an Associate State on 27 February 1967 and uses the flag adopted on that date. This

Arms of Antigua   *Arms of Dominica*   *Arms of St Kitts*

consists of three vertical stripes of the colours of green, yellow and blue, at that time common to several West Indian islands. In the centre is a black palm tree, often omitted in the flag for popular use.

St Kitts also adopted a new Coat of Arms in 1967. This is white with a red chevron, two poinciana flowers, and a schooner. On a blue chief is the head of a Carib between a *fleur-de-lys* and an English rose. The supporters are two pelicans, holding a cocoa palm and a sugar cane, and the crest is a torch held up by a white and a brown arm. The motto is *Unity in Trinity*. The trinity of the island was however upset on 12 July 1967 by the secession of Anguilla, which is referred to separately below.

St Lucia became an Associate State on 1 March 1967. Its flag may be taken to represent the Pitons, the volcanic peaks of the island, rising from the golden sands in the midst of

Flag of St Lucia   *St Vincent: Ensign Badge*

the azure sea. The Arms are based on those granted in 1939, with the colours reversed so that they are now black on gold, and crest and supporters and motto added. The motto is *The Land, The People, The Light*.

St Vincent became an Associate State on 27 October 1969. A flag in the colours of green, yellow and blue with a white diamond in the centre, bordered in blue and charged with a sprig of leaves, was granted in 1967 but was never brought into use. Instead St Vincent has retained the British Blue Ensign with the circular flag badge in the fly. The badge is based on the Arms, and shows two figures representing Peace and Justice attending an altar.

OTHER DEPENDENCIES

Anguilla, as mentioned above, seceded from St Kitts in 1967, and for a long time her future was uncertain, until she reverted to the status of a British colony on 10 February 1976. During this period the islanders used a handsome flag designed by Martin Oberman. The turquoise strip represents the sea, and three dolphins (also found in the previous Arms of St Kitts) represent friendship, wisdom and strength. This flag is still in use locally, but the official flag is the Union Jack, and at sea the Red Ensign.

Bermuda is unusual among British colonies in that she uses the Red Ensign as an official flag. This has the Arms in the centre of the fly. The Arms consist of a white shield charged with a red lion affronté on a green mound, and supporting a scrolled shield upon which is represented the wreck of the *Sea Venture*, which in 1609 under the command of Admiral Sir George Somers came to grief on the Sea Venture Flat.

The Governor's flag is the Union Jack with the Arms in the centre, and the government flag for use at sea is the Blue Ensign with the Arms in the fly.

The **British Virgin Islands** follow the usual practice of employing the Blue Ensign as an official flag, with the shield from the Arms in the fly. The shield shows the 'wise virgin' with her lamp, and eleven other lamps on a green field. There is also a motto: *Vigilate* ('Be Watchful'). These Arms were confirmed on 15 November 1960.

The **Cayman Islands** also have their Arms on a Blue Ensign, this time within a white disc. The islands were originally a dependency of Jamaica, but when the latter became independent in 1962 they became British colonies. A Coat of Arms was granted on 14 May 1958, and it is this which appears on the Blue Ensign. The Arms show three green stars edged in gold on blue and white wavy lines, representing the three main islands, and

Flag of Anguilla

Bermuda : Ensign badge

British Virgin Islands: *Cayman Islands: Arms*   *Montserrat: Ensign badge*
    Ensign badge

a red chief with a Lion of England. The crest is a turtle and a pineapple, and the motto is
He Hath Founded it Upon the Seas.

Montserrat follows the same pattern as the other colonies, in placing the shield of
Arms in the fly of the Blue Ensign. The shield dates back to at least 1909 but was only
brought into use on the Blue Ensign when the Windward Islands colony was dissolved in
1960.

Like the Cayman Islands, the **Turks and Caicos Islands** were originally
dependencies of Jamaica, but are now dependencies of the United Kingdom. A new Coat
of Arms was adopted on 28 September 1965, and consists of a yellow shield charged with
a Queen conch shell, a spiny lobster, and a Turk's Head cactus. The crest is a pelican and
two sisal plants, and the supporters are two flamingoes. The shield only from the Arms
appears in the Blue Ensign.

Belize was known officially as British Honduras until 1 June 1973. Its Coat of Arms
dates from the mid nineteenth century, and portrays the logging industry. The shield is
divided into three parts, two of which illustrate the tools of the trade, and the lower a ship
at sea. In the Arms as granted in 1907 a small Union Jack appeared in the canton, but this
has now been omitted and other alterations made to the Arms. The Arms now appear in
full colour on a white disc within a green garland in the centre of a blue flag. This was
introduced in 1967 and is for local use on land only. The flag for use at sea is the Blue
Ensign charged with the flag badge in the fly. This is also divided into three parts, one of
which has the Union Jack, another the logging tools, and the third the sailing ship. This
badge, rather than the Arms, also appears in the centre of the Governor's flag.

A Coat of Arms was granted to the **Falkland Islands** on 29 September 1948. In chief
of the shield is a ram on a green mound of tussac grass, and in base is a heraldic ship
representing the *Desire* on a sea of blue and white wavy lines. On a scroll beneath is the
motto *Desire the Right*. The whole arms is used as a badge on the Blue Ensign, within a
white disc, and likewise on the flag of the Governor. The *Desire* was the vessel of John
Davies who discovered the islands in 1592.

Part of the former Falkland Islands Dependencies was formed into the **British
Antarctic Territory** on 3 March 1962. The Falkland Islands Dependencies had previously been granted a Coat of Arms on 11 March 1952, and these Arms were taken as the
basis for those of the new Territory: a helmet, mantling, and the crest of a sailing ship
were added. Survey vessels of the Natural Environment Research Council wear a Blue

Turks and Caicos Islands:
Arms

Belize: Ensign badge

Falkland Islands: Arms

Ensign with the shield only from the Arms in the fly. The shield is white with blue wavy lines in the chief, and a red triangle over all, charged with a gold flaming torch.

St Helena uses the Blue Ensign with its flag badge in the fly without a white disc. The badge shows the rocky coast of the island, with a ship of the East India Company at anchor. This flag is also used for the islands of **Tristan da Cunha** and **Ascension Island,** which are dependencies of St Helena.

Gibraltar has a flag-badge for use on the Blue Ensign, consisting of a red shield with a castle with a gold key depending from its gate. Beneath the shield is a scroll with the motto *Montis Insignia Calpe* ('The Sign of Mount Calpe'). It is hardly necessary to remark that the key symbolizes the Rock as the key to the Mediterranean. There is also a local flag for use on land, which is in effect a banner of the actual Coat of Arms. This is white with the lower third red. On the white part is the triple-towered castle in red, and the gold key hanging down into the red strip.

British Antarctic
Territory: Arms

St Helena: Ensign badge

Gibraltar: Ensign badge

When the Federation of Malaysia was formed in 1963 **Brunei** elected to remain outside it as a dependency of the United Kingdom. The Sultanate has a flag, first adopted in 1906. The field is yellow, representing the Sultan, and diagonally across it with its top edge a little below the top hoist corner and its bottom edge a little above the lower fly corner, is a band divided white over black, representing the people and the government, with the white a little broader than the black. In 1959 the State Arms were added. These consist of a device like a palm tree with wings at the top, and above this a parasol with a flag; this is contained within the horns of an upturned crescent, inscribed in yellow Arabic

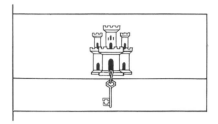

Flag of Gibraltar   Brunei: State Flag

characters with the legend 'The Good Shall Prosper Under God's Guidance'. Beneath this is a scroll with the words 'Brunei City of Peace', and on either side is an upraised arm. The flag for popular use is without the Arms. The British High Commissioner uses a Union Flag with the letters HCB beneath a crown on a white disc in the centre.

The flag of **Hong Kong** is the Blue Ensign with the Arms of the colony on a white disc in the fly. The Arms were granted on 21 January 1959 and show two junks on a sea of blue and white wavy lines, and on a chief 'embattled' a naval crown in gold. The supporters are a British lion and a Chinese dragon and the crest is a further lion holding a pearl.

Britain is responsible in varying degrees for a number of island groups in the Pacific Ocean. One of these, the Solomon Islands, is fully self-governing and moving towards independence, and another, the New Hebrides, is administered as an Anglo-French condominium. The Gilbert and Ellice Islands group recently divided, with the Ellice Islands forming the new colony of Tuvalu. A High Commissioner for the Western Pacific has his headquarters at Honiara in the Solomon Islands and oversees the government of the Solomon Islands, the Gilbert Islands, Tuvalu, the New Hebrides, Pitcairn, and other smaller islands. He is entitled to the use of the Union Flag and the Blue Ensign, in each of which his badge appears on a white disc. It consists of the letters WPHC beneath a crown.

Hong Kong: Ensign badge   Western Pacific   Solomon Islands:
                                 High Commissioner   Ensign badge

The word 'British' was dropped from the title of the **Solomon Islands** in July 1975, and full internal self-government was established on 2 January 1976. The territory still continues to use the British Blue Ensign, with the shield from the Arms on a white disc in the fly. The present Coat of Arms was granted on 24 September 1956, and consists of a shield divided quarterly blue and white with a red chief. In the first quarter is a Sandfordi eagle perched on a branch; in the second a turtle; in the third a Melanesian dancing shield behind which is a trophy of local weapons; and in the fourth two frigate birds. On the red chief is a lion passant guardant in gold.

The **Gilbert Islands** consist of the Gilbert Islands proper, Ocean Island, The Phoenix Islands, The Line Islands, Starbuck Island, Malden Island, Flint Island, Caroline Island, and Vostock Island. The flag is the British Blue Ensign with the shield from the Coat of Arms in the fly, not on a white disc. The shield shows the sun rising over a sea of blue and white wavy lines against a red sky with a gold frigate bird in chief. The Arms also contain a scroll with the motto 'Fear God and Honour the King' in Gilbertese and Ellice. This does not appear on the flag. The Arms were granted on 1 May 1937.

Tuvalu has adopted new Arms which have received Royal approval. They consist of a representation of a *maneapa*, the traditional meeting house. The English translation of the motto is 'Tuvalu for God'. The flag is the traditional Blue Ensign of Great Britain with the whole achievement of the Arms of Tuvalu, but without the motto, set in a white circle in the fly.

The **New Hebrides** group is ruled jointly by British and French Resident Commissioners, and the Union Jack and the French Tricolour are flown side by side, although the islands are moving towards self-government. At sea the British Blue Ensign is used with a badge on a white disc in the fly consisting of a crown with the words New Hebrides around it. This is also used on the Union Flag by the British High Commissioner. The Resident Commissioner has a similar badge with the letters BR beneath a crown. It is not known what flag, if any, is used by the French administrators.

Pitcairn has no distinctive flag for use on land or at sea.

Gilbert Islands:
Ensign badge

Tuvalu: Arms

New Hebrides: Ensign badge

[4] North America

Canada's first truly distinctive National Flag was adopted by a Royal Proclamation on 15 February 1965, thus concluding a controversy which had raged for many years.

The new flag is technically described as a red flag containing a white square the width of the flag bearing in its centre a single red maple leaf, the whole flag being in the proportions of one to two. The square in the centre is sometimes called in heraldry a 'Canadian pale'. The Canadian Parliament resolved on 18 December 1964 that the Union Jack, to be known henceforth as the Royal Union Flag, would continue as a symbol of Canada's membership of the Commonwealth of Nations and of her allegiance to the Crown, and would be flown on the Queen's birthday, on the anniversary of the Statute of Westminster (11 December) and on Royal visits. It would also continue to be flown side by side with the Canadian flag at the National War Memorial and in connection with the anniversaries of events in which Canadian forces took part along with other Commonwealth forces. In fact a good many people in Canada use the flag frequently to express their feeling of a special relationship with Britain.

Prior to 1965 the only flag Canada had for use on land and at sea was the British Red Ensign with the shield from the Coat of Arms in the fly. Its use by Canadian merchant ships was approved by Admiralty Warrant in 1892, although it should be noted that the pattern of the shield in the Arms and in the flag has altered somewhat over the years. During the Second World War the flag was used on Canadian naval vessels in conjunction with the British White Ensign, and on 5 September 1945 it was approved for use by the government, and was hoisted as the flag of Canada at the United Nations and other international occasions.

The first Arms of Canada were granted on 26 May 1868, soon after the Federation had come into existence, and combined the emblems of the four provinces. When further provinces were admitted it became impossible to include them all in the shield, and so a completely new design was established on 21 November 1921, in which the countries of origin of the people of Canada were expressed by the Lions of England, the Red Lion of Scotland, the Harp of Ireland and the Lilies of France. In base was the sprig of maple leaves representing Canada itself. The colour of these was changed from green to red in 1957, in accordance with the livery colours determined by the grant of 1921. These in turn gave rise to the colours of the new flag, although there was an attempt in 1964 to introduce a flag which had blue vertical bands on either side of the maple leaf. A Personal Flag for the use of the Queen in Canada was introduced on 15 August 1962. It is a banner of the Arms, with the Queen's device in the centre. This is a blue disc within a floral chaplet, bearing the Royal Cypher, all in gold.

The Governor General uses the usual blue flag. This is a pattern introduced in 1931,

Canada: National and Merchant Flag and Ensign

Canada: Arms

Queen's Personal Flag for Canada

and is blue with the Royal Crest in the centre, and beneath it a gold scroll with the name of the country thereon. The Lieutenant-Governors of nine of the provinces use the Union Flag with the flag-badge of the province in the centre within a garland. The exceptions to this practice are the Lieutenant-Governor of British Columbia, who uses a light blue flag with the whole Arms of the Province in the centre and the Lieutenant Governor of Quebec who uses a similar flag.

Prior to the adoption of the new National Flag Canadian naval vessels flew the British White Ensign, with the Blue Ensign of Canada (i.e. with the shield in the fly) as a Jack. After 1965 the National Flag was used as Ensign and Jack, but in 1969 the three branches of the armed forces were combined, and a flag known as the Canadian Armed Forces Ensign was adopted. This had been introduced in January 1968 as a distinctive flag for the Governor-General as Commander in Chief, and is white with the combined services emblem in the fly, and the National Flag in the canton. The combined services emblem itself had been approved by the Queen in August 1967, and is very similar to that of the United Kingdom, although in this case there are ten red maple leaves around, for the ten provinces, the whole flag being very similar to that of the Royal Canadian Sea Cadets approved as far back as 11 June 1953. In 1969 a Jack was introduced for use on naval vessels, very similar to this, but with only an anchor, eagle and naval crown as a badge in the fly. The Armed Forces Ensign is now the flag of the Chief of Defence Staff and is flown in conjunction with the National Flag at all defence establishments.

The distinguishing flags of the senior officers are now common to all three services so that, for example, the flag of a Major-General also serves as that of the former rank of Rear-Admiral, i.e. a white swallow-tailed flag with the National Flag in the canton and a badge in the fly.

A special Jack for Coast Guard vessels is like that used before the new National Flag was introduced. It is white with the maple leaf in the centre of the two-thirds nearest the hoist, and a blue fly with two gold dolphins facing in opposite directions.

New Regimental Colours, consisting of the National Flag with a device in the centre of the maple leaf, have been introduced for the army section of the combined defence forces. The illustration shows the Queen's Colour of the Royal Canadian Regiment, and shows that the flag is more nearly square than the National Flag, with a gold fringe and cords and tassels of the type of British Regimental Colours.

The Armed Forces Ensign is also used by the Air Force in conjunction with the National Flag.

A distinctive flag for the Anglican Church of Canada was adopted in 1955. This is the Cross of St George with green maple leaf in each white quarter. The arms of a diocese may be placed in the centre of the cross. The General Synod of the Church also has a flag, a banner of its Arms, which are similar to the Church flag but with a bible and mitre. There is also a flag for the Presbyterian Church of Canada, which betrays its Scottish origins by being a Cross of St Andrew with a representation of the 'burning bush' in green, gold and red.

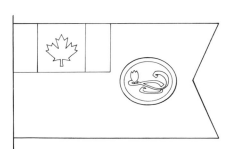

Canada: Armed Forces Ensign

Canada: Naval Jack

Canada: Flag of Major-
General or Rear-Admiral

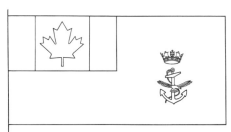

Queen's Colour, the
Royal Canadian Regiment

Canada is a federation of ten provinces, each of which has a considerable degree of autonomy. Each has in recent years made special provision for a provincial flag, with the exception of Newfoundland, which has so far retained the Union Flag, although it has a local flag tradition. In addition there are two Territories administered by the central government. These also have Arms and flags of their own.

Alberta has Arms granted by Royal Warrant on 30 May 1907. The upper part of the shield is white with a Cross of St George. The lower part is a wheat-field with a landscape

Alberta

British Columbia

of prairie fields and mountains in the distance. The flag of the province was authorized in 1967, known officially as the Banner. This is ultramarine blue with the shield of Arms in the centre. The proportions are one by two.

The Arms of **British Columbia** were granted on 31 March 1906 as a shield only, but a crest, supporters and motto have become established by local usage. The shield has the Union Jack in chief with a gold crown in the centre, and beneath this is a pattern of blue and white lines charged with a setting sun. This refers to the motto *Splendor Sine Occasu* ('Splendour that Never Sets') and also to the province's geographical position. The crest is the Royal Crest, and the supporters are a wapiti and a mountain sheep. A flag which is a banner of the Arms was authorized on 20 June 1960. It is in the proportions three by five, which results in the ungainly stretching of the Union Flag.

Manitoba has a shield of Arms granted on 10 May 1905. This also has a Cross of St George in chief. In base is a representation of a buffalo standing on a rock. The provincial flag was introduced on 12 May 1966, and consists of the British Red Ensign (although not referred to as such), with the shield in the centre of the fly.

New Brunswick has a shield of arms dating from 26 May 1868, consisting of a yellow field with a heraldic ship on a heraldic sea, and a red chief with a lion passant guardant. The provincial flag is a banner of the Arms, in the proportions two by three, thus extending the charges unduly. This was introduced on 24 February 1965.

The official flag of **Newfoundland and Labrador** is still the Union Jack, which was adopted by the then independent Dominion in 1931. Whilst it was a Dominion Newfoundland also had a distinctive Red and Blue Ensign, of the British pattern with the flag-badge in the fly. This was a disc bearing a representation of Mercury, the god of commerce, and Britannia, with a fisherman kneeling and offering the fruits of the sea, referred to in the motto *Haec Tibi Dona Fero* ('I bring you these gifts'). These flags and their predecessors became obsolete when Newfoundland joined the Canadian federation

Manitoba

New Brunswick

Newfoundland: Arms

North-West Territories

on 18 February 1949, but were restored by legislation in 1952 and only finally went out of use when the new National Flag was introduced. It seems that for many years the original Arms of Newfoundland, granted on 1 January 1637 and amongst the oldest in the New World, were forgotten, and they were only restored to common use in 1927.

The Arms consist of a red shield with a white cross, and in the first and fourth quarters a lion passant guardant, in the second and third a unicorn. The crest is a moose, and the supporters two 'savages of the clime armed and apparelled according to their guise when they go to war'. The motto is *Quaerite Prime Regnum Dei* ('Seek Ye First the Kingdom of God'). Newfoundland also has an unofficial provincial flag, of three vertical stripes of pink, white and green, known as the 'Native Flag'. This has been in local use for well over a hundred years, and represents the unity of the Irish, Scots, and English settlers.

The Arms of the **North-West Territories** were granted on 24 February 1956 and are divided diagonally by a wavy line. The sinister side is red with the mask of an arctic fox, and the dexter side green with golden billets: this represents the forests and the mineral wealth. The polar ice and the North-West Passage are represented by the indented chief with wavy blue lines across it. The crest is a compass rose symbolic of the Magnetic Pole, flanked by two narwhals. The crest does not appear on the flag, which has the same proportions as the Canadian National Flag, with blue vertical stripes, and the shield in generous proportions in the centre. It was officially introduced on 31 January 1969.

Nova Scotia

Ontario

Nova Scotia's flag, as befits her origins, consists of the blue St Andrew's Cross on a white field with an escutcheon of the Arms of Scotland in the centre. The flag is a banner of the Arms of the province, in the proportions of three by four. The Arms were originally granted by King James I and VI on 28 May 1625, making them the oldest in the English-speaking New World; they are also the badge of Baronets of Nova Scotia. When the Arms of Canada were formed in 1868 their existence was overlooked, and a new shield was devised to represent the province, consisting of a field of yellow with

Prince Edward Island   *Quebec*   *Quebec: Arms*

three thistles, and a blue wavy fess with a salmon. This remained as a quartering of the Canadian shield until 1921, and as the provincial Arms until 19 January 1929 when the ancient Arms were re-granted. The flag derived from them has been in use for several decades, but has never been specifically authorized for public use.

The Arms of **Ontario** are a green shield with a red Cross of St George in a white chief and in base a sprig of maple leaves in gold. The crest is a bear, and the supporters are a moose and a Canadian deer. The motto is *Ut Incepit Fidelis Sic Permanet* ('Loyal in the Beginning, so it Remained'). These were granted on 26 May 1868. The flag was established on 14 April 1965, and is basically the British Red Ensign with the shield in the fly.

The Arms of **Prince Edward Island** consist of a white shield bearing a green mound on which are an oak tree and three saplings, with a red chief charged with a Lion of England. The motto is *Parva Sub Ingenti* ('The Small under the Protection of the Great'). The provincial flag is a banner of these arms in the proportions two by three, and with a border of red and white pieces around three sides. This again has the effect of drawing out the lion to an exaggerated length. The flag was introduced on 24 March 1964.

The Arms of **Quebec** were introduced on 9 December 1939, replacing an earlier version. The new shield is of three parts: blue at the top with three gold lilies for France; red in the centre with a gold lion for England; and yellow at the bottom with a sprig of maple leaves in green for Canada. The motto is *Je Me Souviens* ('I Remember'), and the crest is a royal crown. The flag of Quebec is known as the *fleurdelisé* flag, and has been the official flag of the Province since 21 January 1948. Its design recalls the emblems of eighteenth century France—the white cross on blue was the general design of the French civil ensign, and the lilies are of course inevitably associated with that country, although they have always been gold in French usage. This design is thought to be derived from the flag of French-Canadian society, known as the *Drapeau du Sacré-Coeur* (Sacred Heart flag) adopted in the mid-nineteenth century. The *fleurdelisé* is perhaps the most widely used of all Canadian provincial flags.

Saskatchewan adopted a new provincial flag on 22 September 1969, based on the design of the one used to celebrate the sixtieth anniversary of the province. The latter was red over green with a large ear of wheat in the hoist and the shield of arms in the upper fly, and was designed for a competition. The present design was also the result of a competition, of 4000 entries. It is green over gold with the shield in the upper hoist and a prairie lily in the fly. The prairie lily was adopted as the plant badge of Saskatchewan in 1941. The Arms consist of a shield with a gold chief with a red lion passant guardant and a green field with three gold wheatsheaves. These were granted on 25 August 1906.

Saskatchewan   *Yukon Territory*

The Arms of the **Yukon** were granted in February 1956 and consist of a shield and a crest, with two sprays of fireweed beneath them. The shield represents the gold-bearing mountains of the country with the Yukon river between them; the Cross of St George represents the early English explorers, and the roundel of *vair* stands for the fur trade. The crest is a husky sledge-dog on a mound of snow. The fireweed is the plant badge of the territory, adopted in 1957. The flag was introduced on 1 March 1968, and has a wide central white panel like the National Flag, although only one and a half times the length of the outer strips, and is charged with the whole arms in full colour. The flanking strips are green at the hoist and blue at the fly. The whole flag has the proportions one by two.

The belief that the Raven Flag of the Vikings (*see* p. 11) was the first flag to fly in what is now the **United States of America** can only be regarded as a pleasing legend which is not supported by any documentary evidence, at any rate so far as the flag is concerned.

The first voyage of Columbus in 1492 was made possible by King Ferdinand and Queen Isabella of the Kingdoms of Aragon and Castile. He discovered islands in the West Indies and took possession of one of them, San Salvador, in the name of his sovereigns on 12 October of that year. Two flags were carried ashore for the ceremony: the Royal Banner displaying the Arms of Castile and Leon quartered, and a special white one, having a swallow-tailed fly, charged with a Latin Cross in green, with the letters 'F' and 'Y' (for Fernando and Ysabel) in gold on either side of the lower portion of the vertical limb, each surmounted by a golden crown. These are generally recognized as being the first European flags in America.

The first authenticated European flags raised on the mainland proper were those hoisted by John Cabot in 1497. They are described as the banners of England and St Mark. The banner of England was probably the Royal Standard of Henry VII (*see* p. 26).

Ponce de Leon landed in Florida in 1512, and planted the Castile-Leon flag. Twelve years later Verrazano the Florentine raised the lilies of France on behalf of King Francis I in North America. They were again hoisted in 1534; this time by the French explorer, Jacques Cartier, when he landed and claimed that portion of land which later became Quebec.

In 1609 Hudson arrived in the *Half Moon* at New Amsterdam (later to be called New York) wearing the flag of the Dutch East India Company, a horizontal tricolour, orange

Flag of Columbus　　　　　　*New England*　　　　　*The 'Bedford Flag'*

(on top), white, and light blue with the letters 'VOC', in black, on the white stripe, these being the initials of the Vereenigde Oost-Indische Compagnie (*see* p. 80).

In 1621 these letters were replaced by the monogram of the Dutch West India Company—'GWC'—(Geoctroyeerde West-Indische Compagnie), the 'G' being on the left outer bar of the 'W', and the 'C' on the right.

The Pilgrim Fathers landed on Plymouth beach, now in Massachusetts, on Christmas Day 1620. The famous *Mayflower* in which they sailed wore the British Union Flag (1606–1801 pattern) at the main, and the red Cross of St George on a white field, at the fore.

As Charles I, on 5 May 1634, had restricted the use of the Union Flag to the Royal Navy, the National Flags of England and Scotland, those of St George and St Andrew respectively were used for public departments and the merchant services; and when in 1643 the colonies of Plymouth, Massachusetts Bay and New Haven became the United Colonies of New England they adopted as their flag the Red Ensign of Britain as it was then, with the addition of a green pine tree in the first quarter of St George's Cross in the canton. Many old flag books show the New England flag as the Blue Ensign, but it is now generally agreed this is not correct, and that the red was the first flag. Although New England came into being in 1643 the flag described above does not appear to have come into general use until 1686. By the year 1707 many of the colonies were using flags of their own; these were probably the forerunners of the State Flags of the present time.

The first Congress met at New York in October 1765, and the organized opposition to the Stamp Act gained such force that in 1766 the Act was repealed. But the issue could not be too long delayed, and in December 1773 came the Boston Tea Party.

The Boston Tea Party is popularly supposed to have been the event that finally triggered off the War of Independence, but in fact it was not until fourteen months after the attack on the East India Company's ships in Boston Harbour, by a party of American Colonials, when the cargoes of tea were thrown overboard, that the first shots of the war were fired. This occurred at the engagement at Lexington on 19 April 1775. Later that day at Concord the colonials carried a banner that was probably made in the 1600s and that had originally served as the colours of a locally-raised troop of cavalry. Its design, an arm carrying a sword, emerging from a cloud, was one that was very popular throughout Europe during the seventeenth century. The original Bedford Flag, as it is called, is now preserved at Bedford, Massachusetts.

Lexington was quickly followed in June by the Battle of Bunker Hill, where the British, although theoretically the victors, found themselves besieged in Boston. A few miles from Boston, at Cambridge, Washington set up his headquarters and began to raise and train the new American Army. And it was here, on Prospect Hill, that the first flag of the emerging country which was to become the United States of America was hoisted. Modern American writers have given this flag many names, of which the most popular is the 'Continental Colors'. They have also advanced as many theories as to the origins and design of this flag. It is, however, worthy of note that a letter, written by an American (and now in the Library of the India Office), suggests that the first flag flown at Cambridge may well have been taken from an East India Company ship during the 'tea-party'. While this must remain a speculation, it is worth noting that this flag would certainly have been familiar to the Americans since it was not only flown by the east-coast trading posts and factories of the company but also, on occasions, by their own ships.

Even before the outbreak of the war, America was a land of many flags, and the war when it came caused still further proliferation. Massachusetts had its tree, inherited from the flag of New England, while the white flag of Rhode Island with its blue anchor of hope remains the State flag today. Many unusual designs appeared, the most popular device being a snake, symbolizing in some cases the native American—not to be trodden on with impunity—and in others the enemy.

The 'Continental Colors'

The first 'Stars and Stripes'

The 'Bennington Flag'

The 'Star Spangled Banner'

During the period 1776–95 merchant ships, with which are included privateers, wore an ensign consisting of thirteen stripes with no Union Flag or other device in the upper canton. There are a number of old prints showing such ships in the National Maritime Museum at Greenwich, and the interesting thing is that while in the majority the ensign is shown as being of red and white stripes, there are quite a few where the stripes are red, white and blue—almost green in one case. It was obvious that none of these flags would, any more than the East India Company Ensign, suffice as a National Flag for a new country proclaiming its independence. No surprise will therefore be felt that some change was soon asked for. The stripes did very well—nothing could be better—but what was to replace the Union in the upper canton? Surely the obvious reply must have been white stars, and as there were thirteen states, there should be thirteen stars.

So the Continental Congress on 14 June 1777 'Resolved, that the Flag of the United States be thirteen stripes alternate red and white, that the Union be thirteen stars white on a blue field, representing a constellation'.

It will be noted that the resolution does not give specific details, such as the proportions of the field and its blue canton containing the thirteen stars. The design of the flag is reputed to be that illustrated here, but documentary evidence proving that this is indeed the case has yet to be brought to light. The first Stars and Stripes to be flown in battle by land forces seems to have been the famous 76 Flag flown in the battle of Bennington, 16 August 1777. Its outer stripes were white and the stars had seven points. There are some who consider that this was the first Stars and Stripes to have thirteen stars, but the evidence is uncertain.

In spite of all that has been written—and it is considerable—about George Washington's Arms being responsible for the Stars and Stripes, or the part Mrs Betsy Ross of Philadelphia is supposed to have played in the construction of the first flag, we cannot perhaps do better than quote the well-known American authority, M. M. Quaife, who wrote, in 1942, as follows: 'Homer, alive, attracted but scant attention; when safely dead, and assured of immortality, numerous Grecian cities eagerly claimed him as their son. A like obscurity shrouds the birth of the Stars and Stripes. No one bothered at the time to record the name of its creator, or claim the honor for himself.'

The thirteen states were New Hampshire, Massachusetts, Rhode Island, Connecticut, Delaware, Maryland, Virginia, North Carolina, South Carolina, Georgia, New York, New Jersey and Pennsylvania. Vermont joined in 1791 and Kentucky (which was part of Virginia formed into a separate state, just as Tennessee was afterwards formed out of North Carolina) in 1792. Here were, therefore, fifteen states, and not thirteen, and to meet the new conditions Congress on 15 January 1794, enacted that 'from and after the first day of May 1795, the flag of the United States be fifteen stripes and the Union be fifteen stars'. This was the flag nicknamed the 'Star-spangled Banner'.

There was little difficulty in dealing with an increase among the stars, though every additional star weakened the artistic effect, but by 1818, when five other states had been brought in, and the future had others in store, it became evident that the original idea of a stripe for each state would simply ruin the appearance of the flag by making it look like a piece of shirting; and on 4 April of that year Congress enacted that the stripes should be reduced permanently to the original number of thirteen, and that the Union should then have twenty stars, and that for each new state admitted a star should be added on the next Independence Day, 4 July, following its admission to the Union. Readers have not infrequently asked for a list showing how the number of stars was increased and when each successive design was brought into use. Since the original design came into use on 14 June 1777, there have been twenty-seven official changes in the number of stars, the last being on 4 July 1960 (*see* Table on p. 69).

Before proceeding, we must first retrace our steps and give a brief account of the ephemeral flags of the Confederacy.

The '*Stars and Bars*'   The '*Southern Cross*'
                                  (*the Confederate Battle Flag*)

When the eleven Southern states seceded from the Union in 1860 and formed the Confederation, the Government made no change in the Stars and Stripes, and did not omit the stars which represented its enemies.

The first Confederate Flag was adopted on 5 March 1861, and was known as the 'Stars and Bars'. It consisted of a field, horizontally red over white over red. A large square canton covered the left-hand halves of the top and middle stripes. It was blue and had a circle of seven white stars upon it. This flag also did duty as the Ensign of the Confederate Navy.

It soon became evident that the Confederate armies needed a more distinctive flag for use in the field, and so the Battle Flag was designed and adopted. An oblong version of this, without a white border, subsequently became the widely recognized 'Flag of the South' or 'Southern Cross'.

On 1 May 1863 it was decreed that the Stars and Bars should be superseded by a new flag. This had a white field, one by two, with the aforementioned Battle Flag as a square canton which occupied two-thirds of the depth of the hoist, and became known as the Second Confederate Flag. Nearly four weeks later the Secretary of the Navy signed an order (dated 26 May 1863) instructing warships to hoist this flag as the Ensign, and the Battle Flag mentioned above as a Jack. However, the proportions of the Ensign were two by three, not one by two.

In certain circumstances—i.e. in bad or indifferent visibility—the Second Confederate Flag was extremely difficult to recognize at a distance, so on 4 March 1865 a large red stripe was added to it down the edge of the fly. At the same time it was decided to alter the proportions of the field to two by three, slightly reduce the size of the canton, and make the width of the red stripe equal to one half of the flag, measuring from the canton. This, however, became obsolete almost immediately when the Confederacy laid down its arms later that year.

The way that the National Flag of the United States developed has been explained on pages 66–7, and it can be seen from the table opposite that by the year 1912 it had acquired forty-eight stars, but although the number of the stars and stripes had been fixed this did not apply to the other details of the flag. For instance the proportions of the flag were not laid down, neither were there any instructions which defined how the stars were to be arranged in the canton, with the result that there were many variations of the flag. This chaotic state of affairs was ended by President Taft who by executive orders, dated 24 June and 29 October 1912, limited flags to certain sizes, defined the proportions and furnished a plan, which was published by the Navy Department, showing the exact configuration of the National Flag. The dimensions prescribed in these orders were:

Hoist (breadth of flag)	1 unit
Fly (length of flag)	1·9 units
Hoist of canton	7/13 unit
Fly of canton	·76 unit
Width of each stripe	1/13 unit
Diameter of each star	·0616 unit

There have been some minor variations since, but the basic design introduced under President Taft has been retained, although it was not until 1934 that the exact shades of colour were standardized.

The forty-ninth and fiftieth stars were added for Alaska and Hawaii on 4 July 1959, and 4 July 1960, respectively. Thus the flag assumed its present form.

THE STARS AND STRIPES FROM 1777–1960

DESIGN	NUMBER OF STARS	DATE WHEN BROUGHT INTO USE	ADDITIONAL STATES REPRESENTED
1st	13	14 June 1777	—
2nd	15	1 May 1795	Vermont and Kentucky
3rd	20	4 July 1818	Tennessee, Ohio, Louisiana, Indiana, and Mississippi
4th	21	,, 1819	Illinois
5th	23	,, 1820	Alabama and Maine
6th	24	,, 1822	Missouri
7th	25	,, 1836	Arkansas
8th	26	,, 1837	Michigan
9th	27	,, 1845	Florida
10th	28	,, 1846	Texas
11th	29	,, 1847	Iowa
12th	30	,, 1848	Wisconsin
13th	31	,, 1851	California
14th	32	,, 1858	Minnesota
15th	33	,, 1859	Oregon
16th	34	,, 1861	Kansas
17th	35	,, 1863	West Virginia
18th	36	,, 1865	Nevada
19th	37	,, 1867	Nebraska
20th	38	,, 1877	Colorado
21st	43	,, 1890	North Dakota, South Dakota, Montana, Washington, and Idaho
22nd	44	,, 1891	Wyoming
23rd	45	,, 1896	Utah
24th	46	,, 1908	Oklahoma
25th	48	,, 1912	New Mexico and Arizona
26th	49	,, 1959	Alaska
27th	50	,, 1960	Hawaii

This flag is something more than the National Flag to the citizen of the United States of America—it is the symbol of the nation to which he or she owes allegiance, just as we owe ours to the Throne. The *Pledge to the Flag* is as follows: 'I pledge allegiance to the Flag of the United States of America, and to the Republic for which it stands, one nation under God, indivisible, with liberty and justice for all.' The *Flag Code*, which is a very strict one, consists of a comprehensive set of rules governing the display and use of the flag.

There are a large number of official flags in use in the United States; the space available will allow for the mention of but a few of them.

USA: National and Merchant Flag and Ensign, 1960–

USA: President

The President's Standard is dark blue; in the centre thereof is a representation of the Seal of the President of the United States surrounded by a circle of small white five-pointed stars—one for each state. In October 1975, an executive order was issued which introduced a new Vice-Presidential Flag. This is almost the same as that used by the President, except that the field is white (instead of blue), and bears four blue stars, one in each corner of the flag (which replace the ring of fifty stars that represent the states of the Union on the Presidential Flag).

Heads of Executive Departments with civilian status have four stars, one in each corner of their respective flags.

The Secretary of Defense flies a blue flag charged with a central device, in proper colours, which is taken from the Seal of his Department; in each corner of the flag there is a small white five-pointed star.

The Ensign of the US Navy and also the US Merchant Navy is the National Flag. The dark blue canton with the fifty stars is used by the Navy as the Jack; it is called the 'Union Jack'. Naval vessels in commission fly the Warship Pennant at the masthead. This is dark blue at the hoist and is charged with seven five-pointed stars; the remainder is divided horizontally, red over white, with a long slit in the fly.

The flag of the Secretary of the Navy is dark blue with in the centre a large white foul anchor with four white stars, one in each corner. Each of the Flag Officers of the Navy has his distinguishing flag. Fleet or five-star Admirals have five stars disposed in a pentagon on a dark blue field; that of an Admiral has four stars in a diamond formation, the Vice-Admiral's three stars are in a triangle, and the Rear-Admiral's two vertically one above the other. The Broad Pennant of the Commodore has one star. The colour of the field of all sea-going Admirals is dark blue with white stars; the flags of Vice-Admirals and Rear-Admirals not eligible for a command at sea have white flags with blue stars.

In addition to the flags described above the Navy has a Ceremonial Flag or Colour.

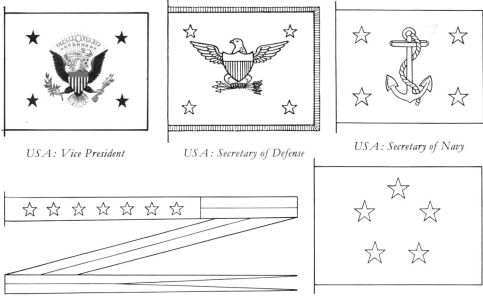

USA: Vice President   *USA: Secretary of Defense*   *USA: Secretary of Navy*

USA: Warship Pennant   *USA: Fleet Admiral*

This has a dark blue field with a golden fringe; in the centre there is a three-masted ship, a conventional anchor and the American eagle, the whole enclosed in a cable-laid rope.

The Army of the United States has very many flags. The flag of the Secretary of the Army has a red field with the four white stars in the corners and in the centre the bald-headed American eagle with a breast plate of red and white vertical stripes.

The flags of the Army can be roughly divided into four main categories, (1) Colours, (2) distinguishing flags, (3) flags of individual high ranking officers, (4) guidons.

Colours are defined as a specific flag indicative of the spirit and tradition of the United States, or the office, position or organization represented. The following are among those authorized to bear Colours: the President and Vice-President of the United States, Cabinet Members and senior officials of the Armed Forces such as the Chairman of the Joint Chiefs of Staff.

USA: Ceremonial Flag of Navy

USA: Secretary of Army

Regiments and separate battalions whose organization is fixed by the tables of organization are authorized Colours symbolic of their branch and history. These are known as Colour Bearing Organizations. Other branches of the Army have distinguishing flags.

When the term Colour, in the singular, is used this implies the National Colour. This is the National Flag, but with a golden fringe and proportions modified to three by four (width by length). Colours, in the plural, implies both the National and Organizational Colour paraded together. All Colours are silk flags with gold fringes. The colours of the fields of the flags are laid down according to the branch of the Army to which the organization belongs, i.e. Armour, yellow; Artillery, scarlet; Infantry, dark blue; and so on. In the case of distinguishing flags, they bear the insignia of the branch and unit identification in numbers and symbols. If the unit is designated 'Colour-bearing', then the colour of the field is the same as that of the distinguishing flag but the device consists of the bald American eagle with on its breast the arms of those units with an authorized coat of arms, and beneath on a scroll the designation of the unit, i.e. 1st Infantry, 5th Artillery etc.

The Ceremonial Flag, or Colour, of the Army has a white field with a complicated device in the centre and a gold fringe.

Guidons are swallow-tailed flags and are used as markers for companies, batteries etc. The design is generally similar to the distinguishing flag of the unit, and of the same colour and bearing the insignia of the unit in the centre.

Senior Officers in the Army have a red flag with the number of stars in white appropriate to their rank. A five-star General, whose title is General of the Army, has his stars arranged in the form of a pentagon. The others have their stars displayed in a

USA: Ceremonial Flag of Army

USA: Ceremonial Flag of Air Force

*USA: Ceremonial Flag
of Marine Corps*

*USA: Ceremonial Flag
of Coast Guard*

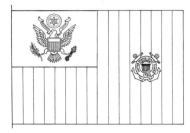

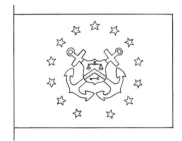

U.S.A: Coast Guard Ensign

U.S.A: Secretary of the Treasury

horizontal line; thus, a General has four, a Lieutenant-General three, a Major-General two and a Brigadier-General one.

The flags of the Air Force of the United States follow the same general pattern as those of the Army, except that the colour of the field is generally blue instead of red. Thus the Secretary of the Air Force has a dark blue flag with four white stars, one in each corner, and in the centre the Arms of the Air Force in full colour.

There are distinguishing flags for all the many Air Commands, Major Air Divisions, Wings, etc. The flags of the Senior Officers of the Air Force are similar to those of the other services; they are dark blue in colour and in order to distinguish them from those of the Navy the stars are arranged in the same pattern as those of the Army.

The Ceremonial Flag of the Air Force is very similar to that of the Secretary of the Air Force except that it does not have the four stars in the corners; the Arms are circled by thirteen white stars and on a scroll beneath is the title *United States Air Force*.

The United States Marine Corps has its own series of flags, the basic colour of which is red. The Standard of the Corps is thus a red flag with in the centre the Arms of the Marines, a gold anchor over which is a globe and the crest is the American eagle with a scroll in its beak bearing the motto *Semper Fidelis* ('Ever faithful'); beneath on a scroll *United States Marine Corps*. The flag of the Commandant is similar to the Standard, but it has no scroll and has four white stars disposed symmetrically round the arms in the centre. The other senior officers have red flags, but the stars are disposed in the same fashion as those of the Navy so as to distinguish them from the Army.

Although the organization is on naval lines, the Coast Guard Service of the United States is strictly a civilian service and comes under the Secretary of the Treasury who has a blue flag with a badge in the centre of a shield and two crossed anchors surrounded by a circlet of thirteen stars; these charges are all white.

The Coast Guard Ensign is an interesting flag. It has sixteen red and white vertical stripes, starting with a red one at the hoist. In the fly is a crossed anchor badge with the motto *Semper Paratus*, 'Always prepared', and the date *1790* in dark blue. In the white canton is a modification of the Arms of the United States with the eagle in blue.

The Senior Officers of the Coast Guard Service have blue flags with the same device that is in the fly of the ensign, and stars indicative of their rank, four for the Commandant, three for the Assistant-Commandant and two for the Rear-Admiral. The Colour of the Coastguards is white with in the centre the same arms that are in the canton of the ensign, with the motto below, and above: *United States Coast Guard*.

The Customs Service Ensign is similar to that of the Coast Guards except that there is no badge in the fly.

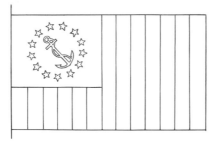

USA: Power Squadron Ensign   *Alabama*

Yachts fulfilling certain requirements are authorized to wear the Yacht Ensign in lieu of the Stars and Stripes. It is clearly distinguishable from the latter in that the blue canton contains a large white anchor inclined at an angle of forty-five degrees, encircled by thirteen white five-pointed stars.

In addition to the Yacht Ensign there is a special ensign for the US Power Squadron. The field of this ensign, the proportions of which are three by two, consist of seven blue and six white stripes arranged vertically. The canton is red and in it is placed an inclined anchor and thirteen white stars, the same as that in the Yacht Ensign.

Each of the states has its own flag. Some of them are very beautiful; some of them are plastered with devices which can only be compared with the ugly badges used by some colonies of the British Commonwealth.

Three main strands in the development of the state flags can be discerned. One is the adoption of Colours for militia called up to fight in the Civil War, or other wars, when flags were hurriedly made up, often by simply placing the state seal on a blue field. The second is the activities of the patriotic 'Daughters of the American Revolution', especially in the Centennial year of 1876, when state flags were needed to fly at exhibitions. A third and very important source is the Confederate flag tradition. Nearly all the states on the Confederate side now use flags which recall directly or indirectly their former allegiance.

The square flag of **Alabama** is white with a red saltire cross, intended to recall the Battle Flag of the Confederate States. It was introduced on 16 February 1895.

Alaska, admitted as the forty-ninth state of the Union on 3 January 1959, retained its original flag, dating from 2 May 1927. This is blue with the constellation of the Great Bear and the North Star, and was designed by a thirteen-year-old schoolboy.

Arizona has a flag adopted on 27 February 1917. The thirteen rays of red and gold refer to the original thirteen states, and their colours to the period of Spanish rule. They express sunset over the desert. The copper coloured star stands for the mineral resources.

Of the four stars in the centre of the flag of **Arkansas,** as modified on 10 April 1924, the top one stands for the Confederate States, and the three lower ones the nations that have ruled the area: France, Spain, and the USA. The twenty-five stars in the blue frame represent the order of admission to the Union. The flag was originally adopted on 26 February 1913.

The flag of **California** was originally used by a breakaway group of Americans at

Alaska   Arizona   Arkansas

California   Colorado   Connecticut

Delaware   Florida   Georgia

Sonoma on 14 June 1846, prior to the occupation of the country by the USA. A revised version was adopted on 3 February 1911. The central feature is the grizzly bear.

The flag of **Colorado,** which also contains the red and gold of Spain in the form of a letter C, was originally introduced on 5 June 1911, and a revised version, more nearly in line with the intentions of the designer, was adopted on 31 March 1964.

Connecticut, like many other states, has a flag derived from the Colours of the militia raised during the Civil War, these very often being, as in this case, a blue flag with the Arms in the centre. The Arms date back to the earliest days of the Colony. The motto is *Qui Transtulit Sustinet* ('He who brought us over will sustain us').

The colours of the flag of **Delaware** date back to the War of Independence, being those of the soldier's uniforms. Originally plain blue the buff diamond was added when the flag was made official on 24 July 1913. The Arms date back to 1777, and the date 'December 7, 1787' is that of the ratification of the US constitution, which Delaware was the first to do.

The present flag of **Florida** was adopted after the state was re-admitted to the Union following the Civil War. Originally, in 1868, plain white, with the seal in the centre, the red saltire was added on 6 November 1900. As with Alabama, this recalls the Battle Flag of the Confederate States.

Georgia is another state whose flag keeps alive the memory of the Civil War. The flag was originally based on the 'Stars and Bars', the first flag of the Confederacy, but then the blue strip was extended to the full width of the hoist; later the state seal was added to the centre of this, and finally on 1 July 1956 the fly of the flag was altered to the same design as the 'Flag of the South'.

| Hawaii | Idaho | Illinois |

| Indiana | Iowa | Kansas |

Hawaii was admitted as the fiftieth state of the Union on 21 August 1959, and retained the flag it had originally adopted on 20 May 1845. The King of Hawaii had received a British flag, of pre-1801 pattern, from Captain George Vancouver in 1793, and flew the British flag until 1816. A flag of nine red, white and blue stripes with the Union Jack in the canton was then adopted. The version of 1845 was claimed to have been designed by a Captain George Beckley, although others also claimed the honour. In this the stripes were set at eight, to stand for the eight islands. The monarchy was overthrown in 1893, but the flag remained in use as the group became first a republic, then a territory of the USA, and finally a state.

The state flag of **Idaho** was adopted on 15 March 1927 on the basis of the Colours of its military forces, but the letter of the law and the pattern of the flag differed so considerably that the legal specifications were altered to fit the flag on 1 March 1957. The device in the centre, as with many other state flags, is the seal in full colour.

The basic design of the flag of **Illinois** was introduced on 6 July 1915, and shows the central emblem from the state seal which dates back to 1810. The name of the state was added in 1970.

As in many other cases, the flag of **Indiana** is based on military Colours, in shape if not in design. The design was the winning entry in a competiton held in 1916, and was officially adopted on 31 May 1917. The outer ring of thirteen stars stands for the thirteen original states and the inner ring for those joining subsequently, including Indiana, itself represented by the larger star above the torch.

The central emblem of the flag of **Iowa** is taken from the seal adopted in 1847. The Great War provided the impetus, as in several other states, for a flag and a design was produced by the Daughters of the American Revolution, who were also responsible for many other state flags. It was originally plain white but the blue and red stripes were added when the flag was finally approved on 29 March 1921. The colours recall the fact that Iowa was once part of Louisana, a territory purchased from the French by the USA in 1803.

The official emblem of **Kansas** is the sunflower and the original flag adopted by the state on 27 February 1925 had the seal placed on a sunflower with the name above in yellow, all on a blue field. On 30 June 1953 a state 'banner' was introduced with a large sunflower head only, but in practice its use is restricted to the National Guard. The present state flag dates from 23 March 1927, and has the sunflower as a crest over the seal which now appears on a white disc. The name of the state was added below on 30 June 1963, and this is now becoming a frequent practice on the part of those states whose flag designs are insufficiently distinctive.

The flag of **Kentucky** is another of those derived from the Colours of the state militia in the Civil War, which was blue with the state seal in the centre. The state flag was originally adopted as such on 26 March 1918, but its design was not regularized until 14 June 1962. The name, and a wreath of goldenrod, the state plant-badge, are now included.

The pelican as a symbol of **Louisiana** dates from the early nineteenth century. It is a local bird, and is also an ancient religious symbol. In heraldry it is usually shown in the act of 'vulning' itself to provide sustenance for its young, a device known as a 'pelican in her piety'. A flag with this device was in use in 1861, and was legal on 1 July 1912.

The seal of the state of **Maine** contains the state Arms, and these appear also in the centre of the flag. The seal dates from 1820 when the state was admitted to the Union (it was originally part of Massachusetts). The flag was adopted on 24 February 1909, although there was an earlier version using only the pine tree, the state plant badge, and the North Star, dating from 1901, and a far more distinctive and handsome design. Maine also has a merchant and marine flag of white with a green pine tree and a blue anchor, and the motto *Dirigo* ('I Guide') above, and the state name below, all in blue letters.

One of the most striking of the state flags is that of **Maryland**, for it is pure heraldry. It is taken from the Arms of the Baltimore family which are a combination of those of Calvert (the first and fourth quarters) and of Crossland. At first the Calvert arms alone were used as a local flag, and in the nineteenth century blue flags with state seals were in

Kentucky *Louisiana* *Maine*

use. However the Calvert–Crossland banner was revived in 1901 and officially adopted as the state flag on 9 March 1904.

Massachusetts originally had a flag with a different design on the reverse from the obverse. The latter shows the Arms which date from 1780, although the figure of an Indian dates back to 1629. The star on the shield shows the membership of the state in the USA; the motto *Ense Petit Placidam sub Libertate Quietem* may be translated as 'Searching with a sword for Peace and Liberty'. The reverse of the flag showed a blue shield with a green pine tree, a reference to the most popular local emblem at the time of the War of Independence. This two-sided flag was adopted on 18 March 1908, but the reverse side was made identical with the obverse on 31 October 1971. Massachusetts had a naval ensign adopted in the early days of the War of Independence, of white with a green pine tree and the motto *Appeal to Heaven* in large letters beneath. This dated from 29 April 1776 and was based on the unofficial flag used by the armed vessels of the rebellious Colonies. The flag was revised on 1 November 1971 by the omission of the motto, and the authorization of its use by all public and private vessels registered in the Commonwealth. In both the state and the maritime flags the emblems are set slightly nearer the hoist than the fly.

The Arms of **Michigan** consist of the central devices from the state seal. These are heraldic in form and were adopted on 2 June 1835. The two mottoes are *Tuebor* ('I Will Defend'), and *Si Quaeris Peninsulam Amoenam Circumspice* ('If You Seek a Pleasant Peninsula Look Around You'), a reference to the state's geographical position. As in many other cases the first flag was a military colour with the state seal. The present design was officially adopted on 29 April 1911.

Maryland

Massachusetts

Michigan

Minnesota was at one time the northernmost state of the USA, hence its motto, *L'Etoile du Nord* ('The Northern Star'). The topmost star in the flag adopted on 4 April 1893 represented this also. There were eighteen other stars disposed around the seal on a white field. These indicated that Minnesota was the nineteenth state to join the Union after the original thirteen. Once again this flag was based on that of the state militia. On 19 March 1957 a revised version of the flag was introduced, with the central emblem on a white disc edged yellow all on a light blue field.

Mississippi is another state which makes use of the flags of the Civil War period. The canton of the flag is the Confederate battle flag, and the three horizontal stripes recall the 'Stars and Bars' pattern. This design was adopted officially on 7 February 1894, and a specific finial for the flag staff was prescribed at the same time, in the form of a battle-axe.

Missouri has a flag which combines several of the trends noted above. The central emblem is the state seal; the original flag was a militia colour with the seal in the centre,

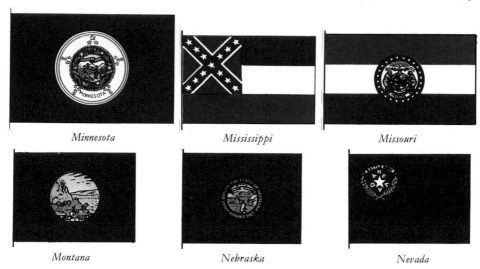

Minnesota   Mississippi   Missouri

Montana   Nebraska   Nevada

and the colours recall those of France and the Louisiana Purchase. The twenty-four stars indicate that Missouri was the twenty-fourth state to join the Union. The flag was adopted on 22 March 1913.

Montana is yet another state with a flag based on militia colours consisting of a blue flag with a coloured version of the seal in the centre. These date from the Philippine Campaign of 1898, and a simplified version became the state flag on 27 February 1905. The seal contains the motto *Oro y Plata* ('Gold and Silver') recalling both Spanish rule and the mineral wealth.

The origins of the flag of **Nebraska** are similar to those of many other states. A seal was adopted in 1867, which was used in the Great War for unofficial flags for troops from the state. This became the basis of a design eventually adopted on 2 April 1925 on the initiative of the Daughters of the American Revolution.

The first flag of **Nevada** was introduced in 1905, and bore the name, the words 'Silver' and 'Gold' and rows of gold and silver stars on a blue field. This was revised on 22 March 1915 by adding the state seal. However, a completely new design was adopted, after a local competition, on 26 March 1929. This includes the state flower, the sagebrush, and the motto *Battle Born* indicative of Nevada's admission to the Union during the Civil War.

New Hampshire follows the flag pattern of many other states, in having a blue flag with the seal in the centre, derived from early military colours. The seal dates from 1784, and the state flag for general use from 24 February 1909. In this the seal is surrounded by a wreath of laurel interspersed with nine stars. The seal and the flag were slightly amended on 1 January 1932.

The buff or light orange colour of the field of the flag of **New Jersey** is derived from the facings of the uniforms worn in the War of Independence. A flag for the state Commander-in-Chief in this colour was created in 1896, with the Arms from the seal in the centre. These in turn date from 1777. The flag was made official for general use in 1938.

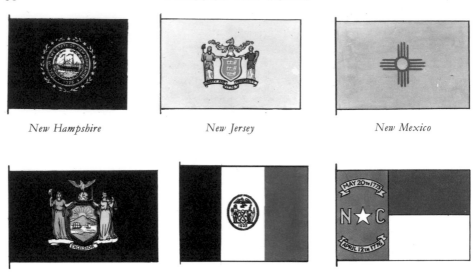

| New Hampshire | New Jersey | New Mexico |
| New York | New York City | North Carolina |

The flag of the state of **New Mexico** is one of the most distinctive in the USA. Its central emblem is the sun symbol of the Zia Pueblo Indians, officially described as the 'symbol of perfect friendship among united cultures'. The colours of red and gold recall the period of Spanish rule. The design was adopted on 15 March 1925, and replaced an earlier much more complicated flag dating from 19 March 1915.

The flag of **New York** state is very similar in origin and appearance to the majority of state flags, being derived from Colours carried in the War of Independence. A state flag with the arms in the centre was sanctioned in 1896 but with a field of buff. This was changed to blue on 2 April 1901. The Coat of Arms dates from 1777. There is also a flag for the City of New York and for the Mayor and for four of the five boroughs. The city flag recalls the Dutch origins, being vertically blue, white, and orange, the colours of the flag of the Dutch East India Company flown by Hendrik Hudson when he founded New Amsterdam, later New York. In the centre are the city Arms. These originated in 1686 and were revised in 1784. Beneath them, within the wreath, is the date 1625 symbolizing the first settlement of the place by the Dutch. This was altered from 1664 on 8 January 1975, and the basic design was originally approved on 27 April 1915. When used by the Mayor it has an arc of five blue stars over the Arms.

The flag of **North Carolina** is in the red, white and blue colours common to all the states which formed the Confederate States of America, although these are also of course the national colours. The original design in fact was adopted on 22 June 1861, a few weeks after North Carolina had seceded from the USA. It was basically the same as the present design, except that the horizontal upper stripe was blue and the vertical one red. The present design was introduced on 9 March 1885. The top date, 20 May 1775, refers to the Declaration of Independence at Mecklenburg on that day, and the lower one, 12 April 1776, refers to the date the Provincial Congress decided on independence.

North Dakota has a flag of the usual type, derived in this case from the Colours of the Dakota Territorial Guard, later the First North Dakota Infantry. The Colours, almost without alteration, were adopted as the state flag on 3 March 1911. There is now also a more orthodox state flag which is gradually replacing the traditional design, introduced on 15 March 1957.

The flag of **Ohio** seems to be based on a US Army cavalry guidon. The flag was officially adopted on 9 May 1902. The thirteen stars nearest the hoist stand for the thirteen original states, and Ohio's status as the fourth state to be admitted subsequently is indicated by the four extra stars. The O formed by the red disc within a white ring stands for Ohio, and the general pattern of stars and stripes recalls the National Flag.

The first flag of **Oklahoma** was adopted on 2 March 1911, and consisted of a white star with the number 46, edged blue on a red field. The number referred to the order of admission of Oklahoma to the USA. Red flags were disfavoured after the Great War, so a competition for a new design was organized by the Daughters of the American Revolution. The winning entry was adopted on 2 April 1925 and is derived almost entirely from Indian sources. The blue field is from a Choctaw flag, the shield is an Osage one, and the calumet is the Indian peace-pipe. This is crossed with an olive branch. On 9 May 1941 the name of the state was added underneath these emblems.

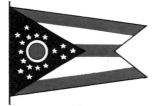

North Dakota   *Ohio*   *Oklahoma*

Oregon has the distinction of being the only state with a flag having a separate design on the reverse side. The observe is based on early military colours, with the Arms all in gold surrounded by thirty-three stars, again standing for the order of the state's admission to the Union. The name appears above and the date of admission below. On the reverse the flag is also blue, with a gold beaver, symbolic of the fur trading in the early days of the Oregon Territory. The flag was adopted on 26 February 1925.

Pennsylvania has a plain flag with the state Arms in the centre. These date from 1777 and were later incorporated into military colours. A flag for general use was approved on 13 June 1907, with the Arms as finally established in 1875. Pennsylvania had a Jack used from 1707 until the Revolution. This was the British Union Jack with the Shield of Pennsylvania, at that time the same as that of William Penn, in the centre.

The emblem of **Rhode Island** has always been an anchor, with the associate motto, *Hope*. The Colour of one of the Rhode Island regiments in the War of Independence was white with a blue anchor and the motto above it. A white flag with a blue anchor, the motto and a ring of blue stars was adopted as the state flag on 30 March 1877. On 1 February 1882 the field was changed to blue, the stars reduced to thirteen, and the design simplified. On 19 May 1897 the present design was established with the original white field.

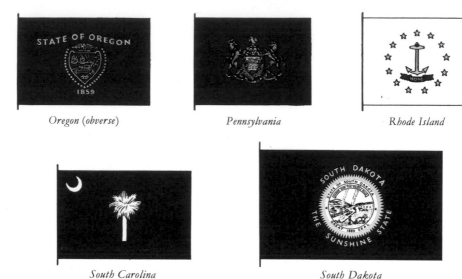

Oregon (obverse)   Pennsylvania   Rhode Island

South Carolina   South Dakota

The flag of **South Carolina** is derived from one made by Colonel Moultrie at Fort Johnson in 1775. His troops had cap badges with a white crescent with the words *Liberty or Death*. The palmetto had also established itself as a local emblem and was incorporated into the state seal. Flags with palmettos were used during the Civil War and the present design was decided upon on 28 January 1861. Unlike those of most other Confederate states it was not altered during or after the Civil War and has remained in use to this day.

South Dakota is known as 'The Sunshine State', and this motto is to be found on its flag. The obverse of the flag originally adopted on 1 July 1909 was very handsome, with a blazing gold sun in the centre of a blue flag, and the name and motto around it. The flag had a reverse side, however, with the highly complicated seal in the centre, in dark blue. A new design with only one side was adopted on 11 March 1963, but by a legislative error the background of the seal could be made either white or blue—the seal now appears in the centre of the sun. In practice the white background is used.

Tennessee is another state, formerly part of the Confederate States, with colours of red, white and blue. The present flag was adopted on 17 April 1905. The three white stars are thought to indicate that Tennessee was the third state to join the Union after the original thirteen.

Texas was an independent republic before it joined the USA, and before that it was part of Mexico. The separatists of the 1830s took their symbolism from 'The Bonny Blue Flag' that had been used by American settlers in Florida, and ultimately the design of this flag—a large white star on a blue field—led to Texas being known as 'The Lone Star State'. The first flag had the name Texas disposed around the points of the star, then a blue flag with a gold star was employed, and a naval ensign like that of the USA but with only one star in the canton. Eventually the present flag was adopted on 25 January 1839, with the Lone Star on a vertical blue strip. This remained in use when Texas became a state in 1845, and during the Civil War, and after that until the present day.

The flag of **Utah** dates from 11 March 1913 and employs the emblems found on the state seal, which was adopted in 1896, although the shield itself dates from 1850. The gold ring around the Arms was added by the first manufacturer, but was liked and officially incorporated in the authorization of 1913.

The independence of New Connecticut, or **Vermont**, as it is now known, was proclaimed on 15 January 1777 and it remained an independent republic until joining the USA as the fourteenth state on 4 March 1791. Vermont originally had a flag like the National Flag, with the name across the top stripe. The present flag, blue with the state Arms, was instituted on 1 June 1923. This was because the soldiers of Vermont had fought under a similar flag.

Virginia is the oldest English-speaking settlement in America and the Arms of the Virginia Company granted by King James I were in use until the War of Independence. A new, more classical and allegorical emblem was adopted in 1776; this is the obverse side of the seal. In full colour this appears in the centre of a blue flag, on a white disc. This was adopted on 30 April 1861 shortly after Virginia seceded from the USA, but has not been altered since.

Washington is the only state to have a green flag. This symbolizes its nickname, 'The Evergreen State'. In the centre is the seal, adopted on 4 July 1889. The flag became official on 7 June 1923, and the seal was given a more precise form in 1967.

West Virginia was formed as a state during the Civil War from the mountain counties which refused to secede from the Union. Hence the motto in its Coat of Arms: *Montani Semper Liberi* ('Mountain Men are always Free'). The arms date from 1863. The first flag of the state was white with a bunch of rhododendron leaves and flowers within a blue border. In 1905 this was restricted to the reverse side of the flag: the obverse bore the Arms and the name on a scroll. The present form of the flag was introduced on 7 March 1929 with the Arms on both sides, although flanked by a wreath of rhododendron.

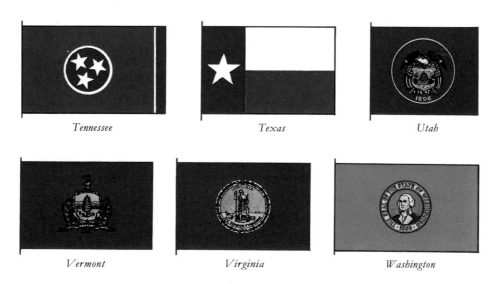

Tennessee   Texas   Utah

Vermont   Virginia   Washington

Wisconsin is another of those states whose flag grew out of its military colours. In fact in 1863 they were almost identical. The flag was inadvertently abolished in 1887 by a legislative oversight, and a new version was enacted on 29 April 1929. This is like the old one, in being blue with the state Arms in the centre. The latter date from 1851 and were revised in 1881.

Wyoming is another state which owes its flag to the activities of the Daughters of the American Revolution, who organized a flag design contest in 1916. The winning entry was officially adopted on 31 January 1917. Since then a number of modifications have been made, altering the bison to face the hoist, and placing the state seal within the outline. The seal was adopted in 1890.

| West Virginia | Wisconsin | Wyoming |

Within the USA is a territory that is not a state, namely the **District of Columbia**, which is the federal district containing the capital, Washington. The district has a flag, approved on 15 October 1938. The flag is a banner of the Arms of George Washington, which were originally granted to the Washingtons of Sulgrave Manor in Northamptonshire in 1592.

Overseas the USA is responsible for a number of dependencies each of which has a distinctive flag flown together with the flag of the United States. **American Samoa** was acquired when the islands were partitioned in 1899. The territory adopted a distinctive flag early in 1960 and it was flown for the first time at Pago Pago on 27 April of that year, the sixtieth anniversary of the first raising of the Stars and Stripes there in 1900. The field of one by two is blue, and has a red-bordered white triangle extending from the fly to the hoist. On this is an American bald eagle in proper colours in flight towards the hoist, looking downwards and grasping in its right talon a *fue*, a Samoan chief's symbol, and in

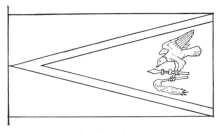

| District of Columbia | American Samoa |

its left an *uatogi*, or war club, both in gold. The blue and red of this design are the colours used on the Stars and Stripes; the American eagle holding in its talons the symbols of Samoan authority and culture indicates the protection and friendship of the United States.

Guam passed to the United States from Spain in 1898, and acquired a territorial flag officially adopted on 4 July 1917. It has the unusual proportions of 21 : 40. It is dark blue with a red border all round, and in the centre of the seal of Guam in colour, on which is depicted an estuary, an outrigger canoe and a coconut tree with the word GUAM over all in block letters.

In the **Panama Canal Zone**, a strip of territory on either side of the canal leased

Guam

Governor of Panama Canal Zone

Puerto Rico: Seal

temporarily to the USA, the flags of the USA and of the Republic of Panama fly side by side, officially since 2 January 1964. The American Governor has a flag adopted on 8 June 1915. This is dark blue with a large white disc in the centre charged with a shield and a scroll with the motto *The Land Divided The World United*. This is the central emblem from the seal of the American administration.

Puerto Rico ('The Rich Port') was discovered by Columbus on 19 November 1493 and he took possession of it on behalf of Spain, naming it San Juan Bautiste. In accordance with a decree dated 8 November 1511 King Ferdinand, joint sovereign of Spain with Queen Isabella, granted the Arms. These are green with a representation of the silver lamb of St John on a book. A border all round the shield contains emblems of the royal house of Spain, the gold castle of Castile on red, the red lion rampant of Leon, a banner of Aragon and Sicily on red, and the cross potent of Jerusalem in gold on white. There is also a seal, a circular version of this, in which the lamb is flanked by the crowned initials F and I, and above it is the yoke and arrows badge of Ferdinand and Isabella.

Puerto Rico: Flag

Trust Territory of Pacific Islands

Virgin Islands of the USA

Beneath it is the quotation *Joannes Est Nomen Ejus* ('His Name is John'). In the circular border are simplified versions of the devices from the shield, except that the royal banner is in fact more complex than that in the shield. Puerto Rico continued to be a Spanish possession until the end of the Spanish-American War of 1898, and became a dependency of the USA on 11 April of the following year in accordance with the Treaty of Paris. It has been a self-governing Commonwealth since 24 July 1952. For several decades up to 1948 the American Governors used a white flag with the seal described above in colour in the centre.

The distinctive flag of the island was chosen when it achieved Commonwealth status. This was the flag adopted in 1895 by the Puerto Rican section of the Cuban Revolutionary Party, which was the spearhead of the movement for the independence of both countries from Spain. It is similar to that of Cuba except that the five horizontal stripes are red and white and the triangle is blue.

The **Trust Territory of the Pacific Islands** consists of a large collection of islands in Micronesia held in trust by the USA for the United Nations. They are gradually moving to self-government, and are being divided into areas, each of which will have its own flag. In the meantime the UN flag, the flag of the USA, and the flag of the Trust Territory are all officially flown. The latter is blue with six white stars, representing the districts of Palau, Yap, Truk, Ponape, the Marshall Islands, and the Marianas Islands. The flag was designed locally and was given official recognition in 1965. There is also a flag for the High Commissioner of white with his seal in dark blue in the centre.

The **Virgin Islands** were bought by the USA from the Danes in 1917 and are known officially as the Virgin Islands of the United States to distinguish them from the British Virgin Islands. There is a local flag, adopted by the then Governor on 17 May 1921. It is white with a version of the United States Arms between the initials V I.

[5] Latin America and the Caribbean

CENTRAL AMERICA

Costa Rica, Guatemala, Honduras, Nicaragua, and El Salvador were once provinces of the Spanish Captaincy-General of Guatemala. The independence of Central America was proclaimed on 15 September 1821 in Guatemala City. For a short period after this the five states were under the domination of Mexico, but an independent federation was finally established in 1823. This lasted for fourteen years. Honduras and Nicaragua left in 1838 and the federation was dissolved in 1839. On 21 August 1823 the Arms and flags of the United Provinces of Central America were adopted. The emblems consisted of a triangle, representing equality, charged with five volcanoes in a row, standing for the five states, a Phrygian cap representing liberty, and a rainbow, symbolizing peace. The name of the United Provinces in gold letters was placed around this. The flag consisted of three equal horizontal stripes of light blue, white, and light blue. The state flag had the emblem in the centre, and the merchant flag had the legend DIOS UNION LIBERTAD in silver capitals. Slight changes were made to the emblem and to the encircling title before they went out of use in 1839.

Costa Rica continued to use the flag of Central America after the break-up of the federation, but with its own emblem in the centre. In 1848 a central band of red was added, with a new Coat of Arms over all in the centre. These were very similar to the present ones, showing a range of volcanoes between two seas, on each of which a ship is sailing. Above is an arc of stars, now seven for the departments of the country. The name *America Central* appears on a blue ribbon over the shield, and the title *Republica de Costa*

Costa Rica: Arms

Costa Rica: National and Merchant Flag

Rica on a white ribbon. On the State Flag and Ensign the Arms now appear on a white oval near the hoist, but are omitted from the National and Merchant Flags. The three volcanoes are Barba, Irazu, and Poás, and the two seas stand for the Atlantic and the Pacific Oceans.

El Salvador also has Arms and flags which recall those of the federation, but these too were only recently re-adopted after a period of experimentation, on 15 September 1912. The present Arms have the Phrygian cap in the triangle surrounded by golden rays with the date *15 de Septiembre de 1821* and emerging from the volcanoes on a staff. Around the triangle are five National Flags, and beneath is the federation's motto *Dios Union Y Libertad* on a small scroll. Around this is a wreath of laurel, tied at the bottom with a blue ribbon. Around the whole is the title *Republica De El Salvador en La America Central*. Following new regulations introduced in September 1972 the flag, when charged with the national emblem in the centre, has the usual proportions of 189:335 and is confined to state occasions and government business. A flag with the motto, in the proportions 3:5, is used for public buildings and official establishments. The colour of the wording is unspecified, but it is to be noted that in the days of the federation silver letters were used for the Merchant Flag. A flag without any central device is used for all other general purposes. There is also a Jack, of blue with a white diamond over all. The flag with Arms was formerly specified as the President's Standard and Naval Ensign, and the flag with the motto was the Merchant Flag. That new law does not, however, specify any flag for these purposes, but it would seem that older usages remain current and have been merely amplified by the new regulations.

| *El Salvador: Arms* | *El Salvador: President's and State Flag* | *Guatemala: National Flag and Ensign* |

Guatemala also uses the colours of Central America, but arranged vertically, a design introduced on 17 August 1871 after several variations. The National Flag and Ensign have the same emblem in the centre. This consists of a golden scroll with the motto *Libertad 15 de Septiembre de 1821* (the original date of independence from Spain) on which is perched a quetzal bird (*Paramocrus mocinno*), the national bird of Guatemala. Behind and around the scroll are crossed swords and rifles and a wreath of laurel. This emblem was also adopted in 1871. It does not appear on the Merchant Flag.

Honduras has also retained the flag of Central America, altering only the devices in the centre. In the state emblem, which dates from 1838, the triangle is set in front of a pyramid and flanked by two towers, with volcanic flames emerging from it; this all appears in the midst of a blue sea and a light blue sky. All around is an oval band with the legend *Republica de Honduras Libre Soberana Independiente 15 Septiembre 1821*. Above this are two cornucopiae and a quiver of arrows, and below is a symbolic landscape with trees,

Honduras: Arms

Honduras: National and Merchant Flag

tools, houses, and cave-dwellings, and beneath this again five stars representing the five original members of the federation. The Arms appear only on the ensign. On the state and merchant flags are the five stars, arranged two, one, and two, symbolic of the hope that the five republics would one day re-unite.

Nicaragua has the flags and Arms which most closely resemble those of the Central American federation. The present Arms were adopted on 5 September 1908 after a period in which various other designs were employed. In adopting these present ones the National Assembly was seeking those which 'as nearly as possible were those which represented the Federation of Central America in view of the aspiration of Nicaragua for the rebirth of the political entity formed by the five nations'. The triangle and its charges are therefore exactly the same as those of 1823, but the encircling title is *Republica de Nicaragua: America Central*. The only National Flag has the emblem in the centre in full colour with the title in gold letters. The basic design has remained that of Central America, and was also resumed in 1908.

The national emblem of **Mexico** is adapted from the Aztec symbol for their capital, now Mexico City, but known to them as Tenochtitlan, 'Cactus Rock'. This in turn derived its name and emblem from the legend that the wandering Aztecs could not settle until they found a place on an island in a lake on which grew a cactus. On this cactus plant there would be an eagle holding a snake in its beak. They found this strange phenomenon about the year 1325, and there established the Empire which was later conquered by Hernán Cortez in 1521. Thereafter Aztec symbols remained in existence but had no significant heraldic rôle until they were resurrected at the time of emancipation from Spain. One of the earliest flags was in the blue and white colours of the House of Montezuma, used in 1812. The present colours of green, white and red, date back to the Iguala convention on 2 March 1821, and are said to signify Independence, Religion and

*Nicaragua: National and
Merchant Flag and Ensign*

Nicaragua: Arms

Unity. The first flag, that of the Three Guarantees, had the colours diagonally, with three stars standing for the three principles, one on each colour. The vertical tricolour was introduced on 2 November of the same year, following the declaration of independence on 21 September (simultaneous with that of Central America). It had the eagle and cactus badge in the centre, beneath a crown. Mexico became an Empire on 21 May 1822 using this flag, except that the snake was omitted. The Empire was replaced by a Republic on 1 February 1823, and the Arms more or less as they are now were established, although subsequent constitutional changes involved alterations in the basic design. The present design was made official on 17 September 1968, and has the device in more authentically Aztec form. The flag with the Arms in the centre is the National Flag, Merchant and Naval Ensign.

The Jack is the flag of the Three Guarantees, slightly modified, with three gold eight-pointed stars and white anchor. The pennant is green, white, and red, without any device. The head of the Ministry of Marine has a square version of the National Flag, with a white saltire over the field. The Secretary of State for the Navy has the National Flag with a white anchor on the green strip; an Admiral has three white stars on the green strip, placed vertically, and lesser Admirals have fewer stars. The Commander-in-Chief of the Navy has four white stars placed vertically.

Ambassadors and Ministers use a square white flag with the national emblem in the centre. The flag for a Consular Officer is similar but swallow-tailed. State Governors all use a plain flag of three horizontal strips of green, white and red. All the states have Arms, but none of them has a distinctive flag.

*Mexico: National and
Merchant Flag and Ensign*

*Panama: National and
Merchant Flag and Ensign*

Secretaries of State other than of the Navy use a square version of the National Flag. Under-Secretaries have the same but swallow-tailed. The General of a Division has the same flag as the Governor of a state but with the Arms in the centre. A Brigade Commander has the same but swallow-tailed, and a Brigadier the same pattern but as a triangular flag. There is now no special flag for merchant ships, other than the National Flag. The Customs Ensign is like the former merchant flag of green, white and red, but with a large black foul anchor in the centre. Mail vessels have a similar flag with the letters CM in the centre.

Panama was formerly a province of Colombia, but it became independent on 3 November 1903. The flag was designed by the first President, Manual Amador Guerrero, and serves as National Flag, Naval Ensign, and Merchant Flag. The white stands for peace, and red and blue for the Liberal and Conservative parties. The National Flag flies equally with that of the USA in the Canal Zone, a strip five miles wide on either side of the Panama Canal which is under the jurisdiction of the USA until the year 2000. .

SOUTH AMERICA

The symbol of **Argentina** is the Sun of May, an emblem derived from the appearance of the sun in the cloudy skies of 25 May 1810 when the first demonstrations in favour of emancipation from Spain began. The colours of blue and white were adopted at the same time and were formed into a flag in 1812 by General Manuel Belgrano. The Sun of May was added to this in 1818 and this basic design has formed the National Flag ever since.

The flag for popular use and the Merchant Flag are without the Sun. The Jack is a square white flag with a blue border all round and the Sun of May in the centre. The pennant is divided horizontally blue, white, blue.

The President's Standard is a darker blue than in the National Flags, and in the proportions 3:4 as opposed to their 2:3. It has the national Arms in the centre and a white star in each corner. The Arms are oval, blue over white, with two hands grasping a staff with a Cap of Liberty. Around is a wreath of laurel, and the crest is the Sun of May. These devices are very similar to those of José de San Martín who led the liberating 'Army of the Andes'. The flag of the Minister of Marine is light blue, in the proportions 50:66, with a device of an anchor crossed with the staff and Cap of Liberty with the Sun of May superimposed in the centre. Around this is a white rectangular frame. The Chief of Naval Operations has a flag of blue with five white stars, one in the centre and one in each corner of the field. An Admiral as Commander-in-Chief has the same but with only the four stars in the corners, otherwise he has three stars placed diagonally across the field. A Vice-Admiral has two stars in a diagonal position and a Rear-Admiral has one star placed centrally.

Argentina: State Flag and Ensign

Argentina: Jack

Bolivia was originally known as Upper Peru, but was renamed after the liberating general Simón Bolivar when independence was achieved on 6 August 1825. The National Flag was established in its present form in 1851. The national Arms are placed in the centre to form the President's flag, and the State Flag. Without the Arms the tricolour is the flag for popular use and the Merchant Flag. The present Arms were adopted by law on 14 July 1888, and consist of an oval cartouche encircled with a border, the upper half of which is yellow and bears the name of the country in red; the lower half is blue and is charged with nine gold stars representing the nine departments of the country. In the centre is a landscape with the sun shining over a mountain—the mountain of Potosí, famous for its mineral wealth—a house, a breadfruit tree, a corn-sheaf, and a llama, these symbols representing the riches of the country, mineral, vegetable and animal. Behind the oval are two crossed cannon and four rifles with fixed bayonets, two on each side. On one side is a cap of Liberty, and on the other an axe, while three of the National Flags appear on each side. On top there is a wreath with a condor alighting thereon.

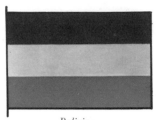

Bolivia: Arms

Bolivia:
National and Merchant Flag

Brazil:
National and Merchant Flag

Although Bolivia has no sea-coast there is a Naval Ensign of light blue, with a small version of the merchant flag in the canton with nine gold stars along its edge, and a larger gold star in the fly, standing for the outlet to the sea it hopes one day to regain.

Brazil was that part of South America once controlled by Portugal, although other European nations tried from time to time to establish footholds there. The French had a settlement at one time near Rio de Janeiro, and the Dutch captured Bahia in 1549 and had a colony known as 'Dutch Brazil' in Ceara and Pernambuco from 1624–54. However Portugal gradually assumed control over the whole country. The capital was established at Rio de Janeiro in 1763. In 1808 the Portuguese royal family fled there, having been exiled by Napoleon. Although they returned home after his downfall, the eldest son remained behind and formed an independent Empire of his own in Brazil on 12 October 1822. A new National Flag was adopted consisting of a green field with a yellow lozenge, and the national Arms in the centre. The Arms contained many elements from those of Portugal, and also a circular blue band with 20 white stars, one for each province. Brazil became a republic on 15 November 1889, and the Imperial Arms were replaced on the flag by the present blue celestial sphere. This has a band across its equator with the national motto *Ordem e Progresso* ('Order and Progress'). The upper part of the sphere has one white star, and the lower part twenty-two other stars arranged in constellations as they appear over Rio de Janeiro, only reversed. The single upper star stands for the state of Pará, and the lower ones for each of the other states together with the Federal District. The latest modification was made on 31 May 1968.

The same law also officially changed the name of the country from *Estados Unidos do Brasil* (the United States of Brazil) to *Republica Federativa do Brasil* (the Federal Republic of Brazil), and this title now appears on the scroll beneath the Coat of Arms. These Arms, which on a green field form the President's Flag, consist of a blue disc containing the five stars of the Southern Cross, with a blue circular band edged in yellow, now containing twenty-two stars. This is contained on a large prismatic star of five points divided green and yellow, and bordered in red; behind this is an upright sword and a wreath of laurel and coffee; at the bottom is a blue scroll with the name as above and the date *15 de Novembro de 1889*. Behind the star and wreath is a sun of gold rays.

The field of the Jack is dark blue, with a cross of twenty-one stars. This is the basic design used for the flag of the Ministry of Marine and other naval flags. That of the Ministry of Marine, or Admiralty, has a simplified version of the national star in the canton and two white crossed anchors in the lower hoist. The Minister himself has this flag without the anchors. An Admiral uses the Jack with five stars in the form of a pentagon in the canton; an Admiral commanding a squadron has four stars in a diamond

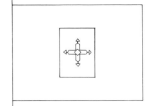

Brazil: President   Brazil: Ministry of Marine   Brazil: Federal District

pattern; a Vice-Admiral a triangle of three stars; and a Rear-Admiral two stars side by side. The pennant is the same dark blue with twenty-one stars arranged horizontally. The Customs flag, hoisted on incoming vessels subject to Customs examination, is dark blue with a large white star.

Each of the states of Brazil and the Federal District has a distinctive flag, many of which are more distinctive and older than those of the USA, although in most cases their use has only recently been officially authorized. The Federal District is the territory containing the new capital, Brasilia. Its flag was adopted on 7 September 1969 and is white with a green rectangle and a device in yellow representing communications in all directions. It has proved impossible to give more than a sample of the flags of the states. That illustrated is the flag of Maranhão, which was officially adopted on 1 December 1971 but which has been in use for several decades. The nine horizontal stripes are alternately red, white and blue and the blue canton bears a white star.

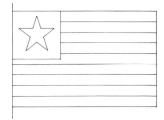

Brazil: State of Maranhão   Chile: Arms   Chile: National and Merchant Flag

Chile has a very handsome flag, although clearly its design is based on that of the USA. It was reputedly designed by Charles Wood, a US citizen serving with the Chilean insurgents, at the instance of the Minister of War, José Ignacio Zentano. It was first used on 18 October 1817, but was preceded by at least two earlier designs. Chile became independent on 1 January 1818. The present design does duty as National Flag, Ensign, and Merchant Flag. The Jack is square, dark blue, and charged with the star as in the National Flag. The pennant is white over red with a blue panel in the hoist with the star.

The President's Standard is the National Flag with the national Arms placed centrally over all. These were designed by Zentano himself in 1834. The shield is based on the National Flag, and is supported by a *huemal* or Andes deer, and a condor. The crest is three plumes of the rhea, another native bird. The motto is *Por La Razon O La Fuerza* ('By Right or Might'), and was used during the war of independence. As used on the President's flag the Arms are usually without the motto.

The flag of the Minister of Defence does have the whole Arms, on a blue field. Generals of a Division and Provincial Governors have a yellow flag with three blue stars arranged one and two. The Commander-in-Chief of the Fleet has a flag of dark blue with four white stars; a Vice-Admiral has three stars; and a Rear-Admiral two.

Colombia, Ecuador, and Venezuela may be conveniently linked together, since they share a common flag history. Independence movements broke out in several parts of what were then the Spanish provinces of New Granada and Venezuela in the second decade of the nineteenth century. Emancipation was secured by Generals Simón Bolivar and Santander and on 17 December 1819 the Republic of Greater Colombia was formed at Angostura. To this Ecuador acceded on 29 May 1822. However, internal rivalries led Venezuela to secede on 30 April 1830, and Ecuador on 13 May 1830. Each republic went its own way with its own flags and Arms. Colombia was renamed New Granada.

The colours used by Bolivar during his campaign were yellow, blue, and red. On the union of Colombia and Venezuela on 17 December 1819 it was decided to adopt these colours in the form in use in Venezuela, i.e. in horizontal bands with the yellow of double width. After Ecuador joined, three stars of blue or white were usually shown in the canton of this flag. The flag had originally been designed by Francisco Miranda in 1806, and its colours symbolized America—gold, separated from Spain—red, by the blue sea.

Colombia: Merchant Flag

Colombia: President

After the dissolution of the confederation **Colombia** had a long and complicated constitutional history. Finally in 1861 the country readopted the Flag of Greater Colombia with a blue oval in the centre, charged with nine stars and bordered in red. In 1890 a single star of eight points was substituted in the centre, and this has remained the Merchant Flag ever since. The Ensign has the National Arms on a small white disc in the centre, and the President's Flag has the Arms on a white disc within a wide red circular band. This is sometimes inscribed with the name of the Republic in gold. The Arms have also gone through many metamorphoses. The basic elements date back to 1834, i.e. the three divisions of the shield, showing in chief a pomegranate (the emblem of Granada) between two cornucopiae, in the centre a Cap of Liberty on a staff, and in base a view of the Isthmus of Panama; the shield is supported by a condor; the motto *Libertad Y Orden*; and the two pairs of National Flags. The specifications were last approved on 9 January 1961. The flag for popular use is still without Arms, and is therefore the same as that of the confederation of 1819.

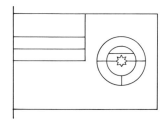

Colombia: Arms   *Colombia: Air Force Ensign*   *Ecuador: Arms*

Many of the provinces of Colombia have their own flags, several dating back to the early days of the independence movement.

The Jack is the same as the National Flag. The pennant is light blue with the National Flag at the hoist. The Air Force Ensign is also light blue, and has the National Flag in the canton. In the fly is the roundel or target—a flag pattern similar to the British RAF Ensign. The flag of the Admiralty is the National Flag with a large black anchor over all, and of the Minister for War the same but with the anchor set lower, and above it a stylized condor, also in black. An Admiral of the Fleet has a flag of the same blue as the National Flag, with a white cross over all, and a white disc in each quarter.

The National Flag of **Ecuador** is the same as that of Colombia, and therefore of the confederation of 1819, although it is distinguished by being slightly longer. For international occasions the State Flag and Ensign is used. This has the Arms over all in the centre.

The Arms were introduced in 1845, and consist of an oval shield which contains a landscape showing a snow-capped mountain rising out of the sea with a steamer thereupon and the sun with four of the signs of the Zodiac in the sky. The snow-topped mountain represents Chimborazo, the highest peak in the country and of historic importance during the war of independence; the steamer stands for commerce, while the four signs of the Zodiac, which cover the months of March, April, May and June, refer to the critical period in the history of the country. Above the oval is a condor, below it is a fasces, and on each side are two tricolours, the heads of which are fashioned like halberds. Each of the provinces of Ecuador has a distinctive flag, although mostly of modern origin; this includes the Galapagos Islands in the Pacific Ocean. Their flag is a horizontal tricolour of green, white and blue. There is also a Communal Flag for use on public buildings. This is the National Flag with a ring of nineteen white stars standing for

Ecuador:
National and Merchant Flag

Ecuador: President,
State Flag and Ensign

the provinces, in the centre of the blue stripe. The Jack is blue, with a white foul anchor beneath a condor in flight, and the pennant is divided vertically, yellow, blue and red.

The yellow, blue, and red colours of **Venezuela** date back before the confederation to 12 March 1806, when Francisco Miranda and others began the liberation of the country. By 1822, as related above, the upper strip had become double the width of the others, but after Venezuela seceded from the confederation the original dimensions were restored. The seven stars representing the seven provinces which formed the original free state of Venezuela in 1811 have appeared in various forms on the flag from time to time. The present flag was last authorized on 19 February 1954, with the stars in an arc in the centre. The national Arms were first adopted in 1836 and were last modified on 15 April 1953. The central emblems have remained unchanged, but the legend on the ribbon of the national colours now reads *19 de Abril de 1810—Independencia: 20 de Febreo de 1850—Federacion: Republica de Venezuela.*

Venezuela: Arms

Venezuela: National and Merchant Flag

The Arms appear in the canton of the State Flag and Naval Ensign. The President's Flag is square, with the National Arms over all in the centre, and a white star, each tilted towards the hoist, above, below and on either side of the Arms. The Minister of Defence has a blue flag with a stylized anchor surrounded by four stars in the centre, and the shield from the Arms in the canton. The Commander-in-Chief of the Navy has the same flag but without the shield. An Admiral has a yellow pennant with three blue stars set horizontally; a Vice-Admiral has two stars, and a Rear-Admiral one. Venezuela now consists of twenty states, two territories, the Federal District, and several federal dependencies. Several of these states have distinctive flags.

Guyana, formerly British Guiana, became independent on 26 May 1966. The National Flag has two forms: in the proportions 3 : 5 for use on land, and 1 : 2 for use at sea. There is otherwise no distinction between National, Merchant Flag, and Ensign. The colours stand for the country's natural resources and the 'dynamic nation-building process' the country is engaged in.

Guyana became a republic within the Commonwealth on 23 February 1970, and a flag was adopted for the President. This is a square banner of the national Arms, with a green shield inset, charged with a cacique's crown of feathers. The Arms show a giant waterlily pad (*Victoria regia*), and a canje pheasant separated by wavy lines of water. The supporters are two jaguars, one with a pick and the other with a sugar cane. The crest has the crown of feathers, and the scroll bears the national motto: *One People, One Nation, One Destiny.*

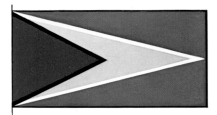

Guyana: National Flag

Guyana: President

Paraguay gained its independence from Spain on 14 May 1811, through a bloodless revolution led by Dr Francia. The following year a horizontal red, white and blue tricolour, charged on one side with the Arms of the King of Spain, and on the other with those of Asunción, was adopted. Francia, who was President from 1816 until 1840, is reported to have been particularly interested in the design of this flag; he also revised the charges, which were adopted by law at the end of 1842. These remain in use today on the tricolour, which is not only the National Flag, but also the Ensign and Merchant Flag. This flag is unique in that it is now the only South American flag having a different charge on each side of the field. These charges are placed in the centre of the white stripe. That on the obverse is the national Arms, and that on the reverse the Treasury Seal. Both are white discs with borders of red, white and blue. The Arms contains the 'May Star' which symbolizes the date of independence, within a wreath of palm and olive branches tied with a ribbon of the national colours, the whole encircled by the name of the country. The emblem on the reverse shows a yellow lion seated in front of a staff with a Cap of Liberty and the inscription *Paz y Justicia* ('Peace and Justice').

The President's Standard is blue, with the National Arms in the centre, and a yellow star in each corner. The title *Republica del Paraguay* does not appear in the Arms on this flag. The flag of the Minister of Defence is also blue, with a yellow anchor in the centre, and a yellow star in each corner. The Chief of Naval Staff has the same without the anchor. A Vice-Admiral has three stars diagonally across the field, and a Rear-Admiral two. A General of the Army has a blue flag with a red cross over all, fimbriated in white, and with a red canton bearing a yellow star. The same flag but with the red and blue reversed is used by diplomatic representatives. Consuls have a flag also with a white cross; the top two quarters are red and the lower two blue. The yellow star appears in the canton.

Paraguay: National and
Merchant Flag and Ensign

Paraguay:
National Emblem

Paraguay:
Treasury Seal

Paraguay: Jack   *Peru: National and Merchant Flag*

The Jack also bears the yellow star, the 'May Star', on a white disc at the centre of two intersecting diagonal stripes: red from upper hoist to lower fly, and blue from upper fly to lower hoist.

Peru has had several different flags in its troubled history, since achieving independence on 28 July 1821, but the flags have nearly always been red and white. These colours are said to have been chosen by José de San Martin during the war of independence. He laid down the pattern of the first National Flag in 1820 as diagonally white and red, and also the first Arms, consisting of a large golden sun rising over the mountains. The present design and the present Arms were introduced on 25 February 1825. The full Arms, illustrated as (A) are only used on certain flags, e.g. that of the President, which is white with the Arms in the centre, and a golden sun in each corner. The Naval Ensign is like the National Flag, but has the full arms in the centre. The lesser Arms, illustrated as (B) appear in the centre of the State Flag, and in the Jack, which is square, with a red-bordered white panel charged with the Arms. The shield of the Arms is divided into three: the top containing a blue field charged with a llama, and a white field charged with a cinchona tree; the bottom is red with a golden cornucopia. The three parts of the shield and the outer border all have a narrow gold edging. The golden sun, now always shown with a human face, represents the Inca race of Peru, and features on a number of subsidiary flags.

Peru: Arms—version A   *Peru: Arms—version B*

Surinam was formerly a part of the Realm of the Netherlands, before becoming an independent republic on 25 November 1975. At midnight 24–25 November of that year the flag of the Netherlands and the former flag of Surinam as a self-governing possession of the Netherlands, with its distinctive design of an oval of stars, were lowered, and the new flag hoisted.

The previous flag was introduced on 29 December 1954 for local use only. Its five stars represented the five racial groups of the country living in harmony. The present flag was chosen by a special commission, and combines the colours of the two main parties (green and red), and the golden star represents hope for the future, as in the Coat of Arms. The Arms date back to the eighteenth century, but were officially introduced on 15 December 1959. The hair of the supporters was changed from blond to black on independence. The Arms appear in the centre of a square white panel replacing the central star on the flag of the President. Members of the Council of Ministers have a plain white flag with the full Arms in the centre.

Surinam:
National and Merchant Flag

Surinam: Arms

Uruguay: Arms

Uruguay was originally a part of the Spanish Vice-Royalty of the River Plate, and took part with the other Argentine provinces in the movement for emancipation and shared with them the emblem of the 'Sun of May' which was in use from 1810. Uruguay took longer, however, to achieve independence, and it was not clear at first that she should be separated from Argentina. José Gervasio de Artigas led a movement for separation, using a flag like that of Argentina, but with a diagonal red stripe from the top of the hoist to the bottom of the fly. A flag like this, in the proportions 4:5 is now the Jack, and was first known on 3 April 1815. Variations on this flag were used during the following period, when Uruguay was annexed by Brazil, itself on the point of becoming an independent state. A further liberation movement was formed under the leadership of the 'Thirty-Three' in March 1825, using a flag of blue, white and red horizontally with their motto *Libertad O Muerte* ('Liberty or Death') in black in the centre. War between Brazil and Argentina followed, but led to the independence of the republic east of the Uruguay on 18 July 1828, although Independence Day is reckoned as 25 August 1825, the day the Thirty-Three landed in the country. A completely new flag was introduced on 16 December 1828, of nineteen horizontal white and blue stripes, with a white canton with a Sun of May thereon. By a law of 11 July 1830 the number of stripes was reduced to five white and four blue, one for each of the departments into which the country was then divided. This flag remains the National Flag to the present day, although the flags of Artigas and the Treinta y Tres are also regarded as National Flags.

Although Uruguay is a republic it has no official President: senior members of the Cabinet take it in turn to carry out the duties of a President, and whilst discharging this office use the Presidental Standard, which is plain white with the Arms in the centre. The Arms are quartered: the first is blue and bears scales of justice in gold; the second is white

Uruguay: National and
Merchant Flag and Ensign

Uruguay: Jack

with a representation of the 'Cerro', the citadel of Montevideo; the third is white with a
black horse; and the fourth blue with a golden bull; the latter symbols represent power,
liberty and wealth respectively. The scales appeared in the Arms of 1815, but otherwise
the Arms date from 1829 and were last revised in 1908. The Minister of Defence flies a
white flag charged with a blue foul anchor between two blue stars. The Inspector
General of the Navy has a white flag with the blue anchor in the hoist and a blue star in
the fly. A Vice-Admiral has a white flag with three blue stars, and a Rear-Admiral two
stars. A Group Commander of the Air Force has a swallow-tailed flag with four blue
stripes as in the National Flag, and the Air Force roundel in the centre. This is a
representation of the flag of Artigas in circular form.

THE WEST INDIES

As on the mainland, all the islands of the West Indies were originally colonies or
dependencies of European countries. Of the British islands, or island groups, five have
become fully independent, and of these the Bahamas, Barbados, Grenada and Jamaica
recognize the Queen as Head of State, whilst Trinidad and Tobago is a republic within
the Commonwealth. The independence of Dominica, St Kitts and St Lucia is envisaged
for 1978.

The **Bahamas** became independent on 10 July 1973, their new flag being hoisted at
midnight on the ninth. It has three horizontal stripes representing the golden sands
between the aquamarine waters, and a black triangle, representing the people. It was
chosen after a local competition had failed to provide a suitable design, and it is to be
noted that the aquamarine colour is a specific part of the official pattern, being that of the
seas around the islands. The flag has the proportions one by two.

There is also a White Ensign, with a Cross of St George, and the National Flag in the
canton; a Blue Ensign, the same with a dark blue cross, used by government vessels, and
a Red Ensign, with a red field and a white cross. There is a flag for the Governor-General,
of the standard type, with the name *Commonwealth of the Bahamas* on the scroll. The flag of
the Prime Minister is the National Flag with a parliamentary mace in the fly, having a
gold sun behind it in the lower stripe. Cabinet Ministers have the National Flag with a
white disc in the centre of the fly, charged with the Arms; Diplomatic Officers have the

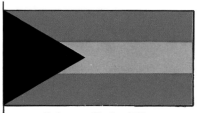

Bahamas: Arms

Bahamas: National Flag

same but with a wreath of laurel around the disc; Consular Officers have a flag of navy blue with the National Flag in the canton and the whole Arms in the fly. There is a large variety of other flags.

The fact that the Bahamas include the first land reached by Columbus in 1492 is commemorated by the main device in the Arms, which is a representation of the *Santa Maria* under full sail. Above this is a rising sun, symbolizing the pleasant climate; the crest is a giant conch shell, also standing for the many beaches; the supporters are a marlin and a flamingo, and the national motto is *Forward, Upward, Onward Together*. These wholly new Arms were adopted on 1 January 1972.

Barbados became independent on 30 November 1966 and her new National Flag was hoisted on that day. It was designed by a local man, Grantley Prescod. As in the case of the Bahamas, the colours represent the sands and the sea. The 'broken' trident, symbolic of the god of the sea, also stands for a clean break with the past, although the previous ensign badge also featured a trident. Barbados continues to use the Coat of Arms granted on 21 December 1965. The shield contains a bearded fig-tree, after which the island is named, and two flowers of the species known as 'Pride of Barbados'. The supporters are a dolphin and a pelican and the crest is an arm and hand holding two canes of sugar. The motto is *Pride and Industry*.

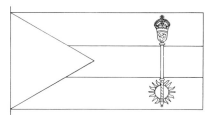

Bahamas: Prime Minister

Barbados:
National and Merchant Flag

The Arms appear in full in the centre of the flag of the Prime Minister, on a white disc in the centre of a flag divided diagonally gold over blue; the disc and the dividing line are fimbriated in a black and white rope pattern. The flag of the Queen of Barbados was displayed when Sir Garfield Sobers was knighted by her in February 1975, being a banner of the Arms, with the royal badge in the centre, as in other Commonwealth countries.

Grenada was formerly one of the States in Association with Britain, and as such had its own distinctive flag, adopted on 3 March 1967. This showed the badge of a nutmeg on a white oval in the centre of a flag striped horizontally blue, yellow and green. However, on independence on 7 February 1974 a completely new Arms and flag were adopted. The colours of red, yellow and green symbolize unity, friendliness and agricultural wealth. Grenada is the world's largest producer of nutmeg, and this in stylized form now appears in the centre of the green triangle near the hoist. The seven stars stand for the seven parishes of the island, which is predominantly Catholic. The flag has the proportions 3 : 5 for use on land, and 1 : 2 for use at sea. The Arms contain a representation of the *Santa Maria* in the centre and the emblem of the Madonna in the second and third quarters. The first and fourth quarters contain a British lion. The compartment portrays the Grand Étang Lake and pods of cocoa and nutmeg; the supporters are an armadillo and a ramier bird; the crest is seven roses, for the seven parishes, and the motto is *Ever conscious of God we Aspire, Build, and Advance as one People*.

Grenada: Merchant Flag

Jamaica: Queen's Personal Flag

Jamaica became independent within the Commonwealth on the night of 5–6 August 1962, and adopted a new National Flag. This consists of a diagonal cross of yellow dividing a field of black at the hoist and fly and green at the top and bottom. These colours stand for hope, natural wealth, and adversity. The Arms of Jamaica have remained virtually unchanged since they were first granted in 1661, shortly after the island had been taken from the Spaniards. They show the Cross of St George with five pineapples. The supporters are a native man and woman, and the crest is a crocodile. This was placed on a royal helmet with mantling in 1957, when the motto was changed from *Indus Uterque Serviet Uni* ('Both Indies shall serve as One') to the present *Out of Many One People*. The Queen's Personal Flag for use in Jamaica was first used in 1966, and consists of a banner of the Arms, with the royal badge in the centre.

The flag of the Prime Minister is blue with a white disc in the centre containing an unofficial version of the Arms, flanked by the letters PM, and within an ornamental white framework. The flag of the Governor-General follows the standard pattern.

The independence of **Trinidad and Tobago** within the Commonwealth was celebrated at a ceremony held on 31 August 1962 when the new National Flag was hoisted. This has a red field with a broad diagonal black stripe fimbriated in white running from the top of the hoist to the bottom of the fly. This is in the proportions 3 : 5 for use on land, and 1 : 2 for use at sea. The Naval Ensign is like the British White Ensign, but with the Trinidad National Flag in the canton. The colours of the flag represent vitality, purity and strength, and also appear on the Arms.

The Arms are divided in two by a white chevron. In the black chief are two golden humming-birds, in the red base are the three ships of Columbus in full sail. The

Jamaica:
National and Merchant Flag

Trinidad and Tobago:
National and Merchant Flag

supporters are a scarlet ibis and a cocrico bird; the crest is a palm tree and a ship's steering wheel, and the motto is *Together We Aspire, Together We Achieve*. The flag of the Prime Minister is white with the Arms within a golden wreath in the fly, and the National Flag in the canton. No flag is known as yet for the President. Trinidad became a republic on 1 August 1976, and the Queen's former personal flag, the banner of the Arms defaced with the royal badge, became obsolete.

Cuba was the first place in the New World settled by the Spaniards, and it remained in their possession until 1898. It was the Venezuelan General Narcisco López who, in 1848, made the first serious attempt to help the Cubans to break away from Spanish rule. He carried the banner known as *La Estrella Solitaria* ('The Lone Star') which was later to become the national flag of Cuba.

The field of the flag consists of five stripes of blue and white, the three blue ones for the three provinces of Cuba. The triangle is for equality, and the star for independence.

The long struggle for independence continued for half a century until, as a result of the Spanish-American War, Cuba was taken under the protection of the United States in 1898. Cuba became an independent republic on 20 May 1902, and López's flag was adopted.

The Arms were also adopted by the liberators in exile, in this case by Miguel Teurbe Tolón. The chief shows Cuba as the key to the Gulf of Mexico lying between Florida and Yucatan; the dexter side has the stripes from the flag, and the sinister side the most beautiful tree among the flora of Cuba, the royal palm, standing in a pleasant landscape. The supporter is a fasces with a Cap of Liberty at the top, which has the white Lone Star on it. The shield is flanked by a wreath of oak and laurel.

The President's Flag is light blue with the Arms in the centre and six stars, three above and three below, in white. The flag of the Minister of Defence is blue with a white anchor within a narrow white rectangular frame. The Jack of Cuba is a flag of historical

Cuba: Arms

Cuba: National and
Merchant Flag and Ensign

Cuba: Jack

Dominican Republic: Arms

Dominican Republic:
National and Merchant Flag

importance, that of Carlos Manuel de Céspedes, used during the liberation struggle of 1868–78. It is in the proportions 2:3 and divided white over blue, with a red canton charged with a white star. Both it and the flag of Narciso López clearly derive their inspiration from that of the USA.

The **Dominican Republic** occupies the eastern and larger half of the island of Hispaniola. Its flag was designed by Juan Pablo Duarte, founder of the society known as *La Trinitaria* ('The Trinitarians'), established on 16 July 1838, with the object of freeing the country from Haiti, and who were responsible for the formation of the republic on 27 February 1844. The flag was originally blue over red, the same as the then flag of Haiti, but with a white cross over all. The cross also appeared in smaller dimensions, and within a ring of white stars, on some early flags, but the present design was definitely established on 14 September 1863.

The State Flag has the Arms in the centre. These are quartered like the National Flag, but with a trophy of flags, a cross, and an open bible in the centre. This is open at the Gospel of St John, Chapter One. The national motto appears on a blue scroll above the shield, and is the same as the secret password of the Trinitarians, *Dios Patria Libertad* ('God, Country, Liberty'). The name of the state is on a red scroll below, and around are branches of palm and laurel. The flag of the President is white, with the State Flag in the canton and a large yellow vertical anchor in the fly. The flag for popular use and the Merchant Ensign is the same as the State Flag but without the Arms.

The Army flag has the white cross over all on a field blue in the canton, which is charged with a row of five white stars, red in the upper fly and lower hoist cantons, and a lower fly canton divided horizontally into four stripes of green, white, red and yellow. The Commander-in-Chief of the Armed Forces has a flag which is basically white, with a small version of the Merchant Flag in the canton, and a blue stripe along the bottom

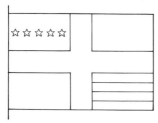

Dominican Republic:
Army Flag

Haiti: State Flag
and Ensign

charged with the Arms with five white stars. The Naval Ensign is now the same as the State Flag, and the former Ensign is now the Jack, i.e. blue with the Arms on a white disc in the centre all within a ring of seventeen white stars.

Hispaniola (Little Spain) was the name given by Columbus to the island he discovered lying south-east of Cuba. It was known to the natives as **Haiti**, and this is still the name of the smaller or western part of the island. By the Treaty of Ryswyk in 1697 this part was ceded by Spain to France, and the lilies of France superseded the red and gold of Spain.

During the French Revolution a movement for independence began in Haiti, and General Jean-Jacques Dessalines adopted a distinctive flag on 18 May 1803, consisting of the blue and red stripes from the Tricolour. These, he said, represented the negroes and mulatoes who were fighting side by side for liberty. Under President Jean-Paul Boyer the blue was changed to black, but this ephemeral flag was superseded by one divided *horizontally* blue over red, charged with the Arms of Haiti which were designed by President Alexandre Sabès Petion, who held office from 1807 to 1818. It was re-affirmed by the Constitution of 1843. On 22 June 1964 Haiti reverted to the black and red flag of 1806 in order to reinforce the concept of Haiti's African heritage. The State Flag and Ensign have the Arms on a white panel in the centre. These consist of a trophy of flags (now the same as the National Flag), a drum, rifles, two cannon, etc., in front of a tree (the emperor palm) thought of as the tree of liberty. This formerly had a Cap of Liberty on a small staff on top. The motto on a scroll beneath is *L'Union Fait La Force* ('Union Makes Strength').

The flag for popular use and the Merchant Ensign are without the Arms.

[6] Europe

Albania's colours are black and red, and her emblem is the black double-headed eagle of Skanderbeg, the great fifteenth century Albanian patriot, who preserved some part of the country from the Turks even after the fall of Constantinople. The eagle has always been the emblem of Albania, due in part to their name for their country, *Shqiperia*, 'The Land of the Eagle'.

The eagle flag was revived when Albania regained her freedom on 28 November 1912. Albania became a republic in January 1925, and a monarchy under King Zog until his country was conquered by the Italians in April 1939. The official day of liberation from the Axis forces is 29 November 1944, since when Albania has been a Communist republic.

Before 1939 the State Flag had a crown, known as the Helm of Skanderbeg, in gold over the eagle's head. During the Italian occupation the flag was red with the Arms all in black outline. On 15 March 1946 the present flag, with a red star edged in gold, was officially adopted. The present State Arms also show the black double eagle, within a border of wheat ears, and with a red ribbon with the date 24 May 1944.

The Merchant Flag consists of three horizontal stripes of red, black and red, with the red star edged in gold in the centre. The Naval Ensign is white, with the eagle and star in the centre, and a red stripe along the bottom edge.

Albania: National Flag

Albania: Merchant Flag

The flag of **Andorra** is a vertical tricolour of blue, yellow, and red. This is the flag for popular use, but the State Flag carries the Arms of Andorra in the centre. With some minor variations in detail these Arms have contained the same elements for many years: the mitre and crozier represent the Bishop of Urgel, one of the 'Co-Princes'; the second quarter bears three red stripes on yellow for the Counts of Foix; the third quarter is the Arms of Catalonia; and the two cows in red on yellow are for the Counts of Béarn. In the Arms of Béarn these face the dexter, but they are sometimes represented the other way

Andorra: State Flag

Andorra: Arms

round, and sometimes with the colours reversed. The motto is *Virtus Unita Fortior* ('United Strength is Greater').

The National Flag of **Austria** consists of three horizontal bands of red, white and red, and these are the original Arms of the country. They are attributed to Leopold Heldenthum, Duke of Bebenberg, whose white surcoat became stained with blood in battle, except for the part kept white by his belt. Although subsequently obscured by emblems of the Hapsburg dynasty, this simple device has been in uninterrupted use ever since.

The plain flag of Austria was retained when the republic was established on 12 November 1918. A simplified version of the Arms was also adopted, an eagle with only one head, a civic crown, and in place of the orb and sceptre, a hammer and a sickle. These Arms and flag remained in use until the forcible annexation of Austria to Germany in 1938.

The republic was restored on 20 October 1945, and the plain flag was brought out again immediately after the defeat of Germany and has remained in use ever since. In 1945 the broken shackles and chains were added to the eagle to symbolize the restoration of freedom, according to Article 1 of the Law of Coats of Arms dated 1 May 1945.

The Arms are borne in the centre of the flag, slightly overlapping the red stripes, by the President, state authorities and departments and on all official occasions.

Each of the nine states, or *Länder*, of Austria has its own Arms and Flag. That of Burgenland is red over yellow with the shield of Arms in the centre. That of Carinthia is horizontally yellow, red and white. The flag of Lower Austria is blue over yellow, and the flags of Upper Austria and of the Tirol are white over red, although the Tirol often places her Arms in the centre of a large white disc in its flag. Salzburg, Vorarlberg, and Vienna all have the same flags: plain red over white. Styria has a flag of white over green. In each case the colours are the predominant ones in the Arms.

Austria: Arms

Austria: National Flag

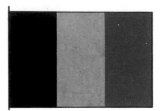

Belgium: Merchant Flag   *Belgium: Royal Standard*

Belgium was established as an independent kingdom on 4 October 1830 and elected Prince Leopold of Saxe–Coburg as its first King. The country had previously been ruled in turn by the Spaniards, the Austrians, the French and the Dutch. The national colours of black, yellow and red had been used for some time in the movement for emancipation: they are those of the provinces of Flanders and Brabant. The form of the flag was established in 1830, and last confirmed in 1936. The shield of the Arms is the same as that of Brabant, but a black lion rampant, that of Flanders, is used in the centre of the State Flag, beneath the royal crown. The Merchant Flag has the proportions 2:3, but the National Flag has the unusual shape of 13:15. The first Royal Standard was adopted in 1858 and had the Royal Arms in the centre of the National Flag. This was intended for use afloat, but the navy was disbanded in 1862, and the flag went out of use. The present Royal Standard, also intended for use afloat, was established in 1921. It is square in shape, with a field the colour of the ribbon of the Order of Leopold, known as *rouge ponceau*, a shade between crimson and aramanth. On the centre is the shield of Arms within an ornate frame of gold. In each corner is the royal cypher, now a crowned letter B, all in gold. The Personal Standard of the Queen and those of other *male* members of the royal family are similar, except that they each have their own cyphers in the corners. Princesses of Belgium have no Personal Standards.

On land the royal family uses the National Flag, except that the King may use a small version of the Royal Standard as a car flag.

The Belgian Royal Navy was re-established in February 1950, with a special Ensign of unusual but handsome design. It is white with a saltire formed by the national colours; in the upper part are two crossed cannon beneath a crown, and in the lower part a foul anchor, all in black. The Jack is the National Flag in square shape.

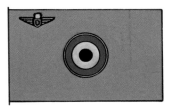

Belgium: *Belgium: Air Force Ensign*   *Belgium:*
Naval and Military Ensign   *finial on military Colours*

All units of the Belgian Army have the same basic colours, also a square version of the National Flag, and have a special finial on the flagstaffs. This consists of a rectangular platform, the longer sides of which are inscribed with the national motto in French on one side and in Flemish on the other: *L'Union Fait La Force* ('Unity is Strength'), and also the designation of the unit to which the Colours belong. The short sides carry the initials of the monarch in whose reign the Colours were awarded. The platform rests on a pillar within a wreath of oak and laurel, and supports the figure of a rampant lion. The whole device, reminiscent of Roman standards, is in gilt bronze. The flags of the Colours vary in size, those of the infantry being 0.9 m square, while the standards of the cavalry and artillery are 0.8 m, and the *fanions* or guidons of the auxiliary services are 0.7 m. Honours and citations are embroidered on the flags in capital letters, and the Colours have golden cords and tassels.

An ensign for the Belgian Air Force was established on 26 April 1950, in the proportions of two by three in air-force blue, with the target in the centre. This is red, yellow and black, and separated from the field by a yellow fimbriation. The target occupies half the width of the flag. In the canton is the Air Force badge: the national shield flanked by a pair of wings beneath a stylized crown. The crown and wings are in gold, and the shield black with a narrow red border. The State Flag is used on vessels owned or operated by the government. The yacht ensign is the same as the Merchant Flag, with the royal crown in gold in the canton.

Belgium: Flemish Flag   *Belgium: Walloon Flag*

The two main national communities of Belgium have flags of their own, now officially recognized. These are for the Flemings and the Walloons, or Dutch and French-speaking ethnic groups. The Flemings have a square version of the banner of Flanders, yellow with a black rampant lion armed red. This has been known since the earliest days of heraldry. The Walloon flag is also yellow and square, with a red rampant cockerel, representing their kinship with the French. This dates from 1913. Each of the nine provinces of Belgium has its own Arms and flag, but these are not seen so frequently as the Flemish lion and the Walloon cock.

White, green and red are the colours of **Bulgaria**, representing the country's love of peace, her agriculture, and the bravery and endurance of her army. In fact the colours are a slight variation of the 'Pan-Slav' colours widely used in Eastern Europe during the emancipation movements of the late nineteenth and early twentieth centuries. Bulgaria was established as an autonomous state within the Turkish Empire in July 1878, and adopted her colours on that occasion. Later Bulgaria became a kingdom, and after the Second World War, a Communist republic.

In accordance with the Constitution of the People's Republic of Bulgaria, dated 6 December 1947, the State emblem was placed in the canton of the flag. This employs the gold rampant lion which dates back to the earliest days of independence, but now on a light blue field, within a wreath of wheat-ears tied with a ribbon of the national colours, and a red ribbon. This originally had the date '9.IX.1944' in gold—the date of liberation from the fascists—but on 21 May 1971 this was altered to '681:1944'. The 681 refers to the date the first Bulgarian state was established in the Danube region. The Merchant Ensign is without the State emblem.

The Naval Ensign is patterned on that of the USSR. It is white with a large red star near the hoist, and along the bottom narrow stripes of green and red. The Jack is red with a large red star, fimbriated in white, in the centre.

Bulgaria has no President as such, but there is a Chairman of the Council of State. He has a flag based on the plain tricolour, but with a flag similar to the Ensign occupying the canton. In this flag the red star is replaced by the State Arms. This flag is in itself the flag of the Chairman of the Council of Ministers, i.e. the Prime Minister.

Bulgaria: Arms

Bulgaria: National Flag

Czechoslovakia also employs the red, white and blue colours of the Slavic emancipation movement, derived ultimately from those of Russia. However, they could also be interpreted as a combination of those of Bohemia–Moravia, red and white, and of Slovakia, white, blue and red. The flag was first established by law on 29 February 1920, and originally placed a triangle of blue over the white and red flag of Bohemia, extending only to one third of the length. This was extended afterwards to half the length, to make the present unusual and striking pattern.

The flag went out of use when Czechoslovakia was partitioned in 1939 and horizontal tricolours were used by the German puppet states. It was restored on 9 May 1945, the day of liberation from the Germans.

The flag of the President of Czechoslovakia is square, with a white field in the centre of which is the State emblem surrounded by a wreath of linden leaves, and with the national motto *Pravda Vitezi* ('The Truth Shall Prevail') in gold on a red ribbon beneath. The new Arms were adopted on 21 November 1960. They preserve the white lion of Bohemia, but this is now placed on a Hussite shield (*paveza*), with a small inescutcheon with a blue outline of Mount Krivan on which is superimposed a quadruple flame, and above the lion is a Communist star. A similar emblem, in which the lion was charged on its shoulder with an inescutcheon of Slovakia (white with a red double cross standing on a base of three blue mountains) was in use until 1960, and appeared on a red star in the canton of the Armed Forces Ensign, now obsolete. The lion with the inescutcheon of Slovakia

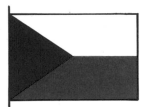

Czechoslovakia:
National Flag

Czechoslovakia: President

was the lesser Arms of Czechoslovakia before the Second World War, and the only ones used afterwards until 1960, except on the previous Presidential Standard, which bore the previous heraldic Arms. No changes were made when the federal constitution was adopted on 1 January 1969.

One of the oldest flags in continuous use is the famous *Dannebrog*, the National Flag of **Denmark,** whose name literally translated means 'Danish cloth', but whose symbolic meaning can best be described as 'The spirit of Denmark'. According to tradition the flag fell from heaven at the Battle of Lyndanisse on 15 June 1219, when King Valdemar was leading his troops into battle against the pagan Livonians. The oldest documentary evidence for its existence as a flag dates from the reign of King Valdemar IV (1340–75) who included it as part of his armorial bearings. In those days the flag was square, with a cross of equal arms, but over the years the 'fly' arm has grown longer until the cross assumed its characteristic 'Scandinavian' form common to all the flags of Scandinavia and associated countries. The *splitflag* shape, i.e. with the fly cut into swallow-tails, has been known since the early seventeenth century, and is reserved for official purposes. The plain *splitflag* is the Naval Ensign; with a white crown in the canton it is the Ensign for government vessels, and with a white square panel in the centre charged with the Royal Arms it is the Royal Standard.

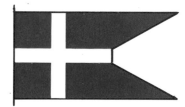

Denmark:
National and Merchant Flag

Denmark: Ensign

Denmark: Royal Arms

The actual proportions were last laid down on 11 July 1848, and decree that the width of the cross is one-seventh of the width of the flag; the rectangles in the hoist are squares with sides three-sevenths of the width, and the rectangles in the fly are twice the length of those in the hoist. In the *splitflag* the fly is extended further: the rectangles in the fly are five-fourths the length of those in the hoist, and swallow-tails are half as much again.

The Arms of Denmark proper, now known as the State Arms, are three blue lions on a field of yellow also containing nine red hearts. These are attributed to King Valdemar the Great, 1157–82, although the number of hearts was only fixed at nine in 1819. In the Royal Arms these are quartered with other Arms of dominion of the Danish sovereigns, which increased in number over the years, but on the accession of Queen Margrethe II on 14 January 1972 it was decided to simplify them. In the new Arms the shield has been increased in size proportionate to the supporters, and the white cross fimbriated red which divides into quarters has been made rectilinear instead of curvilinear as before. The first quarter still contains the Arms of Denmark and the second quarter those of Slesvig. In the third quarter, divided itself into three parts, are updated versions of the three gold crowns commemorating the Union of Kalmar, the united realm of Denmark, Norway and Sweden, of which Margrethe I was Queen; the silver ram for the Faroe Islands; and a silver polar bear for Greenland. On an inescutcheon is the Arms of Oldenburg, the dynasty which has ruled Denmark since 1448. The supporters are two 'wild men' or figures of Hercules, and around the shield are the collars of the Order of the Dannebrog and of the Order of the Elephant. The Arms are contained within a pavilion of scarlet and ermine, and ensigned with the Danish crown. The whole Arms appear on a white panel on the Royal Standard. On the Standard of the Queen Mother the supporters are omitted, and that of the Crown Prince has the State Arms only, with the Order of the Elephant and the royal crown. Other members of the royal family have the royal crown only in the centre of the white panel.

The other flag with a white panel is that of the Minister for the Navy, which has a crowned blue anchor in the centre. An Admiral uses the *splitflag* with three white six-pointed stars, two in the upper hoist canton and one in the lower; a Vice-Admiral has a star in each canton, and Rear-Admiral one star in the upper hoist canton.

The Lights and Buoys Service has a *splitflag* with a crowned anchor all in gold in the canton, and the Postal Flag a bugle surmounted by two crossed arrows beneath the royal crown, all in gold. There is also a special ensign worn by yachts whose owners are members of the Royal Danish Yacht Club. This is the *splitflag* with the letters YF and three stars arranged diagonally, all in gold. The flag of the Ministry of Fisheries is a red triangle, with a crowned foul anchor crossed by a trident, all in gold.

The **Faroe Islands** have a considerable degree of autonomy, and have Arms and a flag of their own. It was introduced in 1931 and officially adopted on 23 March 1948. The blue of the cross was formerly the same as that in the flag of Norway but the present lighter blue was authorized on 5 June 1959. This flag is typical of the many derived from the flag of Denmark itself.

There is no special flag for **Greenland**, although one is under consideration. The Royal Greenland Trading Department uses the *splitflag* with two crossed upright harpoons in the canton in white, a device known since 1795.

Denmark has several interesting flag customs, including that of flying all naval flags at half-mast on Good Friday, and on Remembrance Day, 9 April. Many Danes have a flagstaff in their front gardens, and usually hoist either the National Flag or, if there is no special occasion to do so, a long swallow-tailed streamer. This is because of the prevailing European tradition that it is dishonourable to leave a flagstaff without a flag.

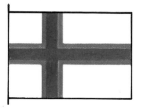

Faroe Islands

Finland: Arms

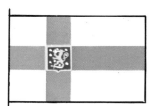

Finland: State Flag

Finland:
the Cross of Freedom

Aaland Islands

Finland was part of the kingdom of Sweden from 1154 until 1809 when it was ceded to Russia. In 1581 King John of Sweden conferred upon Finland the status of a Grand Duchy and a Coat of Arms. These Arms have remained practically the same until this day. The shield is red with a yellow crowned lion rampant, the right forepaw of which is clad in armour and grasps a sword. Also on the shield are nine white roses signifying the then nine provinces of the country, and beneath the feet of the lion is a scimitar on which it treads to signify victory over peril from the east.

The flag of Finland, which has the same kind of cross as that of other Scandinavian countries (although the Finns are not a Scandinavian people), was designed about 1860 by Zakari Topelius, a nationalist poet, who attributed the colours to the snowfields and lakes of Finland. There is some evidence, however, that the colours were used earlier than his time in provincial and military flags. The flag adopted on independence on 20 July 1917 was a banner of the Arms, i.e. a red field with the lion rampant etc., but this was not universally popular, and the blue and white flag was officially adopted on 29 May 1918 for the new republic. The plain flag is the National Flag and Merchant Ensign.

The State or Government Flag has the shield in a square form in the centre of the cross. As a triple-tailed swallow-tail this is the Armed Forces' Ensign. Other service flags have devices in the canton of this flag. The Minister of Defence has a badge of two crossed cannon and two crossed rifles. The Chief of Defence Staff has an upright cannon on which are superimposed a baton crossed with a sword. The Commander-in-Chief of the Navy has two crossed cannon on which is superimposed a blue anchor. The Postal Flag is the same as the National Flag, but with a badge of a bugle beneath a thunderbolt, and the flag of the Customs Service has a badge of two crossed caducei beneath a small version of the shield.

The Jack is a square banner of the shield of Arms, i.e. like the flag first adopted in 1917, but with a narrow white border all round. The flag of the President is the Armed Forces Ensign with the badge of the Order of the Cross of Freedom, a blue cross pattée charged with a gold swastika-shaped cross. The Order is now Finland's highest military award, and was first instituted in 1918.

The **Aaland Islands** constitute an autonomous county of Finland, having a predominantly Swedish population. Their flag dates from about 1920 and was officially adopted on 7 April 1954, for use on land only. It is clearly intended to be a combination of the blue and gold of Sweden with the red and gold of Finland.

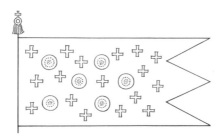

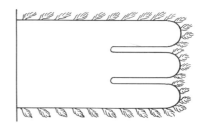

Standard of Charlemagne   *The* Oriflamme

The oldest emblem of **France** is the *fleur-de-lys* and, although abolished during the first French Revolution, the lilies of France have retained the esteem of all French citizens through the ages. As Napoleon Bonaparte himself put it: 'The *fleurs-de-lys*? During eight centuries they have guided France to glory as my eagles do now, and they must always be dear to France and held in reverence by her true children.' The origin of the *fleur-de-lys* is the legend that King Clovis dreamed during the night before the battle of Tolbiac in A.D. 496 that the golden toads in one of his standards had been turned into lilies, thus inspiring him to become a Christian. Despite this story, it was many years before the *fleurs-de-lys* were recorded on any banner in France. After his coronation as Emperor in A.D. 800, Charlemagne is reputed to have had a red standard with three short pointed tails decorated with a number of golden crosses and roundels. Then there was the *oriflamme* of St Denis, which was used intermittently from the eleventh to the sixteenth centuries. This took varying forms, but was essentially a plain red banner with tails of varying numbers. A banner bearing the *fleurs-de-lys* did not appear until the reign of Philippe II, in the year 1191; this was azure blue with the field sprinkled with golden lilies of a heraldic form—a pattern known as *semé-de-lys*. This is the flag, and Arms, known as 'France Ancient', so called after 'France Modern' was introduced in 1365 during the reign of Charles V, in which the lilies were reduced to three only, placed two and one.

The blue colour of the field is thought to be derived from another ancient emblem of France, the Cape of St Martin. This commemorated one of the patron saints of France, St Martin of Tours—the other is St Denis, whose banner was the *oriflamme*. The lilies themselves are thought to be emblems of the Virgin Mary, and to be heraldic representations of the yellow iris, *Iris pseudocorus*. Blue became the predominant colour of French flags, together with white, until the French revolution, and the basic French merchant flag before the Revolution was blue with a white cross over all.

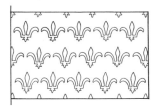

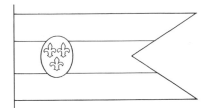

Banner of Philippe II   *French Galley Ensign*

There were other ensigns, or *pavillons* for warships. One of the earliest was a swallow-tailed flag divided horizontally red, white and red, with an oval shield in the hoist charged with the *fleurs-de-lys*. This was used on royal galleys, and went out of use when these vessels were no longer used as fighting ships. Other French warships used a plain white ensign, usually decorated with the Royal Arms and with the field decorated with *fleurs-de-lys*. An Ordinance of 1661 reserved the white flag for the royal ships, and prescribed the blue flag with a white cross, with the shield of Arms in the centre, for merchant ships. However, as in Britain, private ships tried to secure the privileges and protection of the Royal Navy by imitating the royal ensigns or using them illegally, and a further Ordinance was issued in 1670 to remind them of their obligations. This was repeated in 1681 and again in 1689, by which time the authorities appear to have given up trying to make merchant ships wear any specific flag, but merely allowed: 'whatever distinction they think fit, so long as the stern ensign be not entirely white'. This doubtless explains the great wealth of local flags known from harbours all round the coast of France in the eighteenth century, which were nearly all combinations of blue and white.

The Revolution of 1789 led to the abandonment of all these flags. The red, white and blue of the revolutionaries became established at an early stage in Paris, from at least 17 July 1789 when the King was forced to add the blue and red cockade of Paris to the white cockade of the Bourbons that he wore in his hat. The first official use of these colours in a flag was in the Naval Ensign established on 24 October 1790. This was still white, but had a version of the Tricolour in the first quarter. This version, also used as the Jack, was vertical stripes of red, white and blue, with a white inner border and an outer border parti-coloured blue and red. On land various patterns of red, white and blue were used, and even at sea there was little uniformity. Eventually on 24 May 1794 the first Naval Ensign was abolished, and a uniform Tricolour was prescribed for all purposes. This is the flag we know today, of three vertical bands of blue, white and red. Later, on 17 May 1853, the flag for use at sea was given the proportions 30:33:37 in terms of the blue, white and red bands in the length. This was done to make them appear more nearly equal in conditions of difficult visibility. The Tricolour, as it is now universally known, remained the National Flag of France during the Directory, the First Consulate, and the Empire of Napoleon. The royalists abroad continued to use the white flag of the Bourbons, and this was restored on 14 April 1814 when it seemed that Napoleon was defeated. He returned, however, and restored the Tricolour on 9 March 1815, but only for his 'Hundred Days' and it went out of use again when he was defeated at Waterloo. He himself did more to glorify the Tricolour than any other Frenchman has ever done,

France: the Tricolour

France: President's Flag

and of the Colours laid up in Les Invalides nearly all are ones carried by his armies. His own Standard was the Tricolour, strewn with golden bees (an emblem derived from the Frankish kings), with his Coat of Arms in the centre. This of course featured the gold eagle that is the only possible emblem for an Emperor. The Tricolour was re-established on 2 August 1830 and, except for a slight hiatus during the revolution of 1848, has remained in use ever since, even during the German occupation of the Second World War. During the Second World War French patriots abroad rallied round the symbol of the Cross of Lorraine adopted by General de Gaulle, and this was sometimes placed in the centre of the Tricolour to make the flag of the 'Free French'. Later, a Jack with the Cross of Lorraine was adopted for ships which had taken part in the Free French forces. The ordinary Jack is the same as the National Flag, as is the Merchant Ensign.

France has no Coat of Arms as such, but on 3 June 1953 the national emblem that had been in use since the establishment of the Third Republic was officially adopted. This is a blue oval, with a vertical axe and fasces, behind which are crossed a branch of oak and of olive, and across which is a ribbon with the national motto, *Liberté Egalité Fraternité*, all in gold, with black lettering. The axe and fasces, in this context an emblem of republicanism, date back to the earliest days of the Revolution, and were used on many flags of that time, including one worn on the ship of Napoleon when he landed in Malta in 1798. Since the time of Louis-Philippe, and apart from the Second Empire, French Heads of State have used a square version of the National Flag with their initials in the centre. In December 1974, however, President Giscard D'Estaing introduced a new pattern, with a version of the national emblem in the centre, all in gold. In this the axe faces to dexter, and is surrounded only by a wreath of laurel. In practice the flag is 27:38 for use on a car, and 35:45 for use on an aeroplane. As in Britain, the Defence Forces of France have been brought under a single Minister, known as the *Ministre des Armées*. A flag for this Ministry was introduced in 1966, consisting of a square version of the National Flag for use at sea with an emblem representing the *Armées de terre, de mer, et de l'air* in the centre in gold.

A standard type of regimental Colour is used by all three services and by special units of the Navy and units of the Air Force. These Colours, which date from about 1880 but are basically the same as those used by Napoleon, consist of a fringed Tricolour with the name *République Française* on the obverse, and the motto *Honneur et Patrie* on the reverse, all in gold letters. In each corner is a wreath with the initial or number of the unit. The pike has a gilded lance-head finial, and may carry pennants or *cravates* embroidered in more detail with the name of the unit and also its battle-honours. The Colours of the famous French Foreign Legion, *La Légion Étrangère*, follow the same pattern, but it also has its own unit flags consisting of a field divided diagonally green over red, with the Legion's grenade badge in the centre, with a unit number within it, and the motto *Honneur et Patrie* along the top, and *Légion Étrangère* along the bottom, all in gold. The Legion won more battle honours than any other part of the French Army in the First World War, and as a result does in fact have them embroidered on its Colours.

At the end of the Second World War France had a considerable number of overseas possessions, divided into Overseas Departments (Martinique, Guadeloupe, Réunion, and French Guiana), Overseas Territories (French Polynesia, New Caledonia, the Territory of the Afars and Issas, St Pierre and Miquelon, the Southern and Antarctic Territories, and Wallis and Futuna), and the colonies and protectorates in Africa and Asia. Algeria was a part of Metropolitan France. In the course of time the French possessions in Asia achieved independence, as did Tunisia and Morocco, but the independence of Algeria precipitated an internal crisis in France which brought General de Gaulle back to power. In 1958 he offered the larger colonies in Africa the choice of independence or autonomy within the French Community. Guinea was the only one to choose outright independence at that time, although the remainder have since done so. A special flag for the Community was created, consisting of the Tricolour with a gold fringe and a special finial in the form of a wreath containing two clasped hands, and with the motto *Liberté Egalité Fraternité* emblazoned across it in gold. But whilst the former colonies have maintained strong cultural and economic links with France and have retained French as their official language, the idea of the Community itself does not seem to have taken root, and in consequence the banner has fallen from use. Originally several copies were made, of which one remained in Paris whilst the others were sent to the capitals of the member countries.

The Overseas Departments and Territories of France do not have distinctive flags, and all use the Tricolour on land and sea.

France: Emblem of Ministry of Defence

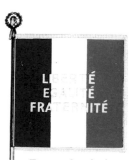

France: Standard of the French Community

France: Military Colours (reverse)

Until just over a hundred years ago, **Germany** was a collection of independent states, some large and powerful, such as Prussia, and others very small. During the Middle Ages they had formed part of the Holy Roman Empire, but this had only a nominal existence and was finally dissolved by Napoleon in 1806. After this two opposing varieties of

Germany: *Germany:*   *German Federal Republic:*
the 'Black-Red-Gold'   *the 'Black-White-Red'*   *State Flag*

nationalism emerged in Germany: the one federalist and democratic, the other, led by the growing power of Prussia, centralist and imperialist. The colours adopted by the federalists first appeared at the all-German Parliament which met at Frankfurt in 1848. The flag then used was of three horizontal stripes of black, red and gold. Its colours are said to be derived from those used by the partisans and students who had fought against Napoleon. The federalist congress was, however, suppressed, and instead a North German Confederation was launched by Bismarck in 1867. This had a flag of three horizontal stripes, but black, white and red, a combination of the black and white of Prussia and the white and red of the Hanseatic League, the medieval German trading organization. This flag was adopted as that of Germany when the Empire was established on 18 January 1871 in the wake of the Franco-Prussian War. A new Naval Ensign and Jack were also adopted, and a whole range of departmental and service flags, all in black, white and red.

After the defeat of Germany in the First World War the democratic colours re-emerged to be adopted by the first federal, or 'Weimar' republic. They were never popular, however, with right-wing groups, and their revival was short lived. When Hitler came to power on 30 January 1933 the Imperial colours were immediately restored, and the Nazi Party flag, the *Hakenkreuz*, was ordered to be flown alongside them. On 15 September 1935 the Swastika became the only National Flag. It had a red field with a black swastika on a white disc, which thus repeated the Imperial colours whilst abandoning the design. After the collapse of Germany in 1945 and its occupation by the four allied powers all swastika flags and emblems were removed. The state of Prussia was finally dismembered, and ultimately two régimes, each claiming to be the heirs of the democratic tradition, were set up in 1949, now known popularly as East Germany and West Germany. Both use the black, red and yellow tricolour, although their emblems and flags differ in other respects.

The **German Federal Republic** was established in the three western zones of Germany on 23 May 1949. The Basic Law adopted on that date included provision for the National Flag to be the German tricolour of black, red and yellow, although the federal colours had already been officially adopted on 9 May of that year. This has remained the National Flag, without any additions, since then. It became the Merchant Ensign on 14 August 1950. A State Flag was also introduced at that time, with the shield of Arms in the centre, or to be precise set slightly towards the hoist. Likewise a flag for the Ministry of Posts and Telecommunications was introduced, like the National Flag but with the central red stripe slightly wider than usual, with the post horn in gold in the centre. This flag was also used during the first republic.

The same is true of the President's Standard, also introduced in 1950. This is square, with a yellow field bordered all round in red, with the German eagle in black in the centre. The eagle is not exactly the same as that used in the Weimar republic, in that it has only ten stylized feathers, as opposed to twelve. The State Arms are also a stylized black eagle with red beak and claws on a gold field. This emblem dates back to the very earliest days of heraldry as that of the Holy Roman Empire, and was also used by the Empire of 1871–1918, but in a much more elaborate form.

On 5 May 1955 the Federal Republic adopted a Naval Ensign, consisting of the State Flag with a swallow-tail. This flag is also the Jack. Auxiliary vessels and naval establishments use the ordinary State Flag, which is also used in the proportions one by two for the Prime Minister or Minister of Defence when embarked upon a warship. The flag of an Admiral of the German Navy is the same as in the days of the Empire, a square white flag with the Iron Cross filling the field. This is a black cross with curvilinear arms with a white border edged in black, and is the badge of the Teutonic Knights. A Vice-Admiral has a black disc in the canton, a Rear Admiral a second disc in the lower hoist canton, and a Commodore a third disc in the upper fly canton. The Broad Pendant, now known as the Squadron Pendant, is like the Admiral's flag, but has a long swallow-tail added. The Division Flag is white and triangular but with the fly cut short, and charged at the hoist with the Iron Cross. The masthead pennant is a long white swallow-tail with the Iron Cross in the hoist. All of these date back to the Empire.

The Army uses the State Flag, and units of the armed forces all have the same basic Ceremonial Colours. These are also the State Flag, but square, with a border of red and black and with a gold fringe on three sides. As in France, cravats are added to the finial to distinguish the various units. These also carry the unit badge, and have fields of blue for the Navy, red for the Army, and white for the Air Force.

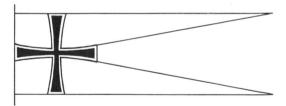

German Federal Republic: *German Federal Republic:*
President   *Squadron Pendant*

The Federal Republic consists of eleven states or *Länder*, including West Berlin, which all have a considerable degree of autonomy, and their own Arms and flags, some of which are of great antiquity. That of Bremen for example dates back in one form or another to at least 1366, and the castle of Hamburg has been in use since at least 1100. Both these cities have maintained their separate identity through all the constitutional changes, and were predominant members of the Hanseatic League. Most of the *Länder* have State Flags, which usually include their Arms, and flags for popular use which are plain.

Baden-Württemberg consists of the former states of Baden and Württemberg and was formed on 9 December 1951. Its Arms are those of the Hohenstaufens, a former

Baden-Württemberg: Arms   *Bavaria: Arms*

Imperial family, three black lions passant on a yellow shield. The flag is in the same colours, black over yellow, and the State Flag has the shield ensigned with a coronet in the centre.

Bavaria is a state which has been in continuous existence since medieval times. Its Arms are those of the Wittelsbach family, a pattern of blue and white lozenges. The State Flag is a banner of these Arms, and the general flag is plain white over blue. An alternative version of the State Flag has this with the shield from the Arms in the centre.

Berlin has a black bear for its emblem. This appears on a flag of white with red bands at the top and bottom. The plain bear, near the hoist, is the City Flag. The State Flag has the bear on a crowned shield.

Bremen has used a flag of this pattern since 1891. The State Flag has a white panel in the centre with the crowned shield of Arms. This is red with the key of St Peter, the city's patron saint, in white.

Hamburg's general flag is red with a white triple-towered castle, having six-pointed stars over the two outer towers. The State Flag is also red with a large white panel bearing the whole achievement of Arms. Hamburg's official title is: *Freie und Hansestadt Hamburg* ('The Free Hanseatic City of Hamburg').

Hesse uses its traditional flag of red over white derived from the colours of the Arms. These show a lion rampant barred in red and white, on a blue shield. This shield appears in the centre of the State Flag.

Berlin: Arms   *Bremen: State Flag*   *Hamburg:* Land *Flag*

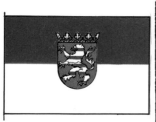

Hesse: State Flag   *Lower Saxony: State Flag*   *Schleswig-Holstein:*
                                                                State Flag

North Rhine-Westphalia: *Rhineland-Palatinate:*   *Saarland: Arms*
Arms   *Arms*

Lower Saxony includes Hanover and Brunswick. Its shield is the white horse of Brunswick which also features in British Royal heraldry, since our present dynasty was derived from Hanover. This shield appears in large proportions on the German national tricolour to form the *Land* flag.

North Rhine-Westphalia has a flag adopted in 1953, in colours taken from the Arms of its main component parts, in the form of a horizontal tricolour of green, white and red, with the shield of Arms in the centre.

Rhineland-Palatinate also uses the national tricolour, with its Arms in the upper hoist. These are in three parts, representing Trier, Mainz, and the Palatinate.

Saarland was detached from Germany after the Second World War, and only returned after a plebiscite on 1 January 1957, when it became a state within the Federal Republic. It had previously used French-inspired flags during its two periods of occupation by that country. Its own flag, officially adopted on 10 September 1956, is the German tricolour with the Arms of Saarland on a large central shield. The shield is divided quarterly: (1) Nassau-Saarbrücken; (2) Trier; (3) Lorraine; and (4) Zweibrucken.

Schleswig-Holstein has a flag dating back to 1843, in colours derived from the Arms of the two Duchies, which are now impaled on one shield. The flag is a horizontal tricolour of blue, white and red, with the shield in the centre. This bears to dexter two blue lions on a field of yellow (see also Denmark), and to sinister a white 'nettle-leaf' on red for Holstein.

German Democratic Republic:
Flag of the Chairman of the Council of State

German Democratic Republic:
National and Merchant Flag

Germany is a country particularly rich in flags, and most cities and districts have distinctive ones. Those of territories now in East Germany or other eastern countries are also still remembered and displayed.

The **German Democratic Republic** was established in the Soviet Zone of Germany on 7 October 1949, and from then until 1 October 1959 it used the unmodified German tricolour. On the latter date the state emblem was added in the centre to make the State Flag more distinctive from that of the German Federal Republic. The state emblem is in the German colours, but follows the typical pattern of a Communist republic. The central device is a hammer surmounted by a pair of dividers, representing the industrial workers and those involved in scientific instrument production. Around this is a wreath of wheat-ears, symbolic of agricultural prosperity, tied in a ribbon of the national colours. This was introduced on 26 September 1955.

The State Flag became the National and Merchant Flag on 1 May 1973. The Naval Ensign is red with the national colours across the centre, and over all a disc with a narrow black fimbriation charged with the state emblem within a further wreath of laurel in gold. The flag of the *Volksarmee* ('People's Army') is like the National Flag, but instead of the ordinary Arms has the emblem from the centre of the Ensign placed centrally.

The flag of the Chairman of the Council of State, an office which replaced that of President on 12 September 1960, is square with a red field charged with the state emblem, and with a corded border of the national colours. The Minister of Defence flies a blue flag in the proportions 3:5 with the state emblem in the centre. There is also a special Ensign for the Fleet Auxiliaries, which is the same pattern as the Naval Ensign, but with a blue field. The Hydrographic Service adds a yellow lighthouse to this in the upper fly.

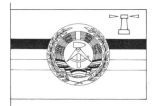

German Democratic Republic:
Hydrographic Service Ensign

German Democratic Republic:
Naval Ensign

and the Salvage and Rescue Service a yellow diver's helmet. The Chief of the Navy has a plain blue flag with an upright foul anchor in the centre and three stars in a vertical row in the fly, all yellow. A Vice-Admiral has the same with two stars, in the lower fly canton, and a Rear-Admiral has one star. The pennant has the Naval Ensign in the hoist, and a red fly for the regular Navy and a blue fly for the Auxiliaries. Ships of the Border Troops use the Army Ensign with a vertical green band at the hoist, and the Coast Guard use the Naval Ensign, also with a vertical green band in the hoist. The flag of the Mail Service is the plain tricolour but with a bugle from which are issuing lightning-flashes in gold in the centre. The central red band is wider than normal on this flag.

Immediately after the war East Germany was divided into five *Länder* or states, Brandenburg, Mecklenburg, Saxony, Saxony–Anhalt, and Thuringia, but the constitution of the German Democratic Republic is not a federal one, and these states with their Arms and flags were dissolved in July 1952.

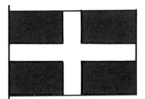

Greece: National Flag

Greece: Merchant and Naval Ensign

Greece: Personal Flag of ex-King Constantine

The simple National Flag of **Greece** dates back to the early part of the nineteenth century when the people fought to obtain their independence from Turkey. According to tradition Bishop Germanos hoisted a blue flag with a white cross at Lavra on 25 March 1821, although the exact form of this is uncertain. But blue and white were established as the national colours when Prince Otto of Bavaria, whose colours these were (*see* p. 120, Bavaria), became King in 1833. There has also been persistent uncertainty about the exact shade of blue to be used in the Greek flag, but an intermediate blue now seems to have become established.

From 1833 until June 1975 the plain flag was restricted to use on land within the boundaries of Greece itself. For a period during which the 'Colonels' were in power, from 18 August 1970 to 23 July 1974, it was abolished altogether. It was restored in its original capacity when the military dictatorship was ended on the latter date, and since 7 June 1975 has been established as the only National Flag. Greece has had another flag, now the Naval and Mercantile Ensign. This has nine stripes of blue and white, with a square canton of blue with the white cross. It seems to have been based on that of the USA, although the stripes are said to stand for the motto used during the independence struggle: *Eleutheria a Thanatos* ('Liberty or Death'). The present National Flag may be used on land both within the country and abroad. The State Arms were also altered in June 1975, and now consist of a shield of the same design as the National Flag within a wreath of silver laurel leaves. The previous emblem, used following the establishment of the republic on 29 July 1973, consisted of a golden phoenix arising from red flames. This still appears on the President's Flag which is blue, in the proportions 20:23, with a gold fringe. The phoenix emblem had been used during the previous republic of 1924–35. The last King of Greece, Constantine II, has lived abroad since 1967. His personal standard is like the National Flag, but with a large shield of the royal arms in the centre, ensigned with the Greek crown, and a small crown in each canton. The shield of Arms is the same as that previously used in Denmark: King Constantine is the great-grandson of Prince George of Denmark who became King of Greece in 1863.

As far as is known, red, white and green made their first appearance as the national colours of **Hungary** at the beginning of the thirteenth century. Later it is recorded that at the coronation of King Mathias II in 1608, 'the wooden bridge leading from the coronation church of Pozsony to the Franciscan church had been covered in a carpet in red, white and green colours'; also that three years later the King gave orders for 'sixty flags in red, white and green silk for warfare'.

Hungary: National Flag
and Ensign

Hungary: State Emblem

The Hungarian colours were suppressed under the Hapsburgs until the revolution of 1848 brought them out again during the short-lived Free State established by Lajos Kossuth. He was also responsible for the restoration of the Arms of Hungary, consisting of a shield of two parts: to dexter seven bars of red and white, and to sinister a white double cross emerging from a coronet on a triple mount, the whole ensigned with the Crown of St Stephen, with its characteristic bent cross. Following the *Ausgleich* or 'compromise' of 1867, the Hungarian colours were incorporated into the Merchant Flag of the Dual Monarchy of Austria–Hungary, and after the fall of this Empire in 1918 they became the National Flag of an independent Hungary. On the State Flag the Arms were placed near the hoist, but in the usual flag they were omitted. This remained the case until the end of the Second World War, in which Hungary fought on the German side. On being occupied by the Red Army a republic was formed, which used the shield from the 'Kossuth' Arms, usually a small version placed in the centre of the white stripe. Hungary became a People's Republic on 18 August 1949, and a completely new emblem was adopted, according to Paragraph 68 of the new Constitution. This consisted of a light blue field with golden rays emanating from a red gold-bordered star above. On the field were a crossed hammer and ear of wheat, and around it were further ears of wheat in a wreath, and below a ribbon of the national colours. This was placed in the centre of the flag.

During the Hungarian revolt of October–November 1956 this emblem was torn out of the flag, and for a few weeks the flag with the 'Kossuth' Arms was restored. After the quelling of this revolt the flag remained without any Arms whatsoever, although a new state emblem was introduced in 1957. This consists of a shield in the national colours, on the same field as the previous emblem, and with a wreath of wheat-ears tied on one side with a ribbon of red, white and green, and on the other with a ribbon of red. The plain tricolour is thus the National and State Flag, and Ensign of Hungary.

Iceland became a separate kingdom in union with Denmark on 30 November 1918, and by a royal decree of 12 February 1919 King Christian X of Denmark approved the use of a special flag for Iceland. This had already been used unofficially since 1913, and since 19 June 1915 officially on land and within Icelandic waters, which were not so extensive as they are today. The National Flag was and is blue with a red cross fimbriated in white. Blue and white were the traditional colours of Iceland (as King, the King of Denmark used a blue flag with a silver crowned falcon). The red cross commemorates the previous union with Norway, and the Scandinavian form of cross links Iceland to the other Scandinavian countries.

Iceland: Arms

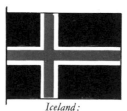

Iceland:
National and Merchant Flag

The Ensign was introduced in 1918, and has the same shape as that of Denmark. When Iceland became a republic on 17 June 1944 these flags were retained, but a new Coat of Arms and a flag for the President were adopted. The Arms consist of a blue shield with the same pattern as the National Flag, supported by four figures: of a bull, an eagle, a dragon and a giant. According to the *Heimskringla*, the saga of the Kings of Norway, these are guardian spirits who defended the island from an attack by the King of Denmark! The President's flag is the Ensign, with a square panel at the centre of the cross, bearing the Arms.

The Posts and Telegraph service also uses the Ensign, but with the addition of the post-horn and thunderbolt emblem, in silver in the canton. The Customs service does likewise, with a silver letter T.

The National Flag of **Ireland** or **Éire** is a vertical tricolour of green, white and orange. It would seem to date from 1848, when meetings were held to celebrate the revolution then going on in France. The Young Ireland movement sent a deputation to Paris and were there encouraged to adopt a tricolour of their own. The colours were to represent 'United Ireland', i.e. both Catholic (green) and Protestant (orange) united by peace (white). The traditional flag of Irish nationalism was however the 'Green Flag', charged with a golden harp. This dates back to at least the mid-seventeenth century, but the harp itself is said to be that of King Brian Boru who flourished in the eleventh century. Green is the colour associated with St Patrick, the patron saint of Ireland.

During the rising of Easter 1916 both the Green Flag and the tricolour were used. Green, white and orange were the colours of the flag of the Irish Citizen Army which

Ireland: National and Merchant Flag and Ensign   *Ireland: President*

took a leading part in the rebellion. The flags flown from the rebel headquarters in the Dublin Post Office were the tricolour and a green banner with the legend 'Irish Republic' in white and orange letters. The actual 'Post Office' flag, captured by the British, was restored to the Irish government on 14 July 1966.

When the Free State was formed, officially on 21 January 1919, the tricolour had so captured the popular imagination as to be the only possible choice for a National Flag. Although at first the arrangement of colours was various, e.g. in 1848 the orange was next to the mast, by 1920 it was definitely established in its present form and was officially recognized as the National Flag by the constitution of 29 December 1937, which states that 'the national flag is the tricolour of green, white and orange'. It continued as such when the Republic was finally established on 18 April 1949. Its official proportions are one by two. It is the National Flag, Naval, and Mercantile Ensign, and its usage is based on a code, itself derived from that of the USA, issued by the government.

The Jack, as in other countries, recalls an early nationalist flag, in this case the 'Green Flag'. The flag of the President, on the other hand, recalls the quartering for Ireland in the Royal Arms of the United Kingdom, and the former Royal Arms of Ireland, being blue with the harp in gold. This harp is however the 'Brian Boru' model, not that used in the British Arms or in Northern Ireland. There are no official state Arms, but the blue shield with the harp in gold is widely used in practice.

Italy was, like Germany, a mere 'geographical expression' until just over a hundred years ago, and was composed of many small states, some included in the Austrian Empire. When Napoleon invaded Italy in 1796 those who wished to free themselves of oppression saw an opportunity for liberation, and hastened to join what was seen as an extension of the French Revolution. Following local revolutions pro-French states were formed in Lombardy (the Transpadane Federation), and in Modena (the Cispadane Federation). In Lombardy the Lombard Legion was formed, with a uniform of green, white and red, and from as early as 9 October 1796 this was equipped with Colours in the form of a vertical tricolour of green, white and red. In the Cispadane Republic these same colours were also adopted, but placed horizontally. They were also used by the subsequent Cisalpine Republic, from 17 July 1797, which had them arranged vertically in green, white and red, and by the Italian Republic, from January 1802, which had a red field with a white diamond over all containing a green rectangle. When Napoleon became King of Italy the central panel was charged with his Arms. This and all his other flags went out of use after 1814–15, and the former flags of the various feudatory states were restored.

However, the tricolour lived on in the popular imagination as the flag of emancipation from both autocratic and foreign rule, and several attempts were made to unite the country as a free, democratic and Italian state. During the Year of Revolutions, 1848, the tricolour was in use in several states which threw off foreign or autocratic rulers. In Savoy–Sardinia the tricolour was adopted without a revolution, on 23 March 1848, but with the shield of Savoy in the centre (a white cross on a red ground with a blue border). The blue border was added on this occasion as a fimbriation. On 15 April the Naval Ensign of Savoy–Sardinia was also changed to the tricolour. Although suppressed in other Italian States the tricolour remained as the flag of Savoy–Sardinia, and the form established on 2 May 1851 is basically the same as that of today, except for the shield and crown of Savoy in the centre.

The new Italian Kingdom was formed under the House of Savoy on 17 March 1861 and used the tricolour until 10 June 1946 when the Republic was declared and the Arms of Savoy were removed from the flag. Since that date the National Flag has been the plain tricolour.

In order to distinguish the Merchant Flag from that of Mexico, which was then also a plain tricolour, a new shield was devised for the centre. This is quartered, and bears the Arms of four of the medieval maritime republics of Italy: Venice, Genoa, Amalfi and Pisa. The shield has a gold corded border. The Naval Ensign is very similar, except that it has a gold naval crown, of the type used by the Romans as a military decoration, above the shield, and there is a slight variation in the Arms of Venice in the first quarter. In the Ensign the lion has his left paw on a closed book and holds a sword in his right. In the Merchant Flag he has an open book, as in the traditional arms of Venice. The shield from the Naval Ensign, in square shape, forms the Jack of the Italian Navy.

Italy: National Flag

Italy: Ensign

Italy: Jack

The flag of the President is also square, in royal blue, with the Arms in gold. The State Arms were adopted in 1948 and consist of a large white star edged in red placed over a blue cogwheel, surrounded by a wreath of olive and oak, and with a red ribbon inscribed *Republica Italiana*.

The Minister of Defence has a flag with a royal blue field with the combined forces emblem in gold in the centre, and a rectangular gold frame. The Chief of Naval Staff has a similar flag, but in place of the emblem four gold stars arranged diagonally from hoist to fly. Admirals have plain blue flags with stars arranged diagonally, varying in number with their rank. The Chief of Defence General Staff has a blue flag with a double white rectangular frame, within which are four white stars arranged diagonally. The Chief of Army Staff has a blue triangular flag with a red border on all three sides and four red stars

Italy: Minister of Defence   *Liechtenstein: National Flag*

in a horizontal row. The Chief of Air Staff has a blue flag with a single red rectangular frame, within which are four red stars arranged diagonally.

The Naval Ensign is the proper flag for yachts of the Yacht Club Italiano and the Naval Yacht Club, and the plain tricolour is used for the President afloat.

Italy is a country rich in civic flags, and the 'Palio' of Siena is an outstanding example of their use, but it has few regional flags, and those of the former States are no longer in use.

The colours of **Liechtenstein** are royal blue and red, divided horizontally. These have been in use since the eighteenth century, but their origin is unknown. A crown was placed in the upper hoist for the Olympic Games of 1936, in order to avoid confusion with the then flag of Haiti. The crown always remains upright, even when the flag is hung vertically, as it often is. The Royal Banner consists of a flag divided horizontally yellow over red, the colours of the inescutcheon on the Prince's Arms. The main shield of the Arms is quartered, with in the first quarter the Arms of Silesia, in the second those of the Künringen, in the third those of Troppau, and in the fourth those of East Friesland and Rietburg; in a small space at the bottom is the Arms of Jägerndorf. These represent the noble families from which the Prince is descended.

All the eleven communes which make up the tiny Principality have flags and Arms of their own.

The Grand Duchy of **Luxemburg** has a flag which is almost identical to that of the Netherlands, except that it has the proportions three by five as opposed to the Dutch two by three, and the blue of the Luxemburg flag is somewhat lighter than the Dutch. Although Luxemburg and the Netherlands are ruled by collateral branches of the same royal family, the similarity in their flags is a coincidence. The colours of Luxemburg can be said to be derived from the Arms, which are bands of white and blue with a red lion rampant over all. This dates from at least 1288. A banner of the Arms has been in use as a

Luxemburg: National Flag   *Luxemburg: Standard of*   *Luxemburg: Merchant Flag*
                               Grand Duke (obverse)

local flag since at least the early part of the seventeenth century, and in recent years the National Flag has often included the shield of Arms, to distinguish it more from that of the Netherlands. The banner of Arms, i.e. a flag in proportions 5:7 with ten stripes of white and blue with the red lion rampant over all, was prescribed as the Ensign for merchant vessels and civil aviation in 1968.

The Personal Standard of the Grand Duke is square, with a blue field charged with a 'modernized' version of the Arms: the shield with the Order of the Oaken Crown around it, and seven gold 'billets'. These are taken from the quartering for the Netherlands in the Grand-Duke's Arms. This Standard was introduced soon after his accession in 1964, and it has the national tricolour on the reverse. The Arms and flags of Luxemburg were all revised and regulated by new legislation on 16 August 1972.

| *Malta: Arms* | *Malta: National Flag* | *Malta: Merchant Flag* |

The Knights of the Sovereign Military Hospitaller Order of St John of Rhodes and Malta established their headquarters on the island of **Malta** in 1530, and were thereafter known as the Knights of Malta. Their Arms and flag consist of a white plain cross on a field of red, and their badge is an eight-pointed silver cross of the type known as a 'Maltese Cross'. White and red have always been used as the colours of Malta, and after the island was acquired by the British, the Knights of St John having been expelled by Napoleon in 1798, ensign badges in various combinations of these colours, with and without the Maltese Cross, were in use. The most recent form was a plain vertical shield of white and red. To this was added by Royal Warrant on 28 December 1943, 'a representation of the George Cross proper'. This decoration was awarded to the people of Malta by King George VI to 'bear witness to the heroism and devotion of its people' during the great siege it underwent in the early part of the Second World War. At first the George Cross was contained in a small blue canton, but when Malta became independent on 21 September 1964 the blue background was removed. This island had already transformed its blue ensign badge into a flag for local use in 1947, and this flag, without the blue background to the George Cross, continued in use on independence. A new Coat of Arms was adopted, also with the same shield as before, but with supporters of two dolphins, a royal helmet and mural crown and a compartment of blue and white wavy water around a rock on which is a Maltese Cross. The motto on a red scroll is *Virtute et Constantia* ('With Courage and Constancy').

A Merchant Ensign was adopted on 12 November 1965, the design of which is based on the flag of the Grand Master of the Knights of Malta, i.e. a red field with the Maltese Cross in white in the centre. In this however there is also a white border around all four sides of the flag. The flag of the Grand Master is still in use in Rome, where the headquarters of the Order are now situated. In Britain the flag of the Order (red with a plain white cross) is flown by the British Association of the Order. There is also a sister-order established by Queen Victoria in 1888, the St John's Ambulance Brigade. This has a flag of black with a large silver Maltese Cross and gold lion and a unicorn between alternate arms of the cross. The Queen's Personal Standard for use in Malta was established on 31 October 1967, with the royal cypher on blue in the centre of a banner of the Arms, but this became obsolete when Malta became a Republic on 12 December 1974. There is as yet no flag for the President of the Republic, but a new national emblem, or 'logo', has been adopted.

The Principality of **Monaco** is situated in the south of France, and contains the famous casino town of Monte Carlo. Its colours are simple red over white, the same pattern as that of Indonesia. Monaco's colours date back to at least 1339, and are derived from the Arms of the ruling family, the Grimaldi. The Arms have a shield of red and white lozenges, surrounded by the Order of St Charles and supported by two monks holding swords, with the motto *Deo Juvante* ('With God's Help'), which is also the name of the Prince's yacht. The Prince's Standard, flown from this yacht and at the palace, is white with the whole Arms in the centre. There is also a car-flag of white, with Prince Rainier's cypher in the centre in red and gold.

Monaco: Arms

Monaco: National Flag

Netherlands: National and Merchant Flag and Ensign

The Netherlands, under their famous leader William I, Prince of Orange and Count of Nassau, started their war of independence against Spain in 1568. Independence was practically achieved by 1581 but not formally recognized until 1648. Under William of Orange the Dutch used tricolours of orange, white and blue, known as the *Prinsvlag*, but towards the end of the sixteenth century the top stripe became red. This was possibly due to the indefiniteness of orange and its liability to fade in the sea air, or it may have been to symbolize that power was passing to the States-General (which used a flag of red with a gold lion) from the House of Orange. Moreover there was at first great latitude of treatment in the flag designs, and the number of bars of each colour and their order was variable. Also during this period Jacks were of a gyronny pattern, i.e. with alternating triangles of the national colours; these usually bore the States-General Arms in the centre. Orange remains a feature of Dutch flag-usage to this day, and the House of Orange still rules the country. Flags with orange streamers above them are very frequently employed. The original Union of Utrecht in 1579 included all seventeen provinces of the Netherlands, but the Catholic ones which now form the Kingdom of

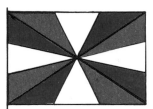

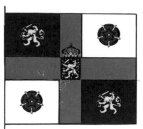

Netherlands: Jack   *Netherlands:*   *Standard of Prince Bernhard*
                             Royal Standard

Belgium were never successfully incorporated, and only seven provinces ultimately formed the Republic of the Netherlands, although others have been organized since. For this reason the lion of the States-General is shown holding a bundle of seven arrows, and these still appear today in the modern Royal Arms.

During the French Revolution the Netherlands became the Batavian Republic. At this time the 'Canton of Liberty'—a white panel with a figure of Liberty and a crouching lion—was added to the flag. This was never popular, and the plain flag under which the Dutch had fought so many successful battles was soon restored. After the fall of Napoleon Belgium was attached to the Netherlands, which then became a kingdom. Belgium, as described on p. 108, achieved her independence in 1830, and Luxemburg has also since separated itself from the Netherlands.

The plain tricolour is the National and Merchant flag, and the Ensign of the Netherlands. The modern Jack, introduced in 1931, is a revival of the gyronny pattern.

The Royal Standard of the Netherlands was established on 27 August 1908. The field is square and orange, charged with a cross over all of 'Nassau' blue. In each quarter is a 'Nassau' blue bugle, garnished with silver and hung on red cords. In the centre is the royal shield, which is blue with a rampant lion holding a sword in one paw and a bundle of arrows in the other, and strewn with billets, all in gold, surrounded by the ribbon and badge of the Order of William and ensigned with the Royal Crown. In addition to the Royal Standard there is also a Coronation Standard, only used at Coronation ceremonies, consisting of a white banner charged with the Royal Arms.

The Standard of Prince Bernhard, the royal consort, was established on 18 June 1937. The field is five by six, and is charged with an orange cross and with the royal shield and crown, but not the Order, in the centre. The first and fourth are blue and bear a lion as in the Arms, and the second and third are white and bear a red rose, from the Arms of Lippe–Biesterfeld. The Standard of Princess Beatrix, established on 10 November 1956, is the same shape as the others but has a triangle cut out of the fly. The field is likewise orange with a blue cross, and has the crowned shield on an orange disc in the centre. In the first quarter is a Nassau bugle as in the Royal Standard, and in the lower hoist a red rose of Lippe. The Standard of Prince Claus of Amsberg, her consort, was introduced soon after their marriage in 1966. It is the same shape as the other Standards, but blue with an orange cross, and in the centre the crowned shield. In the first and fourth quarters is the lion from the Royal Arms, and in the other two a white tower, from the Prince's Arms.

Standard of Princess Beatrix

*Royal Netherlands
Air Force Ensign*

The flag of the Minister of Defence is white with three narrow stripes of the national colours along the top and bottom, and in the centre are two crossed black anchors. The flag for other Ministers is the same, but with a gold lion as in the Royal Arms in the centre. The flag of an Admiral is the National Flag with two crossed white batons in the upper hoist. A 'Lieutenant-Admiral' has four six-pointed stars in place of this, a Vice-Admiral three stars, and a *Schout-bij-nacht*, or Rear-Admiral, two stars. There is a *kerkwimpel*, or Church Pendant, similar to that of the British Royal Navy, with the Cross of St George in the hoist and a fly divided red, white and blue.

All three of the Armed Forces have ceremonial Colours, which with one exception follow the same basic pattern. They are square and orange with a gold fringe. On the obverse is the cypher of the monarch who awarded them, in the base is the name of the unit, and in the cantons the citations or honours. On the reverse are the Royal Arms in blue and gold surrounded by a wreath. The exception is the Naval Cadet Corps, which has a red field and the same pattern on both sides. The Colours have a special finial to the pike: a platform on a column within a wreath, supporting a couchant lion holding a sword, all in gold.

The Royal Netherlands Air Force Ensign was introduced on 17 July 1964, replacing an earlier pattern. It has a field of blue with an orange triangle based on the hoist and charged with the Air Force emblem. The Naval Air Service Ensign is the National Flag, but with a white disc in the centre charged with the badge in full colour. The Naval Reserve Ensign is similar, but has a foul anchor and the royal crown, all in black, in the white disc.

The sole overseas dependency of the Netherlands is now the **Netherlands Antilles**, consisting of islands off the coast of Venezuela and in other parts of the Caribbean. A flag

*Netherlands:
Naval Reserve Ensign*

Netherlands Antilles

was introduced on 2 December 1959, in the Dutch colours, but with six white stars, one for each island group, on the blue horizontal stripe. The vertical stripe is red and the field white. A flag for the Governor was introduced on 14 March 1966. This is like the flag for Ministers, but has a cross in the centre made up of the blue and red stripes from the Antilles flag. One of the islands, Aruba, adopted its own flag in April 1976: this is blue with two narrow yellow stripes across the lower part, and in the upper hoist a red four-pointed star fimbriated in white.

The people of the Netherlands take a great interest in flags, and all the provinces, cities and towns, down to quite small villages, have their own distinctive flags which are in frequent use. In most cases the design and colours of the flags are related to the Coat of Arms, but many modern and ingenious variations are employed.

The province of **Drenthe** has a flag adopted on 19 February 1947. The red and white represent the former Diocese of Utrecht, the black tower stands for the struggle against oppression, and the stars for the tradition of legal independence.

The flag of **Friesland** is perhaps the best-known provincial flag of the Netherlands, due to the independent culture and language of its inhabitants, which it represents. The red shapes on the white bands represent the leaves of the *plompe*, a water plant, and feature on Coats of Arms dating back to earliest times. The flag has been recognized since 1897, and was officially adopted on 9 July 1957.

Gelderland has a simple flag of three horizontal bands of blue, yellow and black, adopted on 13 April 1953; these are the colours of the Coat of Arms.

Groningen also has a flag in the colours of its Coat of Arms, and which also refers to its name. The flag was adopted on 17 February 1950.

A red rampant lion on white is the Arms of the former Duchy of **Limburg**, now shared between Belgium and the Netherlands. The flag of the Dutch province uses all the colours from the Coat of Arms, with the red lion rampant over all near the hoist. This flag was adopted on 28 July 1953.

North Brabant is the Dutch part of the province of Brabant, and shares the same Arms, which are also those of Belgium. The flag however is quite distinct, and dates back to the ancient Duchy of Burgundy. Although only officially adopted on 21 January 1959 it is found on flag charts of three hundred years ago.

The original Arms of the County of Holland were yellow with a red lion rampant. The county now forms two Dutch provinces, of which **North Holland** is one. Its Arms now include the colour blue, and this is combined with the red and yellow to make the provincial flag, officially adopted on 22 October 1958.

Overijssel has a flag based on the Arms, and adopted on 21 July 1948. The blue wavy line represents the river Ijssel.

South Holland has retained the original Arms and colours of Holland, and its flag is a simple combination of the colours. The flag of the County of Holland was six horizontal bands of yellow and red. This flag was adopted on 22 June 1948.

Utrecht employs the colours of the former Diocese, a white cross on red, and the cross also appears in the canton of the flag. The present design was adopted on 15 January 1952.

Zeeland has its crowned shield of Arms in the centre of its flag, which show the lion of Holland arising from the sea. The flag was originally a banner of the Arms, or the Arms in the centre of a Dutch flag. The present design was adopted on 14 January 1949.

Drenthe

Friesland

Gelderland

Groningen

Limburg

North Brabant

North Holland

Overijssel

South Holland

Utrecht

Zeeland

Amsterdam

Amsterdam, the largest city of the Netherlands, also has a distinctive flag: that for popular use is the Arms of the city turned sideways. In the centre are three crosses of St Andrew, the patron saint. The flag of the city of **Rotterdam** is also very ancient: three horizontal stripes of green, white and green.

Norway and Denmark were united in 1397 and both countries used the Danish red flag with a white cross, the *Dannebrog*, until 1814, when Norway was obliged to enter into a union with Sweden as a separate kingdom under the Swedish crown. The flag for use on land only then became the *Dannebrog* with the Arms of Norway: a gold rampant lion grasping an axe, in the canton. Outside home waters Norwegian ships had to use the flag of Sweden with a red canton charged with a white saltire. However, in 1821 a National Flag for Norway was adopted by the *Storting* (the Norwegian parliament), which had a blue cross through the white cross of the flag of Denmark. This was also only for use on land and in home waters. On 20 June 1844 the Norwegian flag was recognized for all purposes, but with a 'Union Canton', consisting of the combined crosses of Norway and Sweden. However, this device was unpopular in Norway, and various attempts were made to get it removed, so that Norway would have her own distinctive range of flags. The Norwegian *Storting* took unilateral action to remove the Union Canton in 1898, and the King assented on 11 October 1899. Norway became a separate independent kingdom on 7 June 1905 and the country's flags, including the National Flag of 1821, were re-adopted. The Union Canton did in fact remain in the Ensign and certain other official flags up to the day of independence.

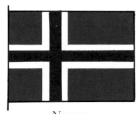

Norway:
National and Merchant Flag

Norway: Royal Standard

The Arms of Norway date back to the Middle Ages, and show a lion bearing the axe of St Olav. In the Royal Arms the axe has a shorter haft and more curvilinear blade than in the State Arms. The Royal Standard consists of a banner of the Royal Arms in the proportions 5:7. The Crown Prince has a similar banner but swallow-tailed.

The National and Merchant flags have the proportions 8:11. The Naval Ensign is swallow-tailed with a tongue, in the proportions 16:17. The Jack is a square version of the National Flag.

The Minister of Defence has the Naval Ensign, with a white version of the lion and axe from the Royal Arms in the canton. The Commander-in-Chief of the Navy has the same, but with two crossed batons in white in the canton. An Admiral has the same flag with three white stars; a Vice-Admiral has two stars, and a Rear-Admiral one.

The Customs flag is the Naval Ensign with a square white panel at the centre of the cross with the word *Toll* in gold letters and the royal crown. The Postal Flag is similar with the word *Post*.

A special Yacht Ensign may be worn by vessels owned by members of the Royal Norwegian Yacht Club. This is similar to the previous flags, with the royal cypher in gold beneath the crown from the State Arms.

Poland has a long and complicated history, but throughout it all her national emblem has always been a white eagle on a red field, and her national colours white and red. These were re-adopted when independence was re-established on 10 November 1918. The Arms and flag were officially adopted on 1 August 1919. At that time the Arms had a white zig-zag border round the shield, and the eagle was crowned. These emblems were also used in exile during the period of German occupation, 1939–45, and before the establishment of the People's Republic. The only change made since Poland became a Communist republic is the omission of the crown from the eagle's head and of the zig-zag border from the Arms. The plain flag of white over red, in proportions 5 : 8, is the general purposes flag for use on land. For use at sea it has the State Arms in the centre of the white strip. The Ensign is similar, but is swallow-tailed. The Fleet Auxiliaries Ensign is light blue with the Ensign in the canton. The Air Force Ensign is also light blue, with a band of white over red diagonally from upper hoist to lower fly, with the Air Force emblem in the centre. The Jack is an old Polish flag restored to use in 1960, although also used for this purpose before 1947. It is horizontally white over red, with a cross 'pattée' countercharged over all in the centre: this is charged with a red disc bearing an arm grasping a sword—a motif very popular with cavalry regiments in the sixteenth and seventeenth centuries.

Poland: National Flag

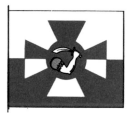

Poland: Jack

Poland has no President as such. This office is fulfilled by the Chairman of the Council of State. Prior to 1952 there was a President, and a Standard for the President, consisting of a banner of the Arms, in proportions 5 : 6, with the zig-zag pattern in white all round the border.

The flag of the Minister of Defence is similar to the Ensign, but with the addition of a yellow cannon crossed with a white anchor in the centre of the red stripe. The Coast Guard Ensign is the same as the Ensign, but with a green border on three sides, namely the hoist, top and bottom. The flag of an Admiral is similar to the Naval Ensign, but in the proportions 3 : 4; there are three white stars on the red strip near the hoist. Lesser admirals have fewer stars. The flag of the Yacht Club of Poland has the same basic design and proportions, but its distinguishing mark is a small white square in the upper hoist charged with a red saltire 'pattée' fimbriated in white and again in blue.

It is interesting to note that on several historical occasions National Flags in the unusual proportions of 3 : 8 (i.e. over twice as long as wide) have been used, and that these proportions were in fact laid down in the Decree of 7 December 1955 (although later rescinded).

The original national colours of **Portugal** were blue and white, but when the country became a republic on 5 October 1910 they were changed to red and green. The previous National Flag was divided vertically into two equal parts, but during the revolution the earlier custom of placing the national emblem near the hoist was reverted to. The pattern then adopted resulted in a flag of proportions 2:3 with the green to red in the proportions 5:8.

The armillary sphere is the main feature of the Coat of Arms, and contains the old shield of Portugal. The sphere—a medieval instrument of navigation—commemorates Prince Henry the Navigator who instigated the Portuguese voyages of discovery in the fifteenth century. It has appeared on Portuguese and Brazilian flags for over four hundred years. The shield in the centre is in two parts. The inner shield contains five smaller ones in blue, each charged with five white discs. The white discs represent the Five Wounds of Christ, and the five shields represent the victory of Alphonso Henriques in 1139 over five Moorish princes at the battle of Ourique. The outer part is red with seven gold castles, known as a 'Bordure of Castile', and commemorates the marriage of Alphonso III to a daughter of Alfonso the Wise of Castile in 1252.

The National Flag is also the Merchant Flag and Naval Ensign. The Jack is square, with the Arms on a red field within a green border all round. The flag of the President is green in the same proportions as the National Flag, with the Arms in the centre. The

Portugal: National and Merchant Flag and Ensign

Portugal: Jack

actual Arms, as opposed to those which appear on these flags, have a wreath of golden laurel leaves around them, tied with a silver ribbon. They appear, with the addition of a motto meaning 'This is My Good and Beloved Fatherland' in a square flag divided vertically and centrally green and red, which is the distinguishing flag of the Army.

A flag for the Prime Minister was adopted on 2 February 1972. This is like the flag of the President, but is white with a green saltire with the Arms (sphere and shield) at the centre. There is a red border on all four sides with a pattern of laurel leaves in gold. This replaces the former flag of the Minister of Defence. An ordinary Minister has the same flag but without the border, except for the Minister for the Navy, who has a white flag with a green cross of St George, with the Arms in the centre. The same flag, without the Arms but with a red disc in the canton, is the flag of a Vice-Admiral. The Minister for War has a flag divided vertically like that of the Army, but with five white stars over all, arranged in a ring.

Portugal has one overseas territory, **Macao,** with a Governor. His flag is white with vertical green bars near the hoist and fly. Over all in the centre is the cross of the Order of Christ, charged in turn with the Arms. In practice only the flag of China is flown in Macao.

There are also two overseas departments, the **Azores** and **Madeira**, which, like Macao, have recently been granted full internal self-government. All the former overseas territories and states have achieved independence and are referred to on other pages, except for East Timor, now integrated into Indonesia.

The National Flag, Merchant Flag, and Ensign of **Romania** is a vertical tricolour of blue, yellow and red. These colours combine those of Moldavia and Wallachia. They first appeared in 1848, arranged horizontally, when the people of these provinces and of Transylvania combined to try to free themselves from Turkish rule. They were used again in 1859 when Prince Alexandru Ioann was elected as Prince of Wallachia and Moldavia, with the addition of emblems of the two provinces. In 1866 Prince Charles of Hohenzollern–Sigmaringen came to the throne and arranged the colours vertically with a Coat of Arms in the centre. This remained the flag of Romania until 1948 when the emblem of the Communist State was inserted in the centre. This shows a scene of forests and mountains with an oil-derrick in the foreground and the sun rising over all. This is contained within a wreath of wheat-ears, tied with a ribbon in the national colours. In 1952 a red star was added at the top of the emblem, and in 1965 the inscription on the ribbon was modified to give the new title of the state: *Republica Socialista Romania*, adopted in the Constitution of 21 August 1965.

The flag of the Chairman of the State Council and President is square with the same pattern as the National Flag, but having the Arms in larger proportions over all in the centre. All around is a border of red, fimbriated on the inner side in white, and with a wide gold fringe on the free sides.

The flag of the Minister of Defence is white in the same proportions as the National Flag, with the National Flag in the canton, and a large red star in the centre of the fly. The Jack is a square version of the National Flag, with two crossed white anchors in the hoist.

San Marino is the oldest independent state in Europe, dating from A.D. 885. Its Coat of Arms expresses its position; a mountain peak with three summits, each with a tower bearing an ostrich plume. The mountain is Mount Titano in the Appenines. The blue and white of the Arms have given rise to the flag. The flag for popular use is plain white over blue, and the State Flag has the Arms in the centre. These were first recorded about the time of Napoleon's attempts to free and unite Italy.

Romania:
State Emblem

Romania: National and
Merchant Flag and Ensign

San Marino: State Flag

The red and gold colours of **Spain** are among the best-known in the world, although the present pattern only dates from 28 May 1785. The colours are the heraldic colours of both Castile (red with a golden castle) and of Aragon (vertical red and yellow stripes), the countries united by King Ferdinand and Queen Isabella. The Kingdom was replaced by a republic in 1931 and the republican flag—a horizontal tricolour of red, yellow and purple—was introduced. The purple in this flag refers either to the *morado* colour of the lion in the Arms of Leon or to the pomegranate in the Arms of Granada. This flag in turn went out of use in 1939 when General Franco eliminated the republic. His own flag was that of the Kingdom, although the monarchy was not in fact restored until his death in 1975. The previous Merchant Flag, of yellow with two horizontal red stripes, went out of use in 1927 and was not restored. The present flag is the National Flag and Merchant Flag.

Spain: Arms *Spain: National and Merchant Flag* *Spain: Jack*

The Arms of Spain are also basically those of the monarchy, although without the Arms of dominion previously included. The first and fourth quarters are themselves divided quarterly into Castile and Leon. This part forms the flag of Spain most frequently seen in medieval times. The second and third quarters are divided vertically into Aragon and Navarre. In base is the pomegranate of Granada. The shield is supported by a black eagle of the Holy Roman Empire and the two pillars of Hercules, with the motto of Charles V: *Plus Ultra*. Around the eagle's head is a nimbus and a scroll with the Falangist motto: *Una Grande Libre*. Below are two other Falangist emblems, the yoke and bundle of arrows—derived from the badges of Ferdinand and Isabella. The motto 'Plus Ultra' ('More Beyond') refers to the former belief that the Pillars of Hercules were the end of the known world: a myth dispelled by the Spanish conquest of the New World. The Arms are placed over all in the hoist to form the State Flag, Ensign and Military Flag.

The Jack is a compendium of quarters from the Arms, those of Castile, Leon, Aragon and Navarre.

The Royal Standard was introduced for Prince Juan Carlos on 22 April 1971. It is very similar to the previous Royal Standard, having a blue field with the Arms in the centre. The new Royal Arms consists of a quartering each for Castile, Leon, Aragon and Navarre, as in the Jack, with Granada in base, and an oval inescutcheon with the Arms of the House of Bourbon: blue with three gold *fleurs-de-lys*. The shield is supported on the saltire raguly of Burgundy, ensigned with the royal crown of Spain, and surrounded by the collar of the Order of the Golden Fleece. Beneath the shield are the yoke and bundle of arrows referred to above. Juan Carlos I, King of Spain, acceded on 22 November 1975.

Spain: Royal Standard   *Spain: Air Force Ensign*

Many of the departmental flags of Spain consist of the National Flag with a small version of the Arms in the centre. The flag of the Prime Minister is in this pattern, and square. That of the Minister of Marine has two crossed blue anchors in place of the Arms. An Admiral has three blue discs, and lesser Admirals fewer discs. The Air Force Ensign has a small version of the Arms with the word *Aviacion* beneath them, and the Air Force emblem on the red stripe above. The wings are silver, the disc is red with a black eagle and ensigned with a naval crown. The Customs Ensign has the Arms flanked by two letters H (for *Hacienda*—'Treasury') beneath mural crowns, in blue. The Ensign of the Naval Reserve is the same but with the letters RN.

The former overseas territories of Spain have now achieved independence, or have been integrated into other countries, as has happened to the Western Sahara. Spain's only overseas provinces are the **Canaries** and the **Balearic Islands,** although Spain still has five small ports in Morocco which fly her flag. In Spain itself the flags of the Basques and of Catalonia are now frequently displayed. The Basque flag is red with a green saltire cross surmounted by a white plain cross, rather like the Union Jack. The Catalan flag has several forms, but it is basically yellow with four horizontal red stripes.

Blue with a yellow Scandinavian cross is the distinctive flag of **Sweden**. This dates from the mid-fifteenth century, and was to some extent created in rivalry to the *Dannebrog* (*see* Denmark, p. 111). The colours are thought to be derived from those of the Royal Arms, known as 'Sweden Modern', i.e. blue with three gold crowns. These Arms date from 1364, and today, ensigned with the royal crown, are referred to as the Lesser State Arms. Early flag records show the Swedish ensign with the whole Royal Arms in the centre. The Ensign, like that of other Scandinavian countries, is swallow-tailed with a tongue, and dates from at least 1600. The Royal Coat of Arms, or Greater State Arms, still appear on a white square panel in the centre of the Ensign to form the Royal Standard. These Arms also form the Royal Command Flag, which is a square banner. The first and fourth quarters are Sweden Modern, and the second and third 'Sweden Ancient', the gold lion rampant of the Folkung dynasty, all divided by a yellow curvilinear cross. In the centre of this is the Vasa Arms impaled with those of Bernadotte, the present dynasty. In the Greater State Arms the shield is surrounded by the collar of the Order of the Seraphim, supported by two gold lions, and contained within an ermine pavilion. There is also a Royal Standard of the same design, but with the Lesser Arms. In this case they too are surrounded by the collar of the Order of the Seraphim. The difference between the two is that the Standard with the Greater Arms is for the King, Queen and Queen Mother only, and the other is for other members of the Royal Family.

The Jack is the same as the Naval Ensign. An Admiral also uses the Ensign, but with three white stars, one and two, in the canton. Lesser Admirals have fewer stars.

The Minister of Defence has a square flag, divided vertically blue and yellow. The blue is charged with three gold crowns, and the yellow with an upright naked sword in blue. The Supreme Commander of the Armed Forces has a flag divided horizontally blue over yellow. The blue again is charged with the three gold crowns, and the yellow in this case with two crossed batons in blue and gold. Each wing of the Royal Swedish Air Force has its own unit flag. The basic flag is light blue with the Air Force emblem, a winged propeller beneath the royal crown, in gold in the centre, and the Arms of the county in which the unit is located in the canton. The flag illustrated is that of the Royal East Gotland Air Squadron based at Linkoping, the emblem consisting of a griffin between four roses, all in gold.

Sweden: National and Merchant Flag

Sweden: Royal Standard

Sweden: Royal Arms

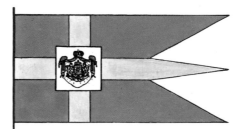

Sweden: Air Force Unit Flag

The flag of the Navigation Authority, or Ministry of Shipping, is a blue triangle charged with a foul anchor beneath a star with rays, all in gold. The flag of the Customs Service is a blue swallow-tail, charged with a lion rampant grasping a portcullis, as on the British Customs Ensign. In this case the lion is gold and the portcullis white. The Postal Service flag is a blue triangle with a post horn beneath the royal crown, all in gold. The Railway Ferry flag is also a blue triangle, but with a gold border, with the device of a winged wheel beneath the royal crown, also in gold.

All of the counties of Sweden have flags, based on their Coat of Arms. In the southern region known as *Skåne* (Scania), a flag of red with a yellow Scandinavian cross is frequently seen.

In Sweden 6 June is celebrated as *Svenska Flaggans Dag* (Swedish Flag Day). It is the anniversary of the accession of Gustav Vasa in 1523. On Flag Day the King donates flags as a mark of honour, and others are given by the Swedish Flag Day Association; a special postage stamp is issued, and the hymn *Sveriges Flagga* is sung. In Scania *Skanska Flaggans Dag* is celebrated on the third Sunday in July.

Switzerland was for long without a National Flag common to all the cantons of the Confederation, and a joint emblem was not chosen until the time of the Battle of Laupen in 1339, when the white cross on red of the Crusaders was adopted. The chronicle of Béarnois records that: 'All were distinguished by the sign of the Holy Cross, a white cross on a red shield, for the reason that the freeing of the nation was for them a cause as sacred as the deliverance of the Holy Places.' As a flag the couped white cross on red was not officially adopted until 1848, although it featured in many historical flags. The National Flag is square, and the Merchant Flag, used on the lakes and rivers, is 2:3. The latter was adopted in 1941. There is also a flag for the Cruising Club of Switzerland: the Merchant Flag with a small anchor placed diagonally in the canton, with the initials CCS, all in gold.

Switzerland: National Flag   *Zürich: flag of canton*   *Berne: flag of canton*

There are now 26 cantons in the Swiss Confederation, the latest one, **Jura**, having been formed in 1975. All use square banners of the Coats of Arms as flags, with one or two minor variations. Thus the flag of **Schwyz** has the white cross in the upper hoist, not in the sinister canton as in the shield, and the flag of **Ticino** has the colours arranged horizontally, not vertically as in the shield. In the flag of **Appenzell** the three white stars are arranged two and one, not as in the Arms. The flag of **Lucerne** has the colours arranged horizontally, not vertically as in the shield. The cantons of Berne and Zürich provide examples of the Arms used as flags. The flag of Berne is the Arms of red with a yellow diagonal charged with a black bear, and that of Zürich is plain white over light blue, diagonally. The flag of the new canton of Jura is divided vertically and equally. The hoist is white with a red crozier similar to that of Basle City. The fly is divided horizontally into four red and three white stripes. Flags in the plain colours of the Arms are sometimes used, as are more elaborate heraldic versions of which the State Flag of Geneva is an example. Every town and commune in Switzerland has its Arms and Flag.

The former Russian Empire possessed a great many flags, based on the white, blue and red colours introduced by Peter the Great, but these all disappeared with the Bolshevik Revolution. However, its successor, the **Union of Soviet Socialist Republics**, also has a very wide range of flags.

These are based on the red flag used by the Bolsheviks. A number of designs for a

USSR : *State Flag*   USSR : *Ensign*

National Flag were tried before the present one was adopted on 12 November 1923. The development was complicated by the fact that the Union of Soviet Socialist Republics was not itself formed until the previous year, although the Russian Soviet Republic and its partners had their own flags, as they still do.

The USSR is now a federation of fifteen soviet republics, and this fact is commemorated in the State Arms, also adopted in 1923. These show the globe surmounted by the hammer and sickle emblem with a red star above, and a wreath of wheat-ears tied with red ribbon. This ribbon bears the Soviet motto: 'Workers of the World Unite!' in the fifteen languages of the constituent republics, all in gold lettering. The red star was the badge used during the Bolshevik Revolution, and the hammer and sickle emblem dates from 1 May 1918, and represents the workers in industry and agriculture.

The State Flag is also the Merchant Flag. The Naval Ensign, introduced on 27 May 1935, is white, with a light blue stripe along the lower edge, one-sixth of the width, and in the white portion a red star and the hammer and sickle placed side by side. This flag has the proportions of 2:3, as do other service flags. The Jack dates from 7 July 1932, and consists of a red flag with a large white star with a red centre on which is a white hammer and sickle. This has the proportions 2:3. The Ensign for the Fleet Auxiliaries is dark blue, with the Naval Ensign in the canton. The Ensign for the Hydrographic Service is similar, but with a white disc edged in black and charged with a black and white lighthouse, in the centre of the fly. The flag of the Minister of Defence is white, like the Naval Ensign, but has an additional blue stripe across the lower third of the flag. Over all in the centre is the State Arms in colour. The Commander-in-Chief of the Armed Forces has a flag of red with the State Arms fimbriated in white in the centre. The flag of an Admiral is red, with the Naval Ensign in the canton, and three white stars in the fly.

There is also a range of flags for the MVD, the Ministry of State Security. Ships and troops of this department use a green Ensign, with the Naval Ensign in the canton. This corresponds to a Coast Guard Ensign. The President of the KGB also has a green flag, with the red flag of a Commander-in-Chief in the canton. The flag of the Army is that used by the famous Red Army in the civil war; a red flag with a red star fimbriated in yellow in the centre. The Sea Rescue flag of the USSR is white, with the badge in the lower fly, and the State Flag in the canton. The badge is a red couped cross surmounting two crossed blue anchors, and with the initials CCCP (i.e. USSR) in gold on the limbs of the cross. Although adopted in 1924 in the Soviet Union this flag has its origins in a flag used in Finland before the Revolution. The USSR also has a special form of the Red

Cross flag, to cater for the fact that a large proportion of its inhabitants are Moslems: this is white with the Red Crescent and the Red Cross side by side.

The flag of *Aeroflot*, the state airline, is red, with a small blue triangle based on the hoist, with the airline emblem in white, and in the canton a small gold star. This is also the flag for civil airports.

The Ensign of the Soviet Air Force is similar in many ways to pre-Revolutionary flags. It is basically light blue, with a gold disc in the upper centre from which emanate gold rays to all sides of the flag. On the disc is a red star charged with a white hammer and sickle, and beneath it is a winged propeller in black and white.

USSR: Jack   *Russian SFSR*

Each of the fifteen republics of the Soviet Union has its own flag, as do the autonomous republics. These flags were originally variations of the State Flag, with initials or inscriptions in gold letters, but between 1949 and 1954 they were all altered to give them a more distinctive appearance.

The **Russian Soviet Federal Socialist Republic** is the largest of the republics and the heartland of the USSR. Its original flag was red with the initials RSFSR in gold in the canton (in Cyrillic letters). This was changed to the present design by an edict of the Supreme Soviet of the RSFSR on 9 January 1954. The design is the same as the State Flag, except for a dark blue vertical strip, comprising one-eighth of the length, immediately next to the hoist. Each of the Autonomous Republics of the RSFSR now has a similar flag, with initials or an inscription beneath the hammer and sickle.

The flag of the **Armenian SSR** was altered on 17 December 1952, and now has a dark blue strip of a quarter of the width running horizontally across the centre.

The flag of the **Azerbaidzhan SSR** was altered on 18 August 1953 to the present design, which has a dark blue strip of a quarter of the width of the flag along the bottom.

The flag of the **Byelorussian SSR** (White Russia) has an interesting design, described as the 'Byelorussian national ornament', vertically in the hoist, and a green strip, equal to a third of the width horizontally across the bottom. In this flag, adopted on 25 December 1951, as in others of the constituent republics, the hammer and sickle are much larger than in the State Flag. The vertical strip in the hoist is one-ninth of the length. White and red were the colours of the independent state of White Russia during the civil war.

The flag of the **Estonian SSR** is the most distinctive of all, with wavy blue and white stripes representing the waves of the sea. It was adopted on 6 February 1953. The blue and white stripes account for three-tenths of the width, the upper red part one half, and the lower red band one-fifth of the width.

Armenian SSR

Azerbaidzhan SSR

Byelorussian SSR

Estonian SSR

Georgian SSR

Kazakh SSR

Kirghiz SSR

Latvian SSR

Lithuanian SSR

Moldavian SSR

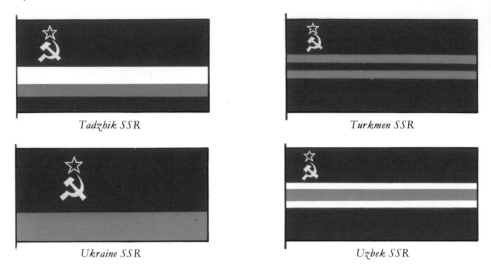

Tadzhik SSR   *Turkmen SSR*

Ukraine SSR   *Uzbek SSR*

The flag of the **Georgian SSR** also has a distinctive appearance: it is the only one in which the hammer and sickle and star are red instead of gold. The canton consists of a blue disc from which emanate twenty-four blue rays, forming a square one half the width of the flag. A horizontal stripe of the same blue equal to a third of the width of the canton runs near the top of the flag. This design was adopted on 11 April 1951.

The flag of the **Kazakh SSR** was altered on 24 January 1953. It has a light blue horizontal stripe two-ninths of the width; the upper red part is two-thirds of the width, and the lower red band one-ninth.

The flag of the **Kirghiz SSR** was changed to the present design on 22 December 1952. It has three bands of blue, white and blue across the centre, dividing the flag into horizontal thirds. The white central strip is one-twentieth of the width.

The flag of the **Latvian SSR** also has wavy bands representing the sea. It was altered on 17 January 1953. The blue and white wavy lines constitute one-third of the width.

The flag of the **Lithuanian SSR** was altered on 15 July 1953. It has a green strip along the bottom comprising a quarter of the width, with a white fimbriation one-twelfth of the width.

The present flag of the **Moldavian SSR** was adopted on 31 January 1952. The green stripe across the centre is one quarter of the width.

The flag of the **Tadzhik SSR** has a larger element of white than any of the other flags. This is one-fifth of the width. The green stripe below it is one-tenth of the width. The upper red part is a half of the width, and lower red part one-fifth. This was adopted on 20 March 1953.

The flag of the **Turkmen SSR** was adopted on 1 August 1953, and is very similar to that of the Kirghiz SSR, except that the blue stripes are of a lighter shade, and the central stripe is red.

Prior to the establishment of the Soviet Republic, the flag of the **Ukraine** was light blue over yellow. Light blue still features in the present flag, adopted 21 January 1949, the first of the new distinctive republic flags. The blue stripe is one-third of the width.

The flag of the **Uzbek SSR** was adopted on 29 August 1952. The horizontal blue stripe and the white fimbration constitute one-fifth of the width.

The flags of Byelorussia and of the Ukraine have international significance, since these republics are individual members of the United Nations, and their flags are shown at its headquarters. In theory, any of the other thirteen republics are free to join the UN.

For centuries the Papal States were the Pope's own temporal domain, but in 1870 they were incorporated into the Kingdom of Italy. The Concordat of 11 February 1929 permitted the establishment of a new temporal authority in the **Vatican City State**, a small area of about a hundred acres in central Rome. Yellow and white were the colours always associated with the Papacy, and the present flag in the colours was formerly the Merchant Flag of the Papal States, although now reduced to square proportions, and with the design modernized. The crossed keys represent the first Vicar of Christ, St Peter, and the 'tiara' or triple crown represents the Pope's superiority to ordinary sovereigns. The Vatican City has its own Arms: a red shield with the crossed keys and tiara, and each Pope has his own personal Arms supported by the keys and ensigned with the tiara. The Vatican City State also retains the famous traditional Swiss Guard, which has its own Colours of medieval origin.

Vatican City State Flag   *Yugoslavia: Arms*   *Yugoslavia: National Flag*

Yugoslavia is now the Socialist Federal Republic of Yugoslavia, although it was established as the united kingdom of the Serbs, Croats, and Slovenes in 1918, when Serbia, Montenegro, Bosnia, Herzegovina and other provinces were united with Croatia and Slovenia. Red, white and blue were the colours of the flags of Serbia and Montenegro and the tricolour of Yugoslavia retained them, in the present arrangement. At the end of the Second World War the monarchy was abolished and a Communist republic on federal lines was established. During the war the Communist partisans had used the red star as a badge, and this was added to the National Flag on 31 January 1946. Most of the present flags date from this time, although there have been several constitutional changes. The State and National Flag is the horizontal tricolour in proportions 1:2, with a large star of red edged in gold over all in the centre. The Merchant Flag is the same but in the proportion 2:3—the reverse of the usual practice. The Naval Ensign has the same proportions, but has a red field with a canton containing the National Flag with a white fimbriation, and with the addition of a gold wreath behind the star. The pennant is red with this canton in the hoist. The Jack is red, in the proportions 2:3, with the State Arms in the centre. The Arms represent the united character of the country: six torches

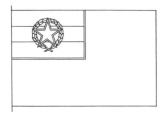

Yugoslavia: President   *Yugoslavia: Ensign*

forming a single flame, within a wreath of wheat-ears tied with a ribbon in one of the national colours. On this is the date '29.XI.1943', the date of the declaration of the Republic, in white.

The Emblem appears in full colour in the centre of the President's Standard, which is otherwise very similar to the former Royal Standard. It is square, with a field of the national colours, and a border on all four sides of red, white and blue triangles. The President of the Federal Assembly has the same flag, but without the decorative border. Members of the Federal Executive Council have a similar flag, but with the device from the canton of the Naval Ensign (star and wreath) over all in the centre. The Secretary of State for National Defence has the State Emblem in the centre of a square white flag, which has a border on all four sides of red, white and blue rectangles. The Commander-in-Chief of the Navy has a similar flag but charged in the centre with a large red foul anchor beneath a red gold-bordered star. An Admiral's flag is similar to this, but has a small yellow plain anchor in the upper hoist. A Vice-Admiral has the same but with a red inner field, and a Rear-Admiral a blue inner field.

Each of the six republics has its own Arms and flag, for internal use only.

Bosnia-Herzegovina has a flag of red in proportions 1 : 2, with a small version of the National Flag within a yellow fimbriation in the canton. This was adopted on 31 December 1946.

Croatia has a flag of red, white and blue in the sequence adopted unofficially in 1848. This now has the red gold-bordered star over all in the centre, adopted on 18 January 1947.

Macedonia also has a red flag, adopted on 31 December 1946. In the canton is a very small red gold-bordered star.

Montenegro has the same flag it has always used, a horizontal tricolour of red, blue and white. The red gold-bordered star was added on 31 December 1946.

Serbia's flag is identical with that of Montenegro, but dates from at least 1835. The red star was added on 17 January 1947.

The flag of **Slovenia** is a horizontal tricolour of white, blue and red, and dates unofficially from 1848. The red star was added on 16 January 1947.

The red, white and blue of all the flags except that of Macedonia are derived from the 'Pan-Slav' colours taken from the flag of the Russian Empire, to which the smaller Slav states looked for support in their struggle to free themselves from the Turks or the Austrians. These colours were nearly always arranged horizontally, but in different combinations, as seen here.

Bosnia-Herzegovina

Croatia

Macedonia

Montenegro

Serbia

Slovenia

[7] Africa

Africa has seen more political changes than any other continent in the last seventy years. During this period the former colonial territories of Britain, France, Portugal, Spain and Belgium, which once comprised nearly the whole continent, have been transformed into a series of modern republics. Only South Africa, South West Africa (Namibia) and Rhodesia are not under the control of their native populations. This chapter relates these widespread changes to the corresponding flag-histories. The African members of the British Commonwealth today are Botswana, the Gambia, Ghana, Kenya, Lesotho, Malawi, Mauritius, Nigeria, the Seychelles, Sierra Leone, Swaziland, Tanzania, Uganda and Zambia. At the time of writing the future of Rhodesia, known as 'Zimbabwe' to the Africans, is uncertain.

Botswana was formerly Bechuanaland, one of the British High Commissioner's Territories in Southern Africa. It became an independent republic within the Commonwealth on 30 September 1966. Its flag is light blue, representing the rain on which the life of the country depends. The black stripe edged in white represents the ideal of racial harmony.

The Arms appear in full in the centre of the President's Standard. On an African shield are symbols for industry, water and the livestock herds. The supporters are two zebra, holding an ivory tusk and a sorghum plant. The motto is *Pula*, the Tswana word for rain.

The Gambia became independent on 18 February 1965, and a republic within the Commonwealth on 24 April 1970. The flag adopted on independence represents the Gambia river flowing through the green country under the sun, and was designed by a Gambian, L. Thomasi.

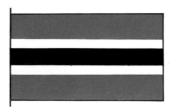

Botswana: National Flag

Botswana: President

Ghana, formerly the Gold Coast, became independent on 6 March 1957, the first British colony south of the Sahara to do so, and a republic within the Commonwealth on 1 July 1960. The colours of the flag adopted on independence deliberately recall those of Ethiopia, the only African country never colonized by Europeans. The black star in the centre is known as the 'lode-star of African freedom', and was intended as a beacon for the decolonization of Africa. Many other countries, particularly in West Africa, have adopted the same colours. In Ghana the yellow stripe was changed to white during the period 1964–66, to make the flag more like that of the ruling party, but the original design was restored when the then President, Kwame Nkrumah, was overthrown. Although there is a Standard for the President it has not been in use since 1966.

The Merchant Flag is like the British Red Ensign, but has the National Flag of Ghana in the canton, with a narrow black fimbriation. The Naval Ensign is also similar to that of Britain, as are those of many Commonwealth countries, but in this case it has the proportions 2 : 3, and has the Ghanaian flag in the canton. The Air Force Ensign is also similar to that of Britain, i.e. a field of 'air force' blue, with the National Flag in the canton, and the target in the fly; this is coloured inwards red, yellow and green. The Civil Air Ensign is similar, but has a large black star in place of the target.

  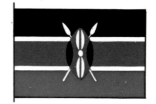

The Gambia: National Flag   *Ghana: National Flag*   *Kenya: National Flag*

Kenya became independent on 12 December 1963 and a republic within the Commonwealth one year later. The colours of her flag are taken from a different source to those of Ghana: the 'Black Liberation' flag of red, black and green. The Kenya African National Union (KANU) which led the country to independence has a flag of black, red and green, and white fimbriations were added to this to make the National Flag, together with the shield and crossed spears. The shield is of African form, also found in the Arms of other African states.

The Naval Ensign of Kenya is white, with the National Flag in the canton, and an upright red anchor in the fly. The Air Force Ensign follows the same pattern as that of Britain, with the National Flag in the canton, and the target, coloured inwards black, white, red, green, in the fly.

The Standard of the President is royal blue, with a small version of the shield crossed by two large assegais in the centre, and near the fly edge a golden cockerel. The latter is the emblem of KANU.

Lesotho was formerly known as Basutoland, a territory of the British High Commissioner in South Africa. It had previously been a native kingdom, and it became independent as such on 4 October 1966. The blue field of the flag adopted on independence is charged with a white representation of the local straw hat. The Royal

Standard is similar to the National Flag, but has the Arms in the centre of the hat. These are an African shield of traditional shape, in yellow, charged with a brown crocodile. The shield is supported by two brown ponies, and stands on a representation of *Thaba Bosiu*, the Mountain of Night, the stronghold of King Moshoeshoe I, with the motto *Khotso*, *Pula*, *Nala* in red letters on a gold scroll. This means 'Peace, Rain, Plenty'. (*See also* **Botswana**, p. 150.)

The Federation of Rhodesia and Nyasaland, comprising the then British colonies of Northern and Southern Rhodesia and Nyasaland, was formed on 1 August 1953 and disbanded on 31 December 1963. The three members went their separate ways: Nyasaland became the independent state of Malawi; Northern Rhodesia was renamed Zambia, and also became independent. Southern Rhodesia became plain 'Rhodesia' and is still in theory a dependency of the United Kingdom (*see* p. 157).

Malawi became independent on 6 July 1964, and a republic within the Commonwealth on 6 July 1966. The flag adopted on independence is that of the Malawi Congress Party, which is also in the 'Black Liberation' colours mentioned under **Kenya** and **Biafra** above. The red sun is adopted from the rising sun which appeared in the

Lesotho: National Flag

Malawi: National Flag

Arms of Nyasaland, and is also found in the modern Arms of Malawi. It is now taken to symbolize the dawn of a new era. The flag of the President of Malawi is similar to the central portion of the shield: red with a lion 'passant' in yellow and beneath this is a yellow scroll with the name *Malawi* in black letters. The Army Flag is also red, with a yellow lion rampant above the rising sun and blue and white wavy bars from the crest of the Arms.

Mauritius passed from French to British colonial rule during the Napoleonic wars, but became an independent member of the Commonwealth on 12 March 1968. On independence Mauritius retained the Coat of Arms granted to the colony on 25 August 1906, but adopted a flag of four stripes in colours taken from the Arms. The Arms represent the island's position, as the 'key' to the Indian Ocean—the sense of the motto *Stella Clavisque Maris Indici*—and its chief produce, sugar. The extinct dodo and the sambur deer are the supporters. Their red and white embattled colours are taken from the arms of the then Governor.

Merchant and Government Ensigns were adopted in 1972. These have red and blue fields with the National Flag in the canton and the Arms in the centre of the fly. In the case of the Merchant Ensign they are contained in a white disc.

Nigeria: National Flag

Nigeria: Ports Authority

Nigeria became independent on 1 October 1960, and a republic within the Commonwealth three years later. The flag adopted on independence was chosen after a competition, and the basic design was by a Nigerian student, Michael Akinkumni. The design stands for the green countryside crossed by the wide Niger river; the proportions are 1:2. The National Flag is also the Merchant Flag and Naval Jack. The Naval Ensign is similar to that of Britain, but has the Nigerian flag in the canton. The Presidential Standard is red, also in proportions 1:2, with a large green shield, fimbriated white, in the centre. This is charged with the shield from the Coat of Arms, which is black, with a wavy-edged 'Y' or 'pall' in white (representing the confluence of the Niger and Benue rivers against the black of Nigeria). Above and below this are three black scrolls containing the legend *President Federal Republic of Nigeria* in gold letters. Although Nigeria has undergone several constitutional changes it is now once more a federation, but now of twelve states. These use squarish versions of the National Flag with their Arms in the centre. The three original states, Northern, Eastern and Western, and the later mid-West State had flags which are now obsolete. The Republic of **Biafra** formed in Eastern Nigeria on 30 May 1967 had a flag of red, black and green, horizontally, with a rising sun from the Coat of Arms in gold in the centre. This became obsolete when the Republic ceased to exist on 15 January 1970.

The flag of the Nigerian Naval Board is green, with a horizontal foul anchor in yellow. The flag of the Ports Authority is green with a white disc in the centre charged with a gold dolphin wearing a naval crown and a chain with a gold hexagram around its neck.

The **Seychelles Islands**, which apart from Rhodesia, were Britain's only remaining dependency in Africa, became independent on 28–29 June 1976. The flag adopted on

Mauritius: National Flag

Seychelles: Arms

Seychelles: Badge

independence had colours representing the two main political parties, or perhaps the British and the French who once ruled the islands. This had the proportion of one by two. A flag for the President was also adopted, consisting of the National Flag with the armorial badge, not the Arms, within a white fimbriation in the centre. The badge is like the former ensign-badge, and shows the tortoise and palm-tree motif within a wreath of palm-leaves. The former ensign-badge, dating from April 1961 and based on an earlier version said to have been designed by General Charles Gordon in the late nineteenth century, was replaced by a new Coat of Arms. This also includes the tortoise, the palm-tree, and a maritime scene in the background. These are now contained in a shield supported by two sail-fish, with a crest of a bird known locally as a *Paille en queue*, and a scroll with the old motto *Finis Coronat Opus* ('The End Crowns the Work').

On the first anniversary of independence the government was removed by a bloodless *coup d'état* and a new flag was introduced. The new régime adopted a new National Flag, red above green horizontally, divided by a wavy white band. The standard of the new President has the full achievement of the country's Arms in the middle of the National Flag, which has a golden fringe.

The British Indian Ocean Territory was formed in 1965, and consisted of the Chagos Archipelago, Aldabra, Farquhar and Desroches. The Blue Ensign with the badge of the Seychelles was used in this territory. When the Seychelles became independent all the islands except the Chagos Archipelago were incorporated in the new republic.

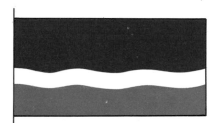

Seychelles: National Flag

Sierra Leone: National Flag

Sierra Leone achieved independence on 27 April 1961, and became a republic within the Commonwealth on 19 April 1971. The National Flag, adopted on independence, has the main colours from the Coat of Arms, which are taken to represent agricultural prosperity, peaceful development, and the harbour of Freetown.

In May 1961 a Personal Flag for the use of the Queen in Sierra Leone was established, consisting of a banner of the Arms, with the royal cypher in the centre. This became obsolete on the creation of the republic. As yet no Standard for the President has been adopted.

The history of the flag of **Swaziland** is interesting. As far back as 1890 a flag was in use bearing a Swazi shield and two battle-axes. Then in 1941 a royal flag was presented to the Swazi Pioneer Corps, then a part of the British Army. This was basically the same as the present National Flag, except that it had the king's name on a scroll. This was revived in 1954 when a new model was made by Emily Shongwe, a cousin of King Sobhuza, and this was adopted as the pattern for the National Flag in 1967. The shield in the centre has a pattern peculiar to the Emasotsha Regiment. Behind the shield are two spears (*tikhali*) and a staff (*umgobo*) decorated with tassels (*injobo*) made from the feathers of the widowbird and the lourie. One of these also hangs from the shield, and they are a prerogative of royalty.

There is also a Royal Standard, which has a small lion 'passant' facing the fly on the upper blue stripe. This was added by King Sobhuza himself and first flown on 5 September 1968. The lion is the symbol of the King whose title it is: *Ingwenyama*. Swaziland became independent on 6 September 1968, but the National Flag was first hoisted on 30 October 1967.

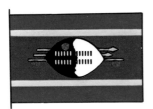

| *Swaziland: National Flag* | *Tanzania: National Flag* | *Tanzania: President* |

Tanzania is an amalgamation of Tanganyika and Zanzibar, formed on 26 April 1964. Tanganyika was originally a German colony, but it was placed under British trusteeship in 1919, and became independent on 9 December 1961, and a republic within the Commonwealth on 9 December 1962. The flag adopted on independence in 1961 was horizontally green, black, green (the colours of the ruling party), with gold fimbriation on the black.

Zanzibar was originally a Sultanate under British Protection, and flew the plain red flag common to many Arab states on the borders of the Indian Ocean. On attaining independence on 10 December 1963 a green disc with two golden cloves (the main product of the islands) was added to the centre. However, the Sultan was overthrown on 12 January 1964 and a new flag, based on that of the Afro-Shirazi party, was adopted. This had three horizontal stripes of blue, green, black, with a narrow white vertical strip in the hoist.

When the two states combined to form the **United Republic of Tanzania** the flags were united to form the present National Flag, which has the green and black of Tanganyika with blue from the flag of Zanzibar, but now arranged diagonally so as to give them each a more equal position. The flags of Tanganyika and Zanzibar are still used as local flags.

The flag of the President is green, with a light blue border all round, and a simplified version of the national Arms in the centre. This shows an African shield supported by two tusks of ivory and a scroll with the national motto in Swahili: *Uhuru Na Umoja* ('Freedom and Liberty'). The shield is divided into sections which were revised when the two states combined. The bottom part has water for Lake Tanganyika, above this is a plain red panel, above this again a representation of the National Flag, and in the top the head of a flaming torch. Over all is an upright spear, crossed with a hoe and a mattock.

Uganda: National Flag

Uganda: President

Zambia: National Flag

Rhodesia: National Flag

Uganda became independent on 9 October 1962, and a republic within the Commonwealth on 8 September 1967. The flag adopted on independence has in the centre a small white disc charged with the African Balearic crested crane which was the flag-badge of the protectorate for seventy years, and which is now one of the supporters in the Coat of Arms. The colours are those of the Uganda People's Congress, and the flag was designed by the then Minister of Justice, Mr Grace Ibingira.

The flag of the President is red with the national colours in six stripes along the bottom, and in the centre the whole Arms. These show an African shield supported by a deer and the crested crane, and having behind it two crossed spears. The shield is mostly black, with a chief of wavy water, standing for Lake Victoria; in the centre is a gold sun, and in base a drum of the kind used in the former kingdoms of Buganda, Toro and Ankole. The compartment is green with samples of local vegetation and a stream representing the source of the river Nile. The motto is: *For God and my Country*.

Zambia, formerly Northern Rhodesia, takes its name from the Zambesi River, and became independent as a republic within the Commonwealth on 24 October 1964. The flag is in the colours of the ruling party, but in an unusual and striking design originating with a European designer. The green field stands for the country and its agricultural wealth, and the three vertical blocks in the lower fly for the people, the struggle for independence, and the mineral wealth. The soaring eagle is taken from the Arms of Northern Rhodesia, which featured a fish-eagle in chief. The flag of the President is orange, the colour referring to the country's wealth of copper, with the whole Arms in the centre. These have a shield which originally formed the main part of the shield of Northern Rhodesia, i.e. black and white wavy 'pallets' standing for the Victoria Falls. The supporters are a Zambian man and woman; the crest is the soaring eagle perched on a crossed hoe and pickaxe; the motto is *One Zambia One Nation*; there is a green compartment containing samples of vegetable, animal and mineral resources.

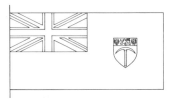

Rhodesia: National Flag
1964–68

Algeria: National Flag

Although theoretically a colony of the United Kingdom, **Rhodesia** declared independence unilaterally on 11 November 1965, and became a republic on 2 March 1970, although without so far securing the recognition of any other state. At the time of the Unilateral Declaration of Independence Rhodesia flew a flag adopted on 8 April 1964, of light blue, with the Union Jack in the canton, and the shield from the Arms in the fly. Like the Americans before them the Rhodesians found the Union Jack something of an embarrassment, and so on 11 November 1968 a new flag was adopted, with the whole Arms in the centre of a flag divided vertically green, white and green. The Arms had to be inserted when it was discovered that the proposed design was identical to the flag of Nigeria. The Arms were granted in 1924, and are related to those of Cecil Rhodes, the founder of the country, and to those of the British South Africa Company which formerly ruled it. The green field with a pickaxe stands for the mineral wealth, and the chief with a lion between two thistles for Cecil Rhodes. The supporters are sable antelopes, and the crest is the soapstone bird found at Zimbabwe, the ruined African city from which the African Nationalists derive their name for the country. The motto is: *Sit Nomina Digna* ('May it be worthy of its Name'). The flag of the President is light blue with the whole Arms in the centre.

OTHER AFRICAN COUNTRIES

Algeria became independent on 3 July 1962 after a long and bitter struggle. The flag adopted on independence was that used by the National Liberation Front after the formation of the government in exile in June 1958, although it appears to have been designed by Messali Hadj in 1928. The green of the flag stands for the Moslem faith, the white for purity of purpose. The long horns of the crescent symbolize prosperity.

Angola became independent on 11 November 1975 and adopted a flag based on that of the party victorious in the short civil war which followed the Portuguese withdrawal, the Popular Movement for the Liberation of Angola. The new flag has an emblem like a hammer and sickle, but made up of half a cog-wheel, and a machete, together with a gold star, placed on the party colours of red and black.

Benin was formerly known as Dahomey, a state which became independent of France on 1 August 1960 and was renamed the People's Republic of Benin on 30 November 1975. The new flag symbolizes the agricultural wealth of the country led by the red star of socialism. The former flag was in the 'Pan-African' colours of red, green and yellow.

Angola: National Flag

Benin: National Flag

Burundi: National Flag

Cameroon: National Flag

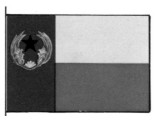

Cape Verde Islands:
National Flag

Central Africa:
National Flag

Chad: National Flag

Comoro Islands:
National Flag

Congo People's Republic:
National Flag

Equatorial Guinea:
State Flag

Burundi was originally part of the Belgian Trusteeship Territory of Ruanda–Urundi. It became an independent kingdom on 1 July 1962. The monarchy was abolished on 28 November 1966. The flag adopted on independence was basically the same as the present one, except that in place of the three stars of red edged in green it had a drum and a sorghum plant. The drum symbolized the monarchy, and so was removed in 1966. A few months later the sorghum also disappeared and the three stars were inserted, to stand for the virtues referred to in the national Arms: Unity, Work and Progress.

Cameroon was originally the German colony of Kamerun, but this was partitioned in 1919 into parts under British and French Trusteeship. The French part achieved independence on 1 January 1960, and was joined by the southern part of the British Cameroons on 1 October 1961, to form the Cameroon Federal Republic. The flag adopted on independence was a plain vertical tricolour of green, red, yellow. When the Federal Republic was formed in 1962 two gold stars were added in the upper hoist to stand for the two regions. However, the country became the United Republic of Cameroon on 2 June 1972, and on 20 May 1975 this was symbolized by the placing of a single gold star in the centre of the flag. The northern part of the British Cameroons was integrated into Nigeria in 1961.

The **Cape Verde Islands** had been a colony of Portugal since the fifteenth century. but they became independent on 5 July 1975 due to the work of the African Party for the Independence of Guinea and the Cape Verde Islands. Like Guinea–Bissau they adopted a flag based on that used by this movement. It is distinguished from that of Guinea–Bissau by having the black star slightly above the centre of the red stripe, and surrounded by a wreath of corn-stalks. At the base of the wreath is a yellow clam-shell.

The **Central African Empire** was originally the French colony of Ubangui–Shari. It became independent as the Central African Republic on 13 August 1960. The flag adopted on independence and still in use today combines the colours of France (red, white and blue) with the Pan-African colours of red, green and yellow. No change was made in the flag when the Empire was established on 4 December 1976.

The flag of **Chad**, which became independent on 11 August 1960, is also a combination of the pan-African colours with those of France: the French Tricolour is the inspiration for the design of the National Flag. As in several other cases the National Flag was adopted when the country became an autonomous member of the French Community prior to actual independence. In this case the flag was first hoisted on 6 November 1959.

The **Comoro Islands** lie off the east coast of Africa, and they too had a flag used before independence. This was green, with a large crescent and four stars standing for the four main island groups, arranged diagonally, all in white. When the islands became independent on 6 July 1975 the design was altered to make the field red, as in the original Arab flags of the area, with a green strip along the bottom, and the crescent and four stars arranged to face the lower fly. Mayotte has remained a dependency of France and uses the Tricolour, although it is represented by a star in the National Flag.

The **Congo People's Republic** was originally the French colony of Middle Congo. This became autonomous on 26 November 1958 with a flag consisting of a diagonal tricolour of green, yellow, red. It became an independent republic on 15 August 1960 and a People's Republic on 30 December 1969, when the present flag was adopted. This follows the usual Communist pattern, and has a device of a crossed hoe and hammer with two larger palm branches and a gold star in the upper hoist.

The former Spanish overseas provinces of Fernando Pó and Rio Muni, or Spanish Guinea, became the independent state of **Equatorial Guinea** on 12 October 1968. The National Flag is without the Arms, which only appear in the centre of the State Flag, and indeed the Arms themselves have otherwise been superseded. Those in the State Flag consist of a silver shield charged with a green silk-cotton tree, and crested with six gold six-pointed stars, standing for the mainland and the five islands. The motto is *Unidad Paz Justicia* ('Unity, Peace, Justice').

The Emperor of **Ethiopia**, Haile Selassie, was deposed by a military revolt on 12 September 1974, since when the country has been ruled by a Junta known as the Dergue. The new rulers have removed all emblems of royalty from the National Flags, but they are otherwise unchanged, and retain the traditional colours of green, yellow and red, known since the late nineteenth century. Because Ethiopia has the distinction of being the only African state never permanently taken over by a European power its colours were adopted by nationalists in many parts of the continent. The present National Flag is the plain horizontal tricolour, but there is also a State and War Flag for official purposes, which replaces the former Royal Standard. This, like the previous standard, has a different design on the obverse and reverse. The obverse has the Lion of Judah in the centre, but now without the crown, and with the cross it formerly carried changed to a spear. On the reverse is a representation of St George slaying the dragon. This also appeared in the previous Standard. The Naval Ensign is blue with the obverse of the State Flag in the canton.

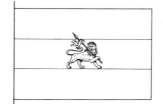

| *Ethiopia:* | *Ethiopia: State Flag* | *Ethiopia: State Flag* |
| *National and Merchant Flag* | *(obverse)* | *(reverse)* |

Eritrea was federated to Ethiopia on 15 September 1952, after a period of British Trusteeship during which a flag of United Nations blue charged with a sprig and wreath of olive leaves in green was in use. It ceased to exist as a separate state on 14 November 1962, but since then several nationalist groups have been fighting for its secession, and one of them, the Eritrean Liberation Front, still makes use of the original flag.

Gabon, formerly part of French Equatorial Africa, became autonomous within the French Community on 28 November 1958, and an independent republic on 9 August 1960. The flag adopted in 1958 was the same as at present, but with the French Tricolour in the canton, and with the central stripe somewhat narrower. The present design was adopted on independence. The President has a flag consisting of a square banner of the Arms. This has a yellow field with a blue wavy base on which is a black ship flying the flag of Gabon. The chief is green with three gold discs. This design, by the Swiss vexillologist Louis Mühlemann, illustrates the mercantile and mineral wealth of the country.

Eritrea   *Gabon: National Flag*   *Gabon: President's Flag*

Guinea was the only part of the French Community to choose outright independence in the referendum of 1958, and became an independent republic on 2 October 1958. The flag chosen is similar to the French Tricolour, but in the colours of the dominant nationalist party, which are also those of Ghana and other West African states. They also correspond to the three virtues in the national motto: *Travail, Justice, Solidarité* ('Work, Justice, Solidarity').

Guinea-Bissau, so called to distinguish it from the other 'Guineas', is the territory formerly controlled by Portugal, which became independent under the leadership of the African Party for the Independence of Guinea and the Cape Verde Islands (*see* Cape Verde Islands above) on 24 September 1973. The flag is the same as that of the PAIGC but without the initials usually placed under the star, and is therefore very similar to that of the Cape Verde Islands, with which union is contemplated in due course. The colours are a further example of the Pan-African colours.

The republic of the **Ivory Coast** was a French colony and part of French West Africa until it became an autonomous republic within the French Community on 4 December 1958. Full independence was achieved on 7 August 1960. As in several other cases the flag is based on the French Tricolour, but in local colours, in this instance making it the same as that of Ireland in reverse.

Guinea: National Flag   *Guinea-Bissau:*
National Flag

The French Territory of the Afars and Issas which was originally French Somaliland became the independent republic of **Jibuti** (formerly spelt Djibouti) on 27 June 1977 and adopted a National Flag. This had a field divided horizontally blue over green, with a white triangle charged with a red star based on the hoist.

Liberia was founded in 1822 by the American Colonization Society as an experiment in the colonization of Africa by Africans. The Society bought land and settled freed American slaves on it. On 26 July 1847 it became the free and independent Republic of

Ivory Coast: National Flag

Jibuti: National Flag

Liberia:
National and Merchant Flag

Liberia: President

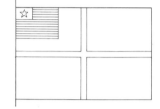

Liberia: Sinoe County

Liberia and adopted a flag which is still in use today. This is based on that of the United States, but in this case the stripes stand for the signatories of the Declaration of Independence. The canton originally had a white cross, but this was altered to a star to represent independence.

The President's Standard is blue and square, with a shield in the centre like that of the USA; it has eleven vertical bars of red and white, and blue chief with a white star, and is edged in gold. In each corner of the flag is a white star.

Each of the nine counties of Liberia has a flag, granted by the then President, William V. S. Tubman, on his seventieth birthday. Each has the National Flag in the canton, and a field with local emblems. That of **Sinoe County** has a green cross on a white field, representing the tropical forests.

Madagascar has had a long and stormy political history. It was first a kingdom, then a French protectorate from 1895, then a French colony from 1896, an autonomous republic from 14 October 1958, and an independent republic on 26 June 1960. The island became the Democratic Republic of Madagascar on 30 December 1975. The National Flag was first adopted on 21 October 1958. The design was chosen after a local competition, but is based on the red and white flags used in the Hova kingdom before 1896. The green was added to represent the coastal peoples.

The flag of the President is like the National Flag, but has the state emblem in gold in the centre of the white stripe. Since the formation of the Democratic Republic this has been changed and it is possible that the Standard is no longer is use. **Diego Suarez**, France's first colony in Madagascar, which was retained by France after independence, was returned to Madagascar on 3 June 1975.

Mali, formerly the French Sudan, is named after one of the great Negro empires of the middle ages. On 17 January 1959 it was linked in a federation with Senegal, known as the Mali Federation, and became independent as such on 20 June 1960. However, the federation was dissolved on 22 August 1960 and the two countries have been separate since then. Their flags are, however, still very similar. The flag of the Federation was the same as that of Mali today, but with a stylized figure of a man, known as the *kanaga*, in the centre in black. This was adopted when Mali became autonomous within the French Community on 24 November 1958. On separating from Senegal the figure was deleted from the flag. The design of the flag is based on the French Tricolour, and the colours, like those of Guinea and Cameroon and other countries, are those of the dominant nationalist party at the time of independence.

Mauritania became autonomous within the French Community on 28 November 1958, and an independent republic on 28 November 1960. The flag was adopted on 1 April 1959, and reflects the country's official title: the Islamic Republic of Mauritania. Part of the former Spanish Sahara was incorporated into Mauritania on 28 February 1976.

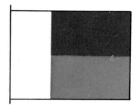
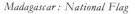

| Madagascar: National Flag | Mali: National Flag | Mauritania: National Flag |

Although divided into French and Spanish protectorates for many years, **Morocco** has never lost its national identity, and was restored as an independent nation in March and April 1956. The former Sultan became King of Morocco on 18 August 1957. The National Flag assumed its present form on 17 November 1915, although during the period of French and Spanish suzerainty this was for local use only. The green pentagram is known as 'Solomon's Seal', and has been known in occult lore for centuries. French ships used the flag with the Tricolour fimbriated in white in the canton, and there was a special flag for ships registered in Spanish Morocco. The flag was, however, used without alteration in the International City of Tangier, 1923–1956. Although Spain still controls certain small ports on the coast of Morocco these now also use the flag of Morocco.

The former Royal Standard has gone out of use, and the only other flag of Morocco is the Naval and Military Ensign, which is the National Flag with the Royal Crown in the upper hoist. The greater part of the former Spanish Sahara territory was integrated into Morocco on 28 February 1976. Each of the provinces of Morocco had its own flag, of heraldic form, with a red streamer across the top charged with the green pentagram. These were introduced on 3 March 1968.

Mozambique secured her independence partly as a result of the political upheaval in Portugal, and partly through the efforts of a number of liberation movements. Of these FRELIMO, the Front for the Liberation of Mozambique, was predominant, and when the transitional government was formed on 20 September 1974 this party's flag was used locally. This consists of three horizontal stripes of green, black, yellow, with the black

Morocco : National Flag

Mozambique: National Flag

fimbriated white, and with a red triangle over all based on the hoist. When the country became independent on 25 June 1975 as the People's Republic of Mozambique, the new National Flag retained these colours but in a new and striking design. In addition, a simplified version of the new national emblem was added in the upper hoist. This shows an open book over which are crossed a rifle and a mattock, within a black cog-wheel, and with a red star above it.

The President's flag is red, and has the whole Arms in the centre. In these the aforementioned emblems are contained within a wreath of corn-stalks and placed on a map of the country. The red star is replaced by a rising sun, and moved to the top of the emblem. The wreath is tied with a ribbon bearing the name *Republica Popular de Moçambique.*

The former French colony of **Niger** became autonomous within the French Community on 18 December 1958, and an independent republic on 3 August 1960. The flag was adopted on 23 November 1959. It is very like that of India, but in this case the orange represents the savannah land, the orange disc the sun, the white strip represents the River Niger, and the green the grasslands of the south. The flag has the unusual proportions of six by seven.

Rwanda, like Burundi, was formerly a kingdom and part of the Belgian Trusteeship territory of Ruanda-Urundi. The republic was established on 28 January 1961, and independence was achieved on 1 July 1962. The first flag dated from January 1961, and was the same as at present but without the initial R. This was added in the following September when it was found that the flag was otherwise identical with that of Guinea.

Niger: National Flag

Rwanda : National Flag

The islands of **São Tomé and Principe** in the Gulf of Guinea were one of Portugal's oldest colonies before they achieved independence on 12 July 1975. A transitional government had been set up on 26 November 1974, employing the flag of the dominant nationalist party. This has two black stars to stand for the two island groups. Originally the horizontal stripes were equal, but on independence they were altered to their present dimensions, and the proportions of the flag became one by two.

Senegal was one of France's oldest colonies on the coast of West Africa. It became an autonomous part of the French Community on 25 November 1958, and a part of the Mali Federation (*see* **Mali** above) on 4 April 1960, and then flew the flag of the Federation, under which it became independent on 20 June. It seceded from the Federation and became an independent republic on 20 August 1960. The flag was then distinguished from that of Mali by the addition of a green star, taken from the national emblem. The flag of the President is like the National Flag but has the proportions three by four, and has the initials of Léopold Sédar Senghor (LSS) around the green star.

São Tomé and Principe:
National Flag

Senegal: National Flag

Somalia, now known officially as the Somali Democratic Republic, was formed from British Somaliland and Italian Somaliland on 1 July 1960. The flag adopted is that flown in the Italian territory when it was under trusteeship of the United Nations, and reflects the flag of that organization, being of United Nations blue with a white star. The five points of this star refer to the five territories inhabited by the Somalis: the former British and Italian Somaliland, the Ogaden province of Ethiopia, Jibuti and the Northern Frontier District of Kenya. The flag dates from 12 October 1954.

Although the Portuguese were the first to discover and lay claim to what is now the coast of the **Republic of South Africa**, the Dutch were the first to make permanent settlements there. In April 1652 Jan van Riebeeck, a ship's surgeon, founded the first European settlement at Cape Town. Although no pictorial record exists it seems likely that the flag used in this settlement was the original flag of the Netherlands, known as the *Prinsvlag* (*see* **Netherlands** p. 130), i.e. a horizontal tricolour of orange, white and blue. It seems, however, that this was changed about two years later to red, white and blue then official in the Netherlands. The orange, white and blue is always referred to in South Africa, however, as the 'Van Riebeeck Flag'. A further Dutch emblem, also to be important in the heraldry of South Africa, was the lion grasping a bundle of arrows and the motto of the Dutch republic, *Eendragt Maakt Magt* ('Unity is Strength').

In 1795 the British occupied Cape Town as part of the struggle against the French and the Union Jack was hoisted over the Castle of Cape Town which had been built on the site of the original Dutch fort. After the Napoleonic Wars the Cape was ceded to Britain, much against the wishes of its Dutch inhabitants, who then began the famous 'Great Trek' which took them further into the interior of the country in search of new settlements where they could be secure and independent. This earned them the name of

Somalia: National Flag

*South Africa:
National and Merchant Flag*

Voortrekkers, 'Pioneers'. A series of settlements were founded, mostly using the Dutch colours, but these were incorporated in turn into the British colony. Further in the interior, the Orange Free State was formed in 1848, and the Transvaal in 1850. These two remained independent until the end of the second South African War in 1902. The flag of the Orange Free State dates from 28 February 1856, when a design was received from King William III of the Netherlands. It has three orange stripes for the House of Orange, and the modern Dutch tricolour in the canton. The flag of Transvaal is known as the *Vierkleur*, and adds a fourth colour, green for youth, to the Dutch tricolour. This was adopted on 6 January 1857.

After the defeat of the Boers the four territories of the Cape of Good Hope, Natal, the Orange Free State and the Transvaal were ruled directly by Britain until 31 May 1910 when they were formed into a new federal dominion, the Union of South Africa. This had a new Coat of Arms, with four quarters representing the four parts, and the shield appeared on the British Red and Blue Ensigns to form the National Flags. However, there was considerable sentiment in favour of a distinctive flag, despite the difficulty of finding a design which would represent all races and traditions. A new flag was finally adopted on 31 May 1928 which is now the flag of the Republic of South Africa, and which does attempt to reconcile conflicting interests. The basic design is the 'Van Riebeeck Flag' with an unusual device in the centre, consisting of the flags of Britain, the Orange Free State and the Transvaal. At first this flag was for use on land only, and then side by side with the Union Jack, but in 1951 it became the Merchant Flag, and the Red Ensign was discontinued. In 1957 the joint use of the Union Jack on land was also discontinued, and finally on 31 May 1961 the country became a republic outside the British Commonwealth, without, however, altering the National Flag or removing the Union Jack from its centre.

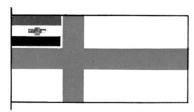

South Africa: President

South Africa: Naval Ensign

The flag of the President of South Africa is dark blue, with the whole Arms in the centre, and the initials SP (for State President) placed over the supporters. The Arms are still much the same as granted in 1910. The first quarter of the shield has a figure of Hope, with her anchor, representing the Cape Province; the second has two galloping wildebeesten for Natal, the third an orange tree for the Orange Free State and the fourth a trek-wagon for the Transvaal. These elements all feature in the Arms of those countries. The supporters are a springbok and an oryx, the crest is a red lion holding a bundle of four rods (the *fasces* of the Roman republic), and the motto is that of the Dutch republic, and of the Transvaal, translated into Latin. The whole Arms are known as the 'embellished' Arms. There is a simpler version which omits the helmet and mantling. This is used on the car-pennants of Cabinet Ministers, which are green. The Administrators of the provinces and of South-West Africa have similar flags with the Arms of those areas.

Until 1 September 1946 the South African Navy wore the British White Ensign, but then a new design was introduced, followed by several others, until the present model was adopted. This has a cross of green (from the Transvaal flag *inter alia*) of Scandinavian pattern, with the National Flag in the canton, fimbriated in white. The National Flag is also the Jack.

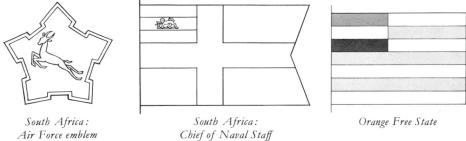

South Africa:
Air Force emblem

South Africa:
Chief of Naval Staff

Orange Free State

The Prime Minister has a green flag of one by two with the simplified Arms in the centre. The flag of the Army is orange-red, with the National Flag in the canton and the Army badge in the lower fly. This is a springbok's head contained within a framework representing the plan of Cape Town Castle, all in yellow. The Air Force Ensign is very similar but has a light blue field. The 'castle' is dark blue outlined in white and charged with a leaping springbok, also in yellow. This device is now the Air Force target. The South African Defence Force (the combined services) flag is a horizontal tricolour of light blue, red and dark blue. The flag of the Chief of the General Staff is the same, but with the simplified Arms over all in the centre.

A further flag with historical links is that of the Citizen Force Units, or part-time Commando Corps. Their flag is green, with an orange saltire fimbriated white. This design is based on the so-called 'Voortrekker Flag', which was blue with a red saltire, later fimbriated white.

In naval flags other than the Ensign, the flag in the canton has the crest from the Arms in the centre rather than the three flags as in the National Flag. This dates from one of the earlier attempts at a distinctive Naval Ensign. Thus the Chief of Naval Staff has a flag like the Ensign but with the special flag in the canton, and a shallow swallow-tail excision. A Vice-Admiral has the same flag with a green disc in the lower hoist.

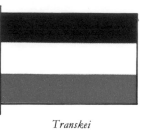

Transkei

Bophuthatswana

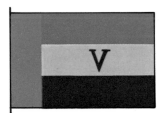

Ciskei

Gazankulu

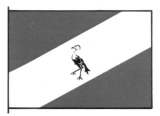

Lebowa

Qwaqwa

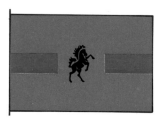

Venda

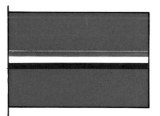

Okavongo

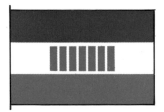

Ovamboland

East Caprivi

Since 1963 the South African government has been creating a series of 'homelands' for the indigenous or 'Bantu' population. These have a limited measure of self-government and are expected to move towards independence. **Transkei** was the first to be created in 1963, and on 20 May 1966 it adopted a distinctive flag: a horizontal tricolour of ochre-red, white and green. On 25 October 1975 the Transkei was officially declared to be independent, and the South African flag was hauled down. No other state has as yet recognized its independence. Other homelands that have been created are **Bophuthatswana, Ciskei, Gazankulu, Kwazulu, Lebowa, Qwaqwa**, and **Venda**, to which the South African government has allocated flags, and **South Ndebele** and **Amaswazi** which do not as yet have flags. **Bophuthatswana** became independent on 6 December 1977, but has not yet been recognized by any other state. **Namibia**, or South-West Africa, is administered by South Africa, although contrary to the wishes of the United Nations, and has set up three 'homelands' there, which also have flags: **Okavongo, Ovamboland** and **East Caprivi**. The immediate future of Namibia is currently subject to negotiation.

The former German colony of **Togo** was partitioned in 1919 into trusteeships administered by Britain and France. The British part was integrated into Ghana in 1957, and the French part became an autonomous republic within the French Community in 1956. A flag of green was then adopted with two gold stars in the fly and the French Tricolour in the canton. The country became independent on 27 April 1960 when the present National Flag was adopted. This has the colours common to many West African states.

Togo: National Flag

Tunisia: National Flag

Tunisia was made a French protectorate in 1881, although it retained its traditional ruler, the Bey, under whom it regained its independence on 20 March 1956. However, on 25 July 1957 the monarchy was overthrown and since then the country has been a republic. The flag of Tunisia pre-dates the French occupation, having been introduced about 1835 by Hassan II, the Bey, or provincial governor, on the basis of the flag of the Ottoman Empire of which Tunisia was nominally a part. The Bey also had a very ornate standard, now obsolete. The modern Presidential Standard is a square version of the National Flag with a wide silver fringe. It is interesting to note that the designs of the crescents and stars on the flags of Moslem countries vary somewhat from country to country, each having a distinctive style. The crescent and star of Tunisia are thus only superficially like those of Turkey.

Upper Volta was formerly a province of French West Africa. It became an autonomous state within the French Community on 11 December 1958, and fully independent on 5 August 1960. Its flag is similar to that of Imperial Germany, but has no

Upper Volta:
National Flag

Zaïre: National Flag

relationship to it: the stripes of black, white and red refer to the three branches of the Volta river which flow through the country. The flag was adopted on 9 December 1959. The flag of the President is a square version of the National Flag with a wide gold fringe.

Zaïre is the modern name of the country once known as the Belgian Congo, or the Congo Free State. It has had a long and complicated flag history. The Congo Free State had a flag of light blue with a gold star in the centre. When the Belgian Congo became independent on 30 June 1960 a vertical row of six smaller stars was added to this to form the National Flag. In 1963 this was modified by placing a red diagonal stripe, edged in yellow, from the lower hoist to the upper fly, and placing one yellow star only in the upper hoist. The country was renamed Zaïre on 1 December 1971 and a new National Flag was adopted. This is a modification of the flag of the ruling Popular Movement for the Revolution, and uses the well-known Pan-African colours. The hand grasping a flaming torch is the emblem of the MPR. The province of **Katanga**, or **Shaba**, as it is now known, existed as an independent state from 11 July 1960 to 24 May 1963. It had its own Arms and flag. The latter was striped diagonally red, green and white, with three red crosses in the lower fly. **South Kasai** was also independent between 9 August 1960 and 2 October 1962. It had a flag of green with a gold 'V' with a red interior, oddly enough the same colours as the present National Flag.

[8] The Middle East

There have been several attempts to form leagues or alliances of Arab countries in the Middle East and North Africa. The first of these arose out of the liberation of the Arab territories formerly part of the Turkish Empire. The initiative was taken by Sherif Hussein ibn Ali of Mecca, who raised the first Arab flag in the Hedjaz in 1916. This had three horizontal stripes of black, green and white, with a red triangle over all based on the hoist. The colours are taken to represent the four famous dynasties of Arab Caliphs, the Ommayads, the Abbassids, the Kharidjites and the Fatimids. When Syria was liberated by the British, an Arab kingdom was set up there using this flag, and a similar design was later adopted in Transjordan and Iraq.

The Hashemites, the dynasty of Sherif Hussein, now rule only the Kingdom of Jordan, and Arab unity has undergone a second phase due to the initiative of the Egyptians. In the 1950s a liberation movement arose which used the colours red, white and black, in a horizontal tricolour. The colours represent progress from past oppression to a shining future through the blood of sacrifice. The eagle, already adopted as an Arab emblem by the Hashemites, was given a modern look, and after the overthrow of King Farouk it became the Arms of Egypt. Subsequently the 'Arab Liberation' colours have spread to several other countries. In 1958 Egypt and Syria formed the United Arab Republic (UAR) under this flag, with two green stars—thus restoring the four colours—and the present Federation of Arab Republics formed in 1972 also uses them. They have also been adopted in the Sudan, Kuwait and the United Arab Emirates, as well as in both parts of the Yemen.

On 1 January 1972 a common flag was adopted by Egypt, Libya and Syria, the members of the Federation of Arab Republics which were to be united under 'One President, One Capital, One Flag'. Only the latter has so far been implemented. It consists of the Arab Liberation flag, with a common emblem in the centre, all in gold. This is a hawk, rather than an eagle, taken from the Arms of Syria. The Hawk of Quraish is the emblem of the tribe of the Prophet Mohammed. In the emblem it grasps a scroll with the title of the Federation in Arabic. Underneath the scroll is a title which varies from country to country, with the name of the country in Arabic. In practice further slight variations from the common pattern occur, as noted below.

The flag-history of **Egypt** is very complicated. A distinctively Egyptian flag was only adopted on 10 December 1923, after the country had secured its nominal independence. This was green, with a single crescent and three white stars within its horns. A wide variety of other flags was also adopted, including the several royal standards. The Naval

Egypt:
National and Merchant Flag

Egypt: Army Flag

Egypt: Naval Ensign

Ensign of this period had two crossed white anchors in the upper hoist, and the Army Ensign two white crossed sabres. After the deposition of King Farouk in 1952 the royal flags disappeared, and the national Arms became the green 'Saladin' eagle. On 1 June 1958 Egypt formed the United Arab Republic with Syria, with the flag of red, white and black, with two green stars in the centre. Syria withdrew from this Union in September 1961, but Egypt retained the name and the flags. These included a flag for the President, and Naval and Army Ensigns of the previous patterns, i.e. the National Flag with the respective emblems in the upper hoist.

These were retained until Egypt entered the Federation of Arab Republics on 1 January 1972 and adopted the flag described above, with the golden Hawk of Quraish in the centre. Egypt was renamed the **Egyptian Arab Republic**. A further new range of flags was adopted, including a new Presidential Standard, which is the National Flag with the emblem in the upper hoist, not in the centre. The Naval and Army Ensigns follow the previous pattern, with the emblems in the upper hoist. In the case of the Army Ensign the federal emblem is distinguished by having the shield of Egypt—vertically red, white, black—on the breast of the hawk. This is the badge of the Army.

Libya was formed as an independent kingdom on 24 December 1951, under King Idris es Senussi, and adopted a flag in the 'Arab Revolt' colours of black, red, green and white. In this case the central part of the flag was black, with a white crescent and star, and this was the flag of the Senussi sect in Cyrenaica. Narrower stripes of red and green were added at the top and bottom to represent the other parts of Libya. The Royal Standard was the Senussi flag with the royal crown in white in the upper hoist. King Idris was deposed on 1 September 1969, and a flag of the Arab Liberation colours of red, white and black was adopted, in the proportions one by two.

When Libya joined the Federation of Arab Republics the federal emblem was placed in the centre, with an added scroll with the name 'Libyan Arab Republic'. The flag had

Egypt: National emblem

Libya: National emblem

Syria: National emblem

the unusual proportions of seven by twelve. The country was renamed the 'Socialist Peoples Libyan Arab Republic' on 22 November 1976. In protest against the visit of the President of Egypt to Israel in November 1977 and his overtures for peace between the Arab countries and Israel, Libya withdrew from the Federation of Arab Republics. As a result the Libyan flag was changed to plain green—which the Libyan authorities say is only temporary.

As recounted above, **Syria** became an Arab kingdom in 1918, under Faisal, a son of Sherif Hussein, but he was deposed in 1920 by the French, who had secured a mandate over the country, and he then became King of Iraq. During the French régime a flag of three horizontal stripes of green, white, green, with the Tricolour in the canton, was used at first, but a distinctive National Flag was introduced on 1 January 1932. This had three horizontal bands of green, white, black, with three red stars on the white stripe. These stood for the three provinces of Damascus, Aleppo and Dar-es-Zor. There were also distinctive flags for Latakieh and the Djebel Druz. Syria became an independent republic on 1 January 1944, and kept this flag, and also adopted a Coat of Arms which now forms the basis of that of the Federation of Arab Republics. This is the Hawk of Quraish, which then bore on its breast a shield with the same pattern as the National Flag, and grasped a scroll with the name of the country.

On 1 February 1958 Syria joined the United Arab Republic, and adopted the flag of red, white and black with two green stars. It left the union on 30 September 1961 and resumed its original National Flag. However, under the new constitution of 8 March 1963 Syria re-adopted the UAR flag, but with three stars in the central strip. The Coat of Arms was also slightly revised at this time.

On joining the Federation of Arab Republics Syria adopted the common flag and emblem. In the latter case the name of the country does not appear under the scroll. The flag is in the same proportions as used by Egypt, i.e. two by three.

Iraq was formed as an Arab kingdom in 1921, but remained under British mandate until 3 October 1932. King Faisal I adopted a flag very similar to that of his father Sherif Hussein, but with a red trapezium based on the hoist, rather than a triangle. On this were placed two seven-pointed stars, whose interpretation was a matter of controversy. His dynasty lasted until 14 July 1958 when the royal family were obliterated and a republic proclaimed. This at first had a vertical tricolour of black, white and green, with a sun-like emblem in the centre said to recall the earlier glorious epochs in Arab history, but in fact almost identical to the emblem of the Babylonian god Shamash. This did not last long, however, and was replaced on 31 July 1963 by the present flag which, it will be noted, is very similar to that of the United Arab Republic and to the former flag of Syria, except that it has the proportions two by three. The new national arms are also practically identical with those adopted by the UAR in 1958.

Jordan alone now retains a Hashemite monarchy, founded by Abdullah, the second son of Sherif Hussein. The country was at first under British mandate, but became independent on 22 March 1946. The flag is based on that of the Hedjaz, and only distinguished by a white star of seven points on the red triangle. The star represents the seven fundamental beliefs of the Mohammedan. The country was renamed the Hashemite Kingdom of the Jordan on 17 June 1946, and in 1948 parts of Palestine, known as the 'West Bank' were incorporated, but these have since been occupied by

Iraq: National Flag

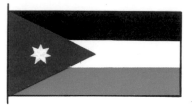

Jordan: National Flag

Israel. The Royal Standard is of unusual design, originally intended to distinguish it from those of the Hedjaz and Iraq. The flag in the centre is the same as the former Royal Standard of Iraq.

The Army Flag is similar to that of the former Arab Legion. It has the Army badge in green in the fly of a red flag with the National Flag in the canton. The Military Ensign is similar, but has a white field, and the badge is a foul anchor with a crown, superimposed on the two crossed swords. The Air Force flag follows the British pattern, with a light blue field and the National Flag in the canton, and the target in the fly: this is green, fimbriated white and black, with a red segment at the top with the white seven-pointed star.

The kingdom of Hedjaz, set up by Sherif Hussein in the First World War, did not have a long existence. It came into conflict with the state of Nejd, established by Abdul Aziz ibn Abdur-Rahman al-Sa'ud, and was defeated and annexed in 1926. The Sultan of Nejd was the leader of the Wahabi sect, devotees of the Fatimid or Shi'a branch of Islam, which has always used the colour green. To this the Wahabis added the *shahada*, the phrase expressing the central creed: 'There is no God but Allah and Mohammed is the Prophet of Allah'.

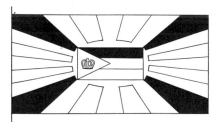

Jordan: Royal Standard

Sa'udi Arabia: National Flag

The kingdom of **Sa'udi Arabia**, including the Nejd, Hedjaz, and other territories, was formally constituted on 23 September 1932, and the present flag was brought into use. This includes the *shahada* in white, and also an Arabian sword. For a period two crossed swords appeared on the flag, but the official design is now as shown. The Royal Standard adds the national Arms in the lower hoist: these are a palm-tree above two crossed swords. The former merchant flag, which was triangular, with the two crossed swords only, and a small white anchor in the upper hoist, is now obsolete.

Moslem etiquette demands that inscriptions on flags should read correctly on both sides, and therefore Sa'udi flags are usually made double-sided with the inscription starting on the observer's right on both sides. Arabic reads from right to left. Sa'udi flags are now primarily distinguishable from each other by their dimensions: the Royal Standard is almost square (23 : 25); the Ensign, which is otherwise identical with the National Flag, is completely square, and the National and Merchant Flags are two by three.

Before achieving independence in modern times nearly all the Arab states in the Persian Gulf and on the shores of the Indian Ocean used flags of red, often plain, but usually with their name in white characters, or with white additions, such as vertical strips in the hoist with plain, wavy, or serrated edges. Red is the colour associated with the Sunni sect of Islam. Such flags were formerly in use in Kuwait, Bahrein, the Trucial States, Oman, Yemen, Zanzibar, the Maldives, the Comoros and even in Indonesia. In modern times they have, in the Middle East, been gradually replaced by flags in the 'Arab Revolt', or 'Pan-Arab' colours of black, green, red and white, which unite all sects and traditional loyalties.

Bahrein formerly had a flag of red, and this was retained when independence was achieved on 15 August 1971. When the island first came under British protection a red flag was specified, and in the course of time this came to acquire the white serrated vertical strip in the hoist that distinguishes it today. Bahrein was nominally a member of the Federation of Arab Emirates in the Persian Gulf from 30 March 1968, but when the United Arab Emirates was formed it opted for independence.

The Royal Flag is like the National Flag, but has a white strip along the top and the bottom, reducing the serrations to five white points. The National Flag has eight white points.

Bahrein: National Flag

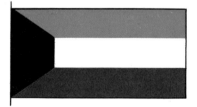

Kuwait: National Flag

Kuwait, formerly a British protectorate, became independent on 19 July 1961. A new National Flag was adopted on independence (Decree 26 of 1961). This is in the Pan-Arab colours, but in the same pattern as that of Iran, i.e. green, white and red, although with a black trapezium over all based on the hoist, and in the proportions one by two.

The Army Ensign is the same, but has the army badge in the upper hoist. The Air Force Ensign is light blue and has the target—green, white, red, black inwards—in the upper hoist and the Air Force badge in the centre in gold.

Qatar formerly had a flag of red with a white strip in the hoist, but in the course of time, and due to the influence of the sun on local vegetable fabric dyes, the red became a dark crimson or maroon, which has now been officially adopted. Qatar became independent on 1 September 1971, but its flag has existed for several decades. In former times the name of the country was added on the red, or maroon section. The flag may be distinguished from that of Bahrein by its having nine whole white points in the serration, its maroon colour, and its unusual proportions of eleven by twenty-eight.

The **United Arab Emirates** (UAE) is a union of the states formerly known as the Trucial States, or Trucial Oman. These consist of seven emirates which came under British protection from 1820 onwards. They were all obliged to use a red flag for their ships, and not those of any other European power under which several of them had been pirating (hence their nickname, the 'Pirate Coast'). Thus all seven states used a red flag with variations, of which two main ones eventually emerged: a long red flag with a white vertical strip in the hoist, and a square red flag with a white border all round. These were known to Britain as No. 1 and No. 2 and were attributed, No. 1 to Ajman, Dubai, and Umm-al-Qawain, and No. 2 to Sharjah and Ras-al-Khaimah. There was also a plain red flag used only by Fujairah.

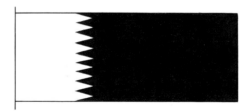

Qatar: National Flag   *United Arab Emirates: National Flag*

In recent decades certain alterations have been made. **Abu Dhabi**, the largest and richest of the oil-bearing emirates, has a flag of red with a small white canton. **Ajman** and **Dubai** have retained the No. 1 flag but reduced to proportions one by two. **Ras-al-Khaimah** and **Sharjah** have retained the No. 2 flag, but increased its proportions to 3:5 and 1:2 respectively. **Umm-al-Qawain** has retained the No. 1 flag but in the proportions 3:5 and with a crescent and star in white facing the hoist.

The formation of the UAE was preceded by a Trucial States Council which had a flag of red, white and red horizontally in 1:2:1, with a green seven-pointed star in the centre. The UAE was officially formed as an independent state, being a federation of the seven emirates, on 2 December 1971. The flag adopted was in the Pan-Arab colours, being a horizontal tricolour of green, white and black, with a red vertical strip in the hoist, with the proportions one by two.

The flags of the emirates have been retained for local use, and are much the same as before except that Fujairah has added its name in white Arabic characters to its previously plain red flag, and Sharjah has announced the abandonment of its flag in favour of the UAE flag.

Oman is one of the few Arab countries never subjected to the Europeans. Its flag was originally plain red and was the inspiration of those used in Zanzibar, the Maldives and

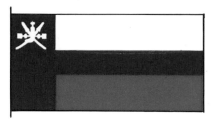

Oman: National Flag

Oman: National emblem

other Arab colonies. In 1970 the name of the country was officially declared to be the Sultanate of Oman, and a new suite of National Flags was adopted on 17 December 1970. These add panels of white and green to the red flag, with the national emblem in white in the upper hoist. The white represents the Imam of Oman, and the green the Djebel al Akhdar (the Green Mountains) of the interior. The national emblem has been in use for some time, and is composed of two crossed scimitars surmounted by a *gambia*, or native dagger, and the chain-like buckle of a belt. The flag of the Sultan has a green field with a red panel in the centre, fimbriated white. In the centre of this is the national emblem in gold. This flag has the proportions one by two and was adopted in 1976.

The Merchant Flag is still plain red, with the national emblem in the upper hoist. The Naval Ensign is blue, with the new National Flag in the canton, and a vertical foul anchor in the fly in white. The Air Ensign is light blue, with the National Flag in the canton and the target in the lower fly. This is red, fimbriated white, with the national emblem in white in the centre. The Chief of Air Staff has a flag of light blue with the target only in the centre. All these flags have the proportions two by three, except the last which is four by five.

The **Yemen Arab Republic** was established on 27 September 1962 following the death of the Imam. The flag used prior to this was red, with a white sword horizontally in the centre, and five white stars representing the five duties of the devout Mohammedan. A civil war followed, in which the royalist forces continued to use this flag, but they were finally eliminated by October 1969. The flag adopted by the republicans was based on that of the then United Arab Republic, but with only one green star in the central white stripe. The Yemen Arab Republic was officially federated to the UAR between 8 March 1958 and 26 December 1961, but no special flag was ever used for this 'Union of Arab States'.

Yemen Arab Republic:
National Flag

Yemen People's Democratic
Republic: National Flag

The former British colony and protectorate of Aden is now the **Yemen People's Democratic Republic**, and flies a flag based on the Arab Liberation colours, i.e. red, white, black, with a light blue triangle over all based on the hoist, charged with a red star. When the country became independent on 30 November 1967 it was known as South Yemen, but the name was changed in 1972 when an agreement in principle to unite with the Yemen Arab Republic was signed. Prior to independence the British had formed a federation of the native states and the Colony of Aden, known as the Federation of South Arabia (11 February 1959). This had a flag of three horizontal stripes of black, green and blue, with the green fimbriated yellow, and over all in the centre a white crescent and star. Each of the member states had a flag and arms of its own. Aden also had its own flag, as well as an ensign-badge used on the British Blue Ensign. The flag was horizontally blue, white, blue, with a red trapezium over all in the hoist, and a green star in the centre.

All these flags became obsolete when the Arab nationalists took power, and the country became independent. The new flag reflects the influence of Egyptian ideas and expresses the intention to unite with the northern Yemen. The Arms are also identical with those of the United Arab Republic, except for a shield in the national colours. These are placed in the upper hoist of the National Flag to form the President's flag.

The **Sudan** was formerly one of the world's few condominiums, being ruled jointly by Britain and Egypt, but it became an independent republic on 1 January 1956. The flag then adopted was a horizontal tricolour of blue, yellow and red, symbolizing the river Nile, the desert and the fertile area. The Sudan became a Democratic Republic on 25 May 1969, and a competition was held to choose a new National Flag which more fully expressed the Sudan's links with other Arab countries. The present design was chosen, patterned closely on the 'Arab Liberation' colours. It was adopted on 20 May 1970.

The flag of the President is the same, but with the National Arms in the centre of the white strip. These consist of a secretary bird with outspread wings bearing a shield of Sudanese traditional shape. Over its head is a scroll with the name *Al Sudan*, and beneath is a scroll with the national motto: 'Victory is Ours'.

Sudan: National Flag

Israel: National Flag

The **Republic of Israel** was formed on 14 May 1948 in the former British mandated territory of Palestine. The Jewish community had been working towards a national homeland for half a century, and its symbolism reflects that of the early Zionists led by Theodore Herzl. The National Flag adopted on independence is very like that of the Zionists, although other variations have been in use for some time. The blue and white edges of the flag recall the *tallith*, or *tallis*, the Jewish prayer shawl, and the central device is the *Magen David*, the Shield of David, a device also appearing on the Zionist flag, but well-known in occult lore.

Other new flags of modern design were adopted in 1948. These include the Merchant Flag which is blue, with a white oval near the hoist, charged with an elongated version of the *Magen David*. The Naval Ensign is also blue, with a white triangle based on the hoist, bearing the Shield of David. The flag of the President is square and blue with a white border all round. It is basically a banner of the State Arms, and has in the centre the seven-branched candelabra known as the *Menorah*. The original of this stood in the Temple of Jerusalem but was carried off by the Romans in A.D. 70. Beneath this is the name *Israel* in Hebrew characters, and it is flanked by two olive branches. Afloat the President uses a version of the Naval Ensign, with gold borders along the top and bottom and a small gold anchor in the upper fly.

The flag of the Defence Force is light blue, with the National Flag, also light blue, in the canton, and the Defence Force badge in the lower fly in gold. This flag has a gold fringe on three sides. The Minister of Defence has a similar flag, but with a gold border on all four sides, and the national shield with a sword and olive branch behind it in the lower fly, all in white. The Commander of the Navy has a flag like the Naval Ensign but with a gold badge of an upright sword and an anchor crossed with an olive branch in the lower fly.

Israel: Merchant Flag

Israel: President

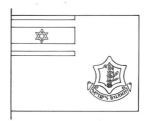
Israel: Defence Force

The Air Force Ensign is light blue, with the target in the centre. This is a white disc edged in dark blue, with the Shield of David in solid blue. Near the top and bottom, as in the National Flag, are stripes of dark blue and white; three of each, with the uppermost and lowermost dark blue stripes twice the width of the others.

Those working for the creation of an Arab state in Palestine use a flag based on that of the 'Arab Revolt', but with the horizontal stripes coloured black, white, green. This flag is used in the West Bank and in other parts of the country occupied by Israel.

A cedar tree has appeared on flags of the **Lebanon** for many years, and is the particular emblem of the Maronite Christian community. When Lebanon was under French mandate the cedar tree was placed in the centre of the Tricolour. The country became fully independent on 1 January 1944, but a National Flag, consisting of the cedar tree on a white field with red stripes along the top and bottom, had already been adopted on 7 December 1943. Lebanon has no official Arms, and no other flag except the Naval Jack, which is like the National Flag but with white vertical strips at the hoist and fly, each of which bears a red vertical anchor.

The present design of the flag of **Turkey** dates back to the early nineteenth century, but a red flag in some form or other has been used for centuries. Turkey, or the Ottoman

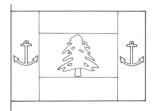

Lebanon: National Flag   *Lebanon: Jack*

Empire as it then was, was the first Moslem country to adopt the crescent and star emblem and, as mentioned before, this has now become a very widespread symbol, especially in lands which once formed part of the Empire. Turkey became a republic on 29 October 1923, and the emblems of the Sultan and Caliphate were abolished, but the National Flag remained unchanged.

The flag of the President is a square version of the National Flag, with a gold device consisting of a sun surrounded by sixteen stars in the upper hoist. The Commander-in-Chief of the Navy also has a square flag, with a white sun in each corner, an upright foul anchor in the centre, and an upturned crescent beneath the anchor. A Senior Admiral has the same, but with the four white suns only, and an Admiral has three suns, arranged one and two. The flag of the Customs Service is a square version of the National Flag with a white border all round.

Turkey: National Flag   *Turkey: President*   *Cyprus: National Flag*

Cyprus has passed through many hands in its long history. In 1571 it passed to the Ottoman Empire, and Turks began to settle there alongside the native Greek population. In 1878 the island was ceded to Britain, and remained a British colony and military base until 16 August 1960 when it became an independent republic. No ordinary flag would adequately express the aspirations of the two rival communities, and so one was chosen representing the island itself, above two olive branches. Since 20 July 1974 the northern part of the island has been occupied by Turkish troops, and the aim of the Turkish leaders is to form a federal government. Their part of the island was formed into the 'Turkish Federated State of Cyprus' on 13 February 1975.

In practice the official flag of Cyprus is only used on international occasions. In the Greek part the flag of Greece, and in the Turkish part the flag of Turkey, are the only ones used. In the Sovereign Base Areas leased to Britain the Union Jack is still in use, and the UN flag is used by the international peace-keeping force.

[9] Asia

Bangladesh was formerly the detached eastern province of Pakistan. It was set up on 16 December 1971 following civil war in Pakistan and with the military help of India. As a result Pakistan left the British Commonwealth, although Bangladesh has been accepted as a member.

The flag adopted during the struggle for independence was like the present one, but had a gold silhouette map of the country on the red disc. Later this was omitted for technical reasons, and the present design was introduced on 13 January 1972. The red disc is slightly off-set from the centre towards the hoist. The Merchant Flag is red, with the National Flag in the canton.

India and **Pakistan** became separate dominions within the British Commonwealth on 15 August 1947, and both adopted flags based on those of the predominant nationalist movements.

In the case of **India** this was the Indian National Congress, whose flag was orange, white and green, with a blue spinning-wheel in the centre. The colours of this, like those of Ireland, symbolize the two main religious communities and the peace intended to exist between them.

On independence a new emblem was put in the centre, the blue *Chakra*, a Buddhist symbol representing the Law of *Dharma*, or eternal change. This is found, *inter alia*, on the pillar of Sarnath, whose lion capital has been taken as the State Arms. The pillar was placed by the Buddhist emperor Asoka to mark the spot where the Buddha first announced the doctrine of *Ahimsa* to the four quarters of the universe. India became a republic within the Commonwealth on 26 January 1950, the first state to assume this constitutional status, and a flag for the President and a new range of subsidiary flags were introduced. The President's flag is quarterly, blue and red. The first quarter bears the state emblem in gold, the second a red elephant outlined in gold, taken from the Ajanta frescoes of the fifth century A.D., the third a balance in gold, taken from the Red Fort at

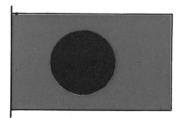

Bangladesh: National Flag

India: National Flag

India: State Arms

India: President

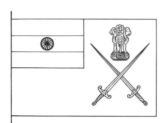

India: Commander-in-Chief of Army

Indian Army Service Corps Colours

Delhi, being of seventeenth century Moslem design, and the fourth a bowl of lotus flowers, also from Sarnath. State Governors were provided with orange flags, with the National Arms in the centre and the name of the state beneath. These have gone out of use in recent years in the process of centralization.

The Naval Ensign of India is based on that of Britain, and still has the Cross of St George in the field, although with the National Flag in the canton, and is in the proportions one by two. The Red and Blue Ensigns, for the Merchant Marine and Naval Reserve, are two by three, but otherwise follow the British pattern. The Air Force Ensign is one by two, with a light blue field, the National Flag in the canton and the target (orange, white, green inwards) in the fly. The Army Flag is also like that of Britain: red with two crossed swords, but in this case the state emblem in place of the royal crest, all in gold in the centre. The Commander-in-Chief of the Army has a flag like the Red Ensign, but with a version of the Army badge in the fly. The Ensign for Government vessels is the Blue Ensign with a horizontal gold anchor in the fly in generous proportions.

The Naval Jack is the same as the National Flag. The flags of naval officers were introduced on 22 April 1958, and are the same as those of the Royal Navy, except that the *Chakra* is placed at the centre of the St George's Cross.

Flags of officers of the Air Force are also very similar to those of the United Kingdom, except that the colours are orange, light blue and green. The flag of an Air Marshal is five horizontal stripes of orange, light blue, green, light blue and orange. The light blue is slightly wider than the other stripes.

Units of the Indian Army still use Regimental Colours which were in many cases granted prior to the country becoming a republic. However, new ones are gradually being introduced, as for example the Indian Army Service Corps as illustrated here.

Although India is a federal state very few state flags are in use. **Jammu and Kashmir** is the only one officially permitted, a usage confirmed in March 1953. Its flag is red with three vertical white couped bars in the hoist, and a representation of a native plough in the fly, also white. **Sikkim**, formerly a protectorate of India, was incorporated as the twenty-second state of the union in May 1975, and the office of the hereditary ruler, the *Chogyal*, was abolished. Sikkim has, or had, a flag of white with a red border all round, and a yellow *Chakra* in the centre. **Nagaland** has several flags used by the nationalists who are seeking complete independence. These are mostly blue, with a rainbow running from the lower hoist to the upper fly, and one or more white stars in the upper hoist. **Manipur**, a former 'native state', now a state of the union, had its own flag, bearing a cobra in intricate coils, on a white or red background. Many, if not all, of the several hundred former native states of India had flags of their own, but they no longer have any official status.

Jammu and Kashmir   *Sikkim*

Malaysia is also a country with a long and complicated flag-history. The core of the country is the Federated Malay States: Pahang, Perak, Negri Sembilan, and Selangor, to which the other 'unfederated' states of Johore, Kedah, Kelantan, Perlis and Trengganu were added after the Second World War. The Straits Settlements—Singapore, Penang and Melaka—continued to be administered separately for a time, but in May 1950 the mainland states together with Penang and Melaka formed the Federation of Malaya. This adopted a flag similar to the present one, but with only eleven stripes of red and white, and eleven points on the star in the canton. The crescent and star were yellow to stand for royal authority, since the state was then a federal kingdom, with the office of head of state passing in turn to each of the hereditary rulers. On 31 August 1957 the Federation became independent. Singapore had been a separate colony since 1946, but in 1963, together with Sabah (North Borneo) and Sarawak on the island of Borneo, it combined with the other eleven states to form the Federation of Malaysia (16 September 1963). The stripes on the flag were then increased to fourteen, as were the points on the star, and the Coat of Arms was also amended. However, on 8 August 1965 Singapore seceded from the Federation, which since then has had only thirteen members. The stripes, etc. were not altered, except for the removal of the Singapore quarter from the Coat of Arms, but the fourteenth stripe is now said to stand for the federal district of Kuala Lumpur.

The Standard of the Head of State, the *Yang Di-Pertuan Agong*, is yellow, with the federal Arms on a white disc within a wreath of *padi*. The Arms consist of a shield with quarters representing the Federated Malay States, Penang, Sabah, Sarawak and Melaka, together with a space charged with a red hibiscus flower, the national plant. The chief is

Malaysia: National and Merchant Flag

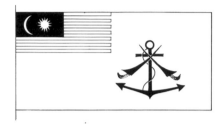

Malaysia: Federal Arms as
in Head of State's Standard

Malaysia: Naval Ensign

red with five *kris*, or Malay daggers representing the 'unfederated' states. The crest is an upturned crescent and a star as in the flag. The supporters are two tigers, and the scroll is yellow with the motto *Bersekutu Bertambah Mutu* ('Unity is Strength') in roman and Jawi characters. The Merchant Ensign is red, with the National Flag in the canton, with a blue fimbriation. The Naval Ensign is white, with the National Flag in the canton, and the military badge in the fly in blue. The badge is two crossed *kris* and an upright blue anchor. There is also a Blue Ensign, blue with the National Flag in the canton. The Jack is the same as the National Flag.

All of the states of Malaysia have their own State Flags, and several have standards for the Head of State and specialized flags as well, and also Coats of Arms.

The flag of **Johore** dates from about 1870. The red canton stands for the state warriors, the *Hulubalang*, the blue field for the government, and the crescent and star the ruler.

Kedah has a flag adopted in 1912. The emblem in the canton is a simplification of the state Arms, which have a shield surrounded by ears of rice.

Kelantan also has a simplified version of its Coat of Arms in white in the centre of its red flag. Each district of Kelantan has its own flag.

Melaka, or Malacca, has a flag adopted in 1961 on the basis of that of Malaya. A new Coat of Arms was also adopted, the central portion of which is a *Pokok Melaka* tree; this is flanked by yellow and red pales. In chief are five golden *kris* on blue. The supporters are mouse-deer, and the crest is a crescent and star. The scroll bears the name and the motto *Bersatu Tegoh* ('Unity is Strength') in roman and Jawi characters.

The yellow field of the flag of **Negri Sembilan** stands for the ruler, the red triangle in the canton the people, and the black triangle the chiefs of the districts.

The flag of **Pahang** dates from about 1903. The white stands for the ruler, and the black the people of the state.

Johore

Kedah

Kelantan

Melaka

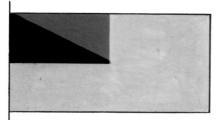

Negri Sembilan

Pahang

Penang

Perak

Perlis

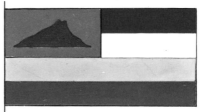

Sabah

Penang, once Prince of Wales Island, is now **Pulau Pinang**. The shield of Arms is the same as that granted on 11 September 1949, with blue and white wavy water, and a yellow chief with the badge of the Prince of Wales in blue. The crest is a *Pinang* tree. The motto, formerly *Ich Dien*, is now *Bersatu Dan Setia* ('United and Loyal'). The flag also dates from 1949, and has the colours of the Arms, with the *Pinang* tree in the centre.

The colours of **Perak** represent the Sultan, the *Raja Muda*, and the *Raja di-Hilir*, the latter being junior members of the royal family.

The flag of **Perlis** was adopted early this century, and the colours stand for the royal family and the people.

Sabah was formerly North Borneo. It became a crown colony in 1946 with its own Arms and badge, and joined Malaysia in 1963, when the Arms were slightly altered and a distinctive flag adopted. The lower part of the shield remains the same: a sailing ship with Mount Kinabalu in the background, but the chief, which formerly had a British lion, now has chevrons in the colours of the flag. The crest had a flag—that of the North Borneo Company—supported by the arms of a native and a white man. Both arms are now those of a native, and the flag is the modern flag of Sabah. This has stripes of red, white, yellow and blue to stand for laudable virtues, and a green canton with a silhouette of Mount Kinabalu in brown. The motto on a scroll beneath is now *Sabah Maju Jaya* ('Progress and Victory to Sabah').

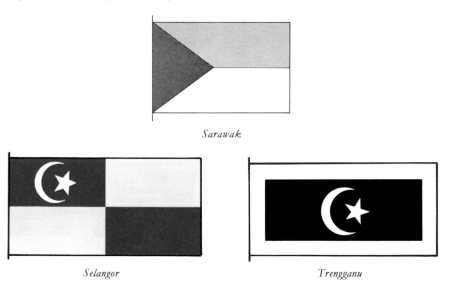

Sarawak

Selangor   *Trengganu*

Sarawak was once ruled by Sir James Brook, the 'White Rajah', and had its own flag. This was yellow with a plain cross throughout divided vertically red and black. In the centre was a gold oriental crown. This later became the badge and Arms of the colony, and remained so until 31 August 1973 when the present flag was adopted. This is based on that of the Federation and is also similar to that of neighbouring Indonesia. A new Coat of Arms was also adopted on this date. The present flag is horizontally red over white with a blue triangle based on the hoist.

The colours of the flag of **Selangor** represent flesh and blood! These are thought of as the life of the state. The crescent and star was altered from yellow to white on 30 January 1965.

The present design of the flag of **Trengganu** dates from 1925, and represents the people—black—enveloped by the protection of the Sultan—white.

Singapore was established as an independent republic within the Commonwealth on 9 August 1965, having been in turn one of the Straits Settlements, a Crown Colony, and one of the states of Malaysia. The flag dates from November 1959, when the island was a self-governing colony. Its proportions are two by three. The colours are said to represent the universal brotherhood and equality of man, and purity and virtue. The crescent stands for a young country, and the stars for the ideals of democracy, peace, progress, justice and equality. In fact the colours are those very frequently found in this part of the world, and are also those of Indonesia. Singapore's flag is only distinguished from the latter's by the crescent and stars. These are the charge on the shield of arms, but with the crescent upturned. The shield is supported by a lion and a tiger (the name means 'City of the Lion'), and the motto is *Majulah Singapura* ('Forward Singapore').

The flag of the President is the same as the canton of the National Flag, i.e. red with crescent and five stars. The Naval Ensign is white, with the same canton, and a red and white compass rose in the lower fly. The ensign for government vessels is the same but with a blue field.

The Merchant Flag, which it is particularly necessary to distinguish from that of Indonesia, is red, with the charge from the Arms on a red disc with a narrow white fimbriation placed in the centre.

Singapore: National Flag

Singapore: Ensign for government vessels

Ceylon had been known to its inhabitants as **Sri Lanka** for many years, but on 22 May 1972 the country became a republic within the Commonwealth, and the name was made official for international usage. Originally a British colony, the island became an independent dominion on 4 February 1948, and a National Flag similar to the present one was adopted in 1946. This consisted only of the red panel with the golden lion grasping a sword, and a yellow border all round. In 1951 two vertical panels of green and orange were added at the hoist to represent the Tamil and Moslem minorities. This flag had small ornamental pinnacles in the corners of the red panel, but when the country became a republic these were also altered. The devices in the corners of the panel are now *bo* leaves, or leaves of the *pipul* tree under which the Buddha sat when he received enlightenment.

Singapore: Merchant Flag   *Sri Lanka: National Flag*

The main part of the flag is based on the flag of Kandy, the central kingdom of Ceylon, and the device of a lion grasping a sword goes back several centuries. New Arms were adopted on the establishment of the republic, and these now appear on the flag of the President. The central part of the Arms remains the same, i.e. the lion device on red within a circle of lotus leaves, but this is now surrounded by a wreath of rice-ears, or *padi*, and the crest has been altered from a native crown to a representation of the *Chakra*. Beneath the disc is a pot of rice, and on either side of this are the sun and the moon. The scroll with the motto has now disappeared, but on the President's flag, which is dark blue, one by two, the Arms have the name of the country in red characters outlined in white beneath them.

So far as is known, no alterations have been made to the ensigns, except for placing the new National Flag in their cantons. The Naval Ensign is like that of Britain, with a red Cross of St George. The Merchant Flag is red, with the National Flag in the canton. The flag for government vessels is blue, with the National Flag in the canton, and two crossed foul anchors in the fly.

The Air Force Ensign has only the original National Flag in the canton of a light blue flag, and the target in the lower fly. This is concentrically red and yellow, with horizontal bars of orange over green on either side.

The Jack is the same as the National Flag. Command flags of the Navy are the same as those of the Royal Navy, except for having the red discs charged with the lion and sword, and edged in yellow.

OTHER COUNTRIES OF ASIA

Afghanistan was recognized as an independent kingdom in 1919, at which time its flag was black with the state emblem in white in the centre. When Nadir Shah became king in 1929 a new flag was adopted, a vertical tricolour of black, red and green, with the emblem in white over all. The state emblem was a mosque, with pulpit and *mihrab* (the recess giving the direction of Mecca), flanked by two flags and a wreath of wheat-ears. Beneath was the date 1348 A.H. (i.e. A.D. 1929), and the name 'Afghanistan' on a ribbon.

Afghanistan became a republic on 17 July 1973, and the royal standard was abolished. A new National Flag was introduced on 9 May 1974, in which the national colours are arranged horizontally. In the upper hoist is the new national emblem, which is a stylized eagle bearing on its breast the combined pulpit and *mihrab* from the previous Arms. The wreath of wheat-ears is also stylized, and the ribbon now bears the title 'Republic of Afghanistan' in Pushtu, and the date *26 Changash 1352* (i.e. 17 July 1973). The eagle is said to represent the legendary bird which brought a crown for the first king of Afghanistan, Yama. The colours of the flag were usually interpreted as standing for progress from the dark times of the past through sacrifice to prosperity.

The National Flag of **Bhutan** is divided diagonally orange over red, with a white rampant dragon facing the upper fly, with a white disc or egg in each of its claws. The vernacular name for Bhutan is 'Land of the Dragon', thought to derive from its frequent thunderstorms, the voice of the dragon. The colours of the flag stand for the king, and the predominant Red Hat sect of Buddhists. The present exact form of the flag was adopted when Bhutan entered the United Nations.

Afghanistan: National Flag

Bhutan: National Flag

Burma: National Flag

Burma was originally a part of the British Empire of India, but became independent outside the Commonwealth on 4 January 1948. The flag then adopted was based on that of the Anti-Fascist Resistance Movement of the Second World War—red with a large white star in the canton. The new flag was red, with a blue canton, with a large white star surrounded by five smaller ones. These represented the racial minorities, the Karens, Shans, Kachins, Chins and Arakanese and Mons. This flag was adopted prior to independence on 24 September 1947, and remained in use until the establishment of the Socialist Republic of the Union of Burma on 2 March 1974. The new constitution made certain alterations to the Arms and flags. The canton of the flags was furnished with a new device based on that of the dominant party, i.e. a cogwheel with an ear of rice, standing for the industrial and agricultural workers of the country. This is surrounded by a ring of fourteen white stars representing the states to be formed within the union.

The Arms have been modified to combine the map of the country with the rice and cogwheel emblem, and to replace the crest of a *chinthe* (a 'sejant' lion) with the large white star. The name of the country on the scroll beneath has also been altered. Prior to 1974 there was a flag for the President, but it is not certain if this is still in use. This was orange, with a peacock 'displayed' in full colour in the centre. This is the ancient national emblem of Burma, and appeared on flags, badges and coins prior to 1948.

The canton of the new flag appears in the subsidiary flags, as follows:
Merchant flag—horizontally blue over red, with the new canton; Naval Ensign— white with a red cross throughout, with the new canton; Government Vessels— blue, with the new National Flag in the canton; Air Force Ensign—light blue, with the National Flag in the canton and the target in the fly. The latter is a concentric triangle of blue, white, orange.

Most of the fourteen states have nationalist movements, each with their distinctive flags, but none of these have any official status. That of the Kachins, for example, is red over green, with two white crossed swords in the centre.

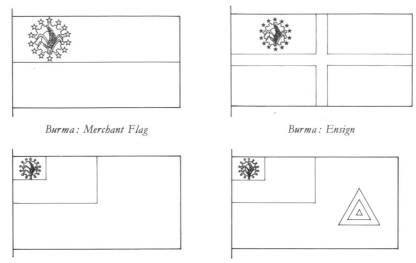

Burma: Merchant Flag   *Burma: Ensign*

Burma: Ensign for government vessels   *Burma: Air Force Ensign*

Cambodia has had a long and troubled history, which has only recently achieved a certain stability. It has, however, always used the famous temple of Angkor Wat as a national symbol. As a French protectorate the flag was red, with Angkor Wat in white in the centre, and a blue border all round. As an independent kingdom the flag had the temple in the centre of a flag striped horizontally blue, red, blue in 1 : 2 : 1. As the 'Khmer Republic' of 9 October 1970 to 17 April 1975, the flag was blue with a red canton bearing the Angkor Wat, and three white stars in the upper hoist. When the Communists finally won control of the country the Angkor Wat emblem did not disappear, but was placed in yellow silhouette in the centre of the new flag adopted on 15 January 1976. Although Prince Sihanouk was first head of state of this régime he has since resigned, and all royal flags and command flags have disappeared. The new flag, with its red field and yellow device, is very similar to that of Vietnam. In the new specifications the temple is not referred to as Angkor Wat, but as a 'monument with three towers'. The official name of the country is now 'Democratic Kampuchea'.

Cambodia: National Flag

*Cambodia:
National Emblem*

Although it is one of the largest and most important countries in the world, the flag history of **China** is not very complicated. In the days of the Empire the principal emblem was the dragon. This appeared on a yellow flag in a rampant posture snapping at a red sun, and there was a range of flags for officials with exactly specified variations on the dragon. When the country became a republic in November 1911 a flag of five horizontal stripes was adopted: red, yellow, blue, white, black. The red stripe stood for China, and the others for its subsidiary racial groups. Red is indeed, *the* Chinese colour, standing not only for the country but for good fortune and happiness, rather like the previous dragon symbol.

China: National Flag
to 1911

China: National Flag
1911–28

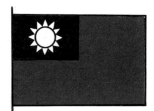

China: National Flag 1928

When the Kuo-Min-Tang (the Nationalist Party) set up the Nanking Government on 10 October 1928 it adopted a new flag of red for China with the party flag (blue with a white sun of twelve rays) in the canton. This was the flag of China until 1949 and still serves as the flag of the Nationalist government on the island of **Taiwan**. The Merchant Flag is similar, but has four zig-zag yellow lines, running across the red field. The flag of the President of Nationalist China is red, with a blue disc with the white sun, and a yellow border all round. The Jack of the Nationalist Navy is the canton from the flag. The Army flag is red, with a blue panel in the centre with the white sun. The Minister of Defence has a white flag, with the combined services emblem in red, consisting of an upright foul anchor over two crossed rifles and a pair of stylized wings. The Chief of General Staff has the same flag but with the emblem in blue. The Air Force Ensign is light blue, with a badge in the centre consisting of a winged disc within a wreath of rice-ears.

China proper was formed into the **Chinese People's Republic** on 1 October 1949. The Chinese Communist régime had long used a red flag, at first with a hammer and sickle, but when the People's Republic was formed the new device of a large gold star and four smaller stars was placed in the canton. The large gold star is said to represent the

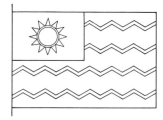

Taiwan: Merchant Flag

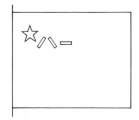

China:
People's Liberation Army

'Common Programme' of the Party, and the four smaller ones the four economic classes of the new state: workers, peasants, petty bourgeoisie and 'patriotic' capitalists. The symbolism of the flag may, however, be much the same as that of the first republic of 1911.

The flag of the People's Liberation Army is similar to the National Flag, but has the characters 8 and 1 next to the large gold star: these stand for the date 1 August 1928 when it was founded.

The only other flag known from Communist China is the Customs flag: this is the same as the National Flag, but with the universal emblem of travel, the staff of Mercury, crossed with a key, all in gold in the lower fly.

People's Republic of China:
National Flag

Tibet

Tibet has an interesting flag, but it has been used only in exile since the flight of the Dalai Lama in 1959. At the base of the flag is a white triangle, not intended to be any specific mountain. On this are two lions outlined in green supporting the 'Wishing gem', a version of the *yang-yin* also found on the flags of Mongolia and Korea, and previously of Tannu Tuva. Above this are three jewels with flames emerging from them, representing **Buddha**, *Dharma* and *Sangha*. *Dharma* is the principle of eternal change, and *Sangha* is the body of guardian saints. Above the mountain is a golden rising sun, and behind this twelve rays of red and blue. There is a gold border on the hoist side and at the top and bottom. The flag was adopted in 1912 when Tibet re-asserted its independence. The country was officially re-incorporated into China on 23 May 1951, and on 9 September 1965 was made into an Autonomous Region, although with no flag of its own. None of the other four Autonomous Regions have flags.

Formerly the Dutch East Indies, **Indonesia** was occupied by the Japanese during the Second World War, and immediately after their defeat was proclaimed an independent republic. Complete sovereignty was transferred to the republic on 27 December 1949, except for the western part of the island of New Guinea. The flag adopted in 1945 is the same as at present, i.e. horizontally red over white. This is said to have been used as early as the end of the thirteenth century by the Majapahit Empire. In modern times it was adopted by the Indonesian Association in 1922, and by the Indonesian Nationalist Party in 1928. The flag is the same as that of Monaco, except for its proportions, which are two by three.

The flag of the President is yellow, the colour of authority, with a gold star within a wreath of rice and cotton. There is a wide gold fringe on three sides, and the flag is used either in square form or in proportions four by five.

The Naval Ensign and Merchant Flag are the same as the National Flag. The Jack has

*Indonesia: National and
Merchant Flag and Ensign*

Indonesia: President

Indonesia: Jack

nine stripes of red and white, and is said to be the flag of the Majapahit Empire. It has the proportions of two by three.

The Indonesian armed forces have ceremonial ensigns. These are of differing colours—green for the army, dark blue for the navy, and light blue for the air force—but all have the same device on the reverse, namely the national Arms in full colour in the centre. The Arms consist of a large displayed bird, the *garuda*, a creature from Hindu mythology which also appears in the Arms of Thailand. On its breast is the national shield, of four quarters. The first is red with the head of a buffalo, the second white, with a green banyan tree, the third white with branches of rice and cotton in yellow, and the fourth red with a golden chain. Over all in the centre is a black inner shield bearing a golden star. The *garuda* holds a scroll with the motto *Bhinneka Tunggal Ika* ('Unity in Diversity'). The obverse sides of the ceremonial flags are illustrated here, and they are all in gold, except for the shield in the Army flag, which is red over white. Each has a motto in the Kawi language, as follows:

Navy: *Jalesveva Jayamahe*—'On the Seas we are Glorious'
Army: *Kartika eki Paksi*—'Strength, Unity, Loyalty'
Air Force: *Swa Bhuwana Paksa*—'The Wings of the Fatherland'.

Although Indonesia was formed as 'The United States of Indonesia' the federal constitution has been inoperative for many years, and the country is now known officially as the Republic of Indonesia. Several states attempted to set up local régimes, with their own flags, in the late 1940s, but the only one to maintain itself in existence is the **South Moluccas**. This has a flag of red, with vertical strips of blue, white and green in the hoist. There is a government in exile in the Netherlands, where this flag is often seen. The flag dates from 25 April 1950.

Indonesia: reverse side
of ceremonial flags

Indonesia: Navy Colours

Indonesia: Army Colours

Indonesia: Air Force Colours

In the period 15 August 1962 to 1 May 1963 the United Nations supervised a transitional government in **West Irian** which used a flag of thirteen horizontal blue and white stripes with a vertical red strip in the hoist charged with a single red star. On the latter date West Irian was integrated into Indonesia, but the flag is still in use by separatists, also based in the Netherlands.

Since the end of 1975 Indonesia has occupied the former Portuguese territory in **East Timor.** The separatist groups there had set up the Democratic Republic of East Timor on 28 November 1975. This had a flag of red with a yellow triangle based on the hoist, on which is superimposed a black triangle charged with a white star. The Indonesians have now incorporated the whole island into Indonesia and it is unlikely that this flag is still in use there.

Although the first recorded flag of **Iran** was the apron of the blacksmith Kava who led the resistance to the Arabs, many standards and flags must have been in use before then. Indeed, the oldest flag known to archaeology was found on the site of Khabis in 1972, dating from about 3000 B.C. It is a metal standard, with a finial in the form of a spread eagle and a square field incised with religious or mythological motifs. The emblem under which the Achaemenians created their empire is thought to be the winged disc of the sun-god, whilst the Sassanids are credited with a winged lion. The flag of Kava was taken by the Arabs at the Battle of Kadisiya which led to their capture of the Persian Empire and the introduction of Islam, in A.D. 636. By that time, according to the Arab writer Ibn Khaldun, it was covered with the signs of the Zodiac and lavishly studded with jewels.

The colour green was used under the Caliphate of Omar and his successors, the colour of the Shi'a sect. The Abbasid Caliphs who originated in and had their headquarters in Persia used black. The lion emblem appeared again with the Ghaznavi Sultans, and the combination of lion and sun—the badge of Iran to this day—can be traced back to the tenth century. From the late thirteenth century onwards it has been used by nearly every dynasty, including that of Tamerlane, and was well established by the reign of Nadir Shah (1736–47). The sword in the right paw of the lion appeared in the seventeenth century, and is now identified as that of Ali, the *zul-faqar*. (The sword of the Prophet's son-in-law split when being drawn from its sheath, but was credited with magical powers.) In fact the sabre held by the lion is of normal shape.

The colours of Iran became gradually established in the nineteenth century, and may perhaps be regarded as a combination of the colours of the Islamic sects, the Shi'a and the Sunni, which have long struggled for the hearts and minds of the people. The National Flag only gradually became regularized. It was first officially adopted in the constitution of 14 August 1905, in the proportions one by three. The long form has gradually diminished to the present four by seven. The lower colour was often shown as pink, but was officially declared to be red in 1933. The State Flag has the lion and sun emblem in the centre. Within a wreath of oak and laurel and ensigned by the crown this badge also appears in the centre of the Naval and Military Ensigns.

Iran: National Emblem   *Iran: National and Merchant Flag*   *Iran: Shah*

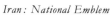

The flag of the Shah is square with a light blue field charged with the Royal Arms in full colour, and with a small canton of the national colours with the badge from the Ensign over all. The Arms have a circular shield divided into four. The first quarter has the lion and sun on blue; the second the figure of the god Fohourhar, representing the Achaemenian dynasty; the third is black with a gold border, charged with the sword of Ali; the fourth is blue with the winged lion of the Sassanids. In the centre is a smaller disc bearing a representation of the mountain Damavand. The supporters are two lions bearing sabres, and the crest is the crown of the Pahlavi dynasty, founded by the father of the present Shah in 1925. Behind the shield is the collar of the Pahlavi Order, and beneath is a scroll with the legend 'He commandeth me to Justice and He is the Judge'. The standard of the Shahbanou (the Empress) is similar, except that in place of the whole Arms is her personal badge in gold, with coloured jewels. The emblem is two griffins whose tails or lower parts merge into a pattern of foliage. Above is the Shahbanou's crown. These Standards replaced earlier patterns in 1974.

The Naval Jack of Iran has also been altered, and is now dark blue with the Pahlavi crown in the centre, within a wreath of laurel, all in gold. The flag of the Minister of War and of Marine is a green square with the lion and sun badge, and four foul anchors, one in each canton with the ring pointing to the corner. Other Ministers have the same flag but without the anchors. An Admiral has a white square flag with an upright foul anchor in the centre in gold, a small canton of the national colours, and a green star in the upper and lower fly cantons. The stars have one point towards the corner of the flag.

Japan is the 'Land of the Rising Sun', and the red sun-disc, known as *Hi-no-maru* is the emblem on its flag. The emblem is the state 'Mon'. 'Mon' are the Japanese equivalent of heraldic emblems, and are in widespread use and have been for centuries. They are generally more stylized and complex in form than Western heraldic devices, and do not have to be shown in any particular colour, although in modern flag usage colours are specified. The State Mon dates back to the Tokugawa Shogunate, if not earlier, but has always been regarded as a royal flag. When the Emperor resumed control of the country on 3 January 1868 (the 'Meiji Restoration') it assumed the status of a National Flag, and this was confirmed in laws issued on 27 February 1870. In the modern design the flag is two by three, and has the disc set slightly nearer the hoist.

The chrysanthemum has always been the Imperial Mon, and also represents the sun. The Imperial Standard in its present form was adopted in 1871, although there was a variant for use at sea with a white emblem on a purple field until 1889. The Imperial Mon is also used as the State Arms of Japan, and is known as *Kiku-non-hana-mon*. The Crown Prince has a similar standard, but with the Mon in smaller dimensions, and contained within a white rectangular frame. The Standard of the Empress is like that of the Emperor, but swallow-tailed, and the Standard for other members of the Imperial family is white, with a red border all round, and a golden Mon in the centre.

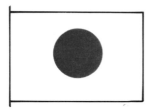

Japan:
National and Merchant Flag

Japan: Imperial Standard

The Japanese Naval Ensign was adopted in 1889, and consists of the sun-disc with red rays extending to the borders of the flag. By the Treaty of San Francisco Japan was precluded from having her own armed forces, but after 1952 'Self-Defence Forces' began to be built up, and the Ensign was resumed in June 1954. The Jack is the same as the National Flag. The flag of the Ministry of Marine is blue with a compass rose of sixteen points in the centre, and a small blue diamond edged in white above it. This was formerly the Ensign of the Maritime Safety Board.

The flag of the 'Ground Self-Defence Force' is square, with the red sun in the centre, with eight red gyrons, and a gold indented border all round. The flag of the 'Air Self-Defence Force' is blue, with the air force emblem in the centre in gold.

The flag of the Prime Minister is yellow, with five Mon in the form of white flowers edged in red arranged in a circle. Mon in the form of red five-petalled flowers are used by naval officers. The flag of the Chief of Maritime Staff is white with three of these, arranged one and two, and a red border all round the flag. A Vice-Admiral has the same but without the red border, and a Rear-Admiral has only two of the Mon, and a Commodore one.

Japan: Naval Ensign

Japan:
Ground Self-Defence Force

Each of the prefectures of Japan has its own flag, often of striking design and unusual colours. The former provinces also had their own flags, most of which bore a Mon of some kind. The prefecture of Okinawa was established on 16 May 1972 when Okinawa and the Ryukyu islands, which had been administered by the United States since 1945, were restored to Japan. Immediately after the Second World War the islands' ships wore a flag of yellow over blue over yellow with the blue of double width and a triangle cut out of the fly. On 1 July 1967 the Japanese flag was restored, but with a white triangular pennant above it with the name *Ryukyus* in Japanese and English in red lettering. When the islands were once more part of Japan, the present flag, which is like that of Japan, i.e. white with a red sun disc in the centre, was established. In this case, however, the Mon is composed of another disc in white superimposed on the red one, and a third red one superimposed on that. The discs are not concentric, but the two latter are 'stepped up' towards the top.

Korea was an independent united kingdom until annexed by Japan on 22 August 1910. After the Second World War it was occupied by the USA and the USSR and rival régimes were established in the North and the South.

In the south the **Republic of Korea** was formed on 15 August 1958, and readopted the flag of the former kingdom, although with some modifications. The flag is now in the proportions two by three, and the device in the centre has been simplified. This particular emblem known as the *yang–yin*, is widespread in Eastern symbolic design, and represents the union of opposites. It is referred to in the writings of the ancient Chinese philosopher Chu-Hsi, and is also similar to the Japanese badge of triumph and honour called the *Tomoye*, which dates from about the twelfth century and is said to have been adopted from the Chinese cosmogony. Around the emblem are four black trigrams, known as *kwae*, representing the four seasons or the four elements of the universe. The original flag was adopted on 22 August 1882 and readopted on 25 January 1950. There is also a flag for the President, adopted on 31 January 1967. This is medium blue, with a Mon in the form of a rose placed just below the centre, and flanking this two birds with ornate tails, known as 'Wonder Birds' all in gold. The Rose Mon is also the basis of the State Arms, with the *yang–yin* superimposed, and a scroll around with the name of the country in blue characters.

The Naval Ensign and Jack is blue, with a white canton charged with the *yang–yin* with two crossed black anchors behind it. This was adopted as early as 11 November 1945. The flag of a Vice-Admiral is also medium blue, with three stars arranged one and two. A

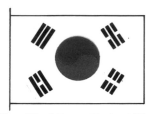

Republic of Korea: National Flag

Republic of Korea: Naval Ensign and Jack

Korean People's Democratic Republic: National Flag

Rear Admiral has two stars arranged vertically. There are also ceremonial flags for the various branches of the armed forces. The Army flag is horizontally white over blue, with the badge in full colour in the centre. The Air Force flag is blue, with the badge in the centre of a silver eagle with a large star within a garland on its breast. The Coast Guard has a flag like the ensign, but with its own badge in the canton. In this the anchors are yellow and the eagle white. A plain blue flag with the same device is flown ashore.

The **Korean People's Democratic Republic** was formed in the northern part on 9 September 1948. The flag adopted on this date is one by two. The *yang-yin* is replaced by the red star of Communism, but the colours of red, white and blue are retained.

Laos, once called Lanxang, the Land of a Million Elephants, was founded as a kingdom in the fourteenth century. It became a French protectorate in 1893, and an associate state of the French Union in 1949. Full independence was achieved on 7 December 1956, but since the Second World War the country has been in the throes of a civil war which only ended in 1975 with the ultimate triumph of the Communists. The Lao Patriotic Front, or Pathet Lao, took over the country, and on 29 November 1975 King Savang Vatthana abdicated and the People's Democratic Republic of Laos was proclaimed. Under the kingdom the flag had been red, with a device of three elephants surmounted by a parasol, symbolizing the three principalities into which the country had become divided. When the republic was established the Pathet Lao flag became the National Flag, the royal Arms were abolished and a new Soviet-style emblem introduced. In the new flag red stands for the blood shed in the liberation struggle, blue for prosperity, and the white disc for the shining future. The flag was officially inaugurated on 4 December 1975.

Four hundred miles south-west of Sri Lanka lie the **Maldive Islands**. In the past they were a protectorate of Great Britain, but on 26 July 1965 they became fully independent and left the Commonwealth. On 11 November 1968 the Sultanate was abolished and the islands became a republic.

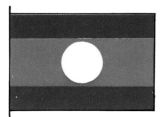

Laos: National Flag   *Laos: National Flag of Kingdom*

For many years the country used a plain red flag, and later one with a white crescent, to which a pattern of diagonal black and white stripes in the hoist was added. The green panel was also added later, but on independence the black and white diagonals were removed. During the first republic the Merchant Flag was without the crescent, but is now the same as the National Flag. The Sultan previously had a flag for use at sea consisting of a double pennant. The upper one was red with a green triangle with a white crescent, and the lower one red with a green rectangle bordered in blue, charged with a white crescent and star. His flag for use on land was like the National Flag but with a star as well as the crescent. This is now the flag of the President. The Ensign is like the National Flag but with a star instead of a crescent. The flag of the Prime Minister is quarterly, green, blue, red, green, with a white star in the first quarter. There is also a range of other flags.

Whilst the British were in occupation of Gan the people of Addu and the southern group of islands formed the **United Suvadivian Republic** with a flag of its own, in opposition to the Maldive Government. This flag was horizontally blue, green and red, with a crescent and star over all in the centre and a star in the upper hoist and lower fly, all in white. The breakaway state was suppressed in late 1963.

Outer Mongolia finally broke away from China's sovereignty when the newly formed **Mongolian People's Republic** was recognized by the Sino-Soviet treaty, which was formally confirmed on 5 January 1946. Its flag was then red with the national emblem, the *soyonbo* in blue in the centre. The Merchant Flag was red with a yellow saltire having the *soyonbo* over all in the centre in blue. The emblem is a compendium of mystical devices surrounding the *yang–yin* disc also found in the flags of Korea and Tibet and other countries under Buddhist influence. The elements above and below this represent fire, earth, water, air and aether, although the whole device is now given a more prosaic interpretation in Communist heraldry, and it now includes the gold

Maldive Islands: National Flag   *Mongolia: National Flag*

star of Communism at the top. In 1940 the colour of the whole emblem, previously blue, the Mongol national colour, was changed to gold, and the present flag design adopted, in which the blue appears as the central vertical strip.

Nepal is the only country in the world which does not have a rectangular National Flag. The shape of its flag is not too easy to describe, and it may perhaps be best thought of as two triangular pennants one above the other. The field is crimson, bordered in blue with the charges in white. These consist of a representation of the crescent moon in the upper part, and of the sun in the lower part. These formerly had faces, but were simplified on 16 December 1962. The crescent represents the royal house, and the sun the Rana family, who were hereditary prime ministers of the country until November 1961. The Royal Standard is rectangular, two by three, with a red field and a narrow white border all round. In the centre is a rampant lion holding a lance with a flag, and in the upper hoist a crescent and in the upper fly a sun with a face, all in white.

The famous Gurkha soldiers are recruited in Nepal, and their well-known badge of crossed *kukri* appears in both the national and royal Arms of Nepal.

The flag of the Commander-in-Chief of the Armed forces has a red field with a white canton containing the National Flag. In the fly is a badge consisting of three crossed *kukri* in white within a golden wreath; above this is a crescent in white and above this again a sun with a face in gold. There is a narrow white border all round except in the hoist where it is gold. Under the Ranas this office was held by the Prime Minister.

Nepal: National Flag   Nepal: Royal Standard   Nepal: Commander-in-Chief
                                                                  of Armed Forces

Pakistan became an independent dominion within the British Commonwealth on the same day as India, 15 August 1947, and an Islamic Republic, also within the Commonwealth, on 23 March 1956. However, after the civil war which led to the formation of Bangladesh in the former detached eastern province, Pakistan left the Commonwealth on 30 January 1972.

No changes have been made in her flags over this period, and the National Flag is that adopted on independence. This is based on that of the Muslim League and has a field of green, known officially as 'tartan green', with a white crescent and star. These are disposed on a diagonal line running from the top of the fly to the bottom hoist corner of the green panel. In the hoist is a vertical white strip equal to a fourth of the length. The crescent and star on green clearly represent the dominant Moslem section of the

Pakistan: National Flag

Pakistan: President

population, and the white strip, added on independence, stands for the religious minorities. The National Flag has the proportions two by three, but the Naval Ensign is one by two.

The flag of the President is blue, with a small version of the crescent and star in the centre, within a wreath of laurel and with the name Pakistan in Urdu, all in gold.

The Naval Jack is dark blue with the naval badge in the centre in white. This badge is a blue shield with an ornate white border, charged with a large foul anchor, also white, with the crescent and star upturned above, and a scroll with the name Pakistan in roman characters beneath. An Admiral of the Fleet has a blue flag with the Navy badge in the hoist and five white stars arranged two, one and two in the fly. An Admiral has four stars two and two, a Vice-Admiral three stars and a Rear-Admiral two.

The Merchant Flag, introduced on 22 October 1958 is red with the National Flag in the canton. The Air Force Ensign is light blue with the National Flag in the canton, and the target of concentric green and white in the fly. The Civil Air Ensign is similar to that of Britain, but instead of a dark blue cross fimbriated in white it has only a horizontal stripe also blue fimbriated white, with the National Flag in the canton. A cross would obviously be out of place in this context.

The Pakistani Army uses colours in pairs, like those of the UK, i.e., National and Regimental Colours. The National Colours are the national flag with the badge of the regiment at the top of the white strip. The Regimental Colours have a field of the regimental colours with the badge and battle honours in the centre. The Chief of Staff of the Army has a flag of green with two crossed sabres above which is the crescent and star facing the upper hoist, and with a narrow white vertical strip in the hoist.

Pakistan controls a part of the state of Kashmir, known as **Azad Kashmir** ('Free Kashmir'). This has a flag of its own, dating from 1947 when Pakistan and India entered into dispute over the state. The flag is one by two, and is divided horizontally. The upper

Pakistan: Jack

Pakistan: Merchant Flag

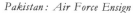
Pakistan: Air Force Ensign   *Azad Kashmir*

half is green, except for a quarter near the hoist which is orange, and the upper fly canton, which contains the crescent and star. The lower half is divided into eight white and green horizontal stripes.

Pakistan now consists of four provinces each with a measure of self-government, and also includes a number of former native states. These all had flags of their own, some of which are still in use, but the modern provinces do not have flags.

In the North-West Frontier Province the Pushtu-speaking people have organized the state of **Pakhtunistan**. Since 1947 this has used a flag of red with a black vertical strip near the hoist. In the centre of this is a disc with a scene of the sun rising over three mountains, and with Pushtu inscriptions above and below.

Although not strictly speaking a Pakistani flag, that of the **Ismaili** sect which has its headquarters in that country, and is led by the Aga Khan, is of interest. It is dark emerald green with a crimson stripe running from the upper hoist to the lower fly, equivalent in width to a quarter of the width of the flag, the proportions of which are one by two. The Ismailis are the descendants of the 'Assassins' who formerly flourished in the Middle East.

The National Flag of the **Philippines** dates from 12 June 1898 when it was raised for the independent republic the Philippinos were trying to form to replace Spanish rule. It was created by the *Junta Patriotico* in exile in Hong Kong and incorporates features of earlier revolutionary flags. Marcella Marino Agoncillo is credited with the design. The white triangle recalls the *Katipunan* movement with its masonic overtones. The three stars stand for the island groups of Luzon, Visayas, and Mindanao. The sun has eight rays, representing the eight provinces where the nationalist movement began, composed of three smaller rays. The flag was taken to the Philippines on 19 May 1898 by General Emilo Aguinaldo and used there from 12 June of that year until 23 March 1901 when he

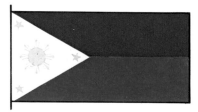

Philippines: National Flag   *Philippines: President*

was defeated and captured by the Americans, to whom the islands had been ceded by the Spaniards on 10 December 1898.

With the agreement of the United States the flag was restored on 26 March 1920, to be flown on land only side by side with the Stars and Stripes, with the latter taking precedence. It was retained when the Philippines was granted Commonwealth status on 15 November 1935 and became the National Flag when the country became an independent republic on 4 July 1946. It should be noted that during hostilities the flag is flown with the red stripe, representing courage, uppermost.

The flag of the President is sky blue, in the proportions twenty-six by thirty-three. In the centre is the sun from the National Flag, with a red triangle superimposed charged with a gold 'sea-lion' (derived from the Arms of Manila), and three gold stars. All round this is a ring of fifty-two white stars.

The National Flag is also the Merchant Flag and Naval Ensign. The Jack is blue with the gold sun and three stars from the National Flag.

As in the USA and some other countries the armed forces have ceremonial flags as well as ensigns. The Navy Standard of the Philippines is blue with a small white diamond in the centre bearing the navy badge. This has two sea-lions, each with a dagger, in the 'respectant' position, with two crossed anchors behind them, all on a white disc edged blue. A Commodore of the Navy has this badge in the canton of a blue flag with a small white star in the centre, and a gold fringe on three sides.

Thailand:
National and Merchant Flag

Thailand: Ensign

Thailand, or Siam as it was known until 1939, is sometimes referred to as the Land of the White Elephant, and this emblem has appeared on its flags throughout the ages. It is associated with Zacca, the founder of the nation, who subsequently achieved divine status. The first National Flag was plain red with a white elephant, but between 1889 and 1926 various changes were made which resulted in the present National Flag. The general purpose flag of today was adopted on 28 September 1917, during the First World War, in order to make the original red and white flag into the colours of the Allies. It is thus now known as the *Trairanga* or Tricolour. The flag had already been modified in 1916 by the inclusion of a horizontal white stripe above and below the elephant. The reform of 1917 omitted the elephant altogether and made the central stripe between the two white ones blue. The elephant does however still appear on the Naval Ensign, on a red disc over all in the centre, and is shown as caparisoned. There is a similar ensign for the Army, which has a gold badge over all in the centre. The caparisoned white elephant standing on a pedestal also forms the national emblem.

The Royal Arms feature in the centre of the Royal Standard, which is a square yellow

Thailand: Jack   *Thailand: Admiral of the Fleet*

flag. In the centre is a representation in red and gold of the *garuda*, the mythological bird of Buddhist lore which also forms the Arms of Indonesia. This was introduced in 1910 and replaced the earlier royal arms. The Queen now flies the same flag as the King, but swallow-tailed in shape, and the Crown Prince has a flag which is like that of the King but with a blue border all round. Royal Princes have a flag of blue, with the Royal Arms on a yellow disc in the centre. The naval Jack is like the National Flag, but has the Navy badge in gold in the centre. The badge is an upright foul anchor around the shank of which is another important Thai emblem, the *Chakra* (*see also* India and Sri Lanka above). In Thailand this takes the form of a 'Catherine' wheel with flame-like blades emerging from the rim. On the Jack this emblem is ensigned with the Royal Crown shaped like a helmet.

An Admiral of the Fleet has a blue flag with two crossed shells within a small wreath, in the centre, surrounded by five silver *Chakras*. An Admiral has the same, but without the central emblem and only four *Chakras* arranged two and two. A Vice-Admiral has three *Chakras*, etc. The Commander-in-Chief of the Navy has a blue flag with the navy badge in gold in the centre. There is another form of badge for the Army, which is the *Chakra* alone within the royal crown, which has gold rays emerging from its peak. The Commander-in-Chief of the Army has this badge in the centre of a square flag, and four gold stars in the canton. The Army Flag has been described above. There is another badge for the Air Force: a shield divided diagonally in the national colours, with the royal crown above with wings depending from it, and wings on either side of the shield, all in gold. This appears in the centre of the national flag of the Air Force Ensign. The Commander-in-Chief of the Air Force has a sky-blue flag with this badge in the centre, and four gold stars in the canton.

The flag of the Minister of Defence is the National Flag, with the combined services emblem (gold anchor, red *Chakra*, green wings) with the royal crown, over all in the centre.

Thailand has a very wide variety of other specialized flags, far too numerous to include in this work, and its flag-history is longer and more complex than briefly sketched in here.

The flag-history of **Vietnam** is another that is long and complex, reflecting the complicated recent history of the country. Basically, it was partitioned by the Geneva agreements in 1954 into a northern and a southern state. The northern state was a Communist republic which had been founded on 29 August 1945, immediately after the surrender of Japan, but had to struggle for its existence until recognized by the French the following year. The south was a republic sponsored first by the French and then by the Americans, which was subject to increasing Communist infiltration from the north

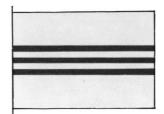

Vietnam   *Republic of Vietnam to 1975*

and from the National Liberation Front. The south was evacuated by the Americans in 1973, and Communist activity increased until the Saigon régime collapsed on 30 April 1975. The Communists resolved to re-unite the country, and this was effected on 2 July 1976.

The flag used in the North is now that of the whole country: plain red with a large yellow star. This dates from the 1940s. The South had used since 14 June 1948 a flag of yellow with three red horizontal stripes across the centre (from the Chinese ideogram for 'The South'). The National Liberation Front had used a flag divided horizontally red over blue with a large yellow star in the centre. This was the flag of South Vietnam from the fall of Saigon until re-unification in July the following year. The country is now known as the Socialist Republic of Vietnam, and the Arms have been amended accordingly.

[10]   Oceania and Australasia

Oceania embraces the whole of the Pacific Ocean, which is scattered over with a vast multitude of islands, only some of which are independent, the others being the dependencies of Britain, France or the USA. However, a great many have moved to independence in recent years, and more may be expected to do so. The two major countries of Australasia are Australia and New Zealand, the latter itself having dependencies in the South Pacific.

Australia adopted a flag based on the British Blue Ensign on 16 September 1901, having become an independent dominion on 1 January of that year. The design was chosen after a competition, and at first no proper regulations were adopted for its use or specifications.

Five separate persons entered the design ultimately chosen, which contains three elements: the Union Jack to represent the links with Britain; the Southern Cross to represent Australia's geographical position; and a large star of six (now seven) points to represent the Commonwealth, i.e. the union of six colonies. The seventh point of the star was added in 1908, and is now taken to stand for the Northern Territory. The diagram shows how the stars of the Southern Cross are arranged. They have been treated rather freely by the designer to get them to fit into the flag, and it is worth comparing this arrangement with those on the flags of New Zealand, Western Samoa and Brazil.

It was not until 20 February 1903 that the National and Merchant Ensigns received royal approval in London, and it was not until 15 February 1954 that the Flags Act, laying down specifications, etc. received the Royal Assent, on an occasion when the Queen was present in Australia.

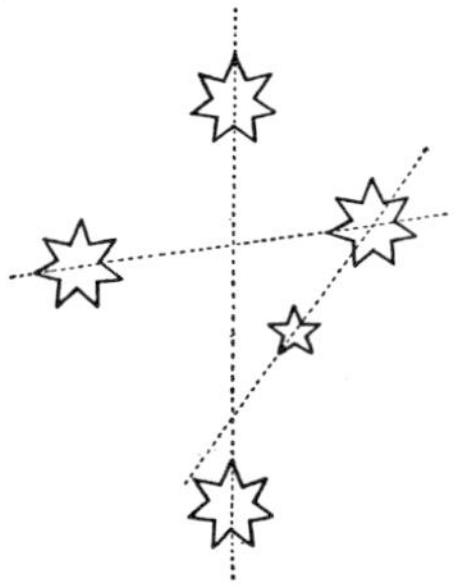

Australia: layout of the
Stars of the Southern Cross

Australia:
National Flag and Jack

Australia: Merchant Flag

Australia: Naval Ensign

Australia: Air Force Ensign

Australia:
Civil Air Ensign

Australia:
Queen's Personal Flag

In 1911 the National Flag became the Jack for the Royal Australian Navy which was then being formed: the White Ensign of the Royal Navy was retained until 1 March 1967 when the present Ensign, which is the same as the National Flag but with blue stars on a white field, was adopted. The National Flag continues in use as the Jack.

On 20 September 1962 royal approval was given to the design for the Queen's Personal Flag for use in Australia. This consists of a banner of the Arms of Australia in the proportions twenty-two by thirty-one, with a large gold seven-pointed star over all in the centre, charged with the royal cypher within a chaplet on a blue disc. The Arms of Australia as used at present were granted on 10 September 1912, and the shield contains quarterings for each of the six states within a border of ermine. The flag of the Governor General is the usual pattern, with the legend 'Commonwealth of Australia' on the scroll. The Federal Prime Minister also has a flag, consisting of the National Flag with the whole Arms in the centre of the lower half of the flag, between the Commonwealth Star and the Southern Cross.

The Ensign of the Royal Australian Air Force is like that of the UK in having a sky-blue field with the National Flag in the canton. On the field the stars of the Southern

Cross are squeezed out of the way to make room for the target in the lower fly. The target is the same as that of the UK but in much smaller proportions. The Civil Air Ensign is also like that of the UK except that the design has the stars from the National Flag arranged over all, in such a way that the smallest star (*Epsilon Crucis*) appears on the horizontal arm of the cross. When first introduced this had yellow stars, but these were altered to white on 4 March 1948.

The Australian Army uses flags very similar to those of the British Army, the regiments having a Queen's Colour and Regimental Colour in the same pattern as those of Britain.

The flag of the Australian Naval Board is like the British 'Admiralty' flag, except that its field is horizontally red over blue with a horizontal foul anchor in yellow over all. The flag for the Secretary of the Navy is like this, but has a countercharged blue and red border on four sides. Naval officers have the same flags as their British counterparts, as do Army and Air Force officers.

The flag of the Minister for Air is sky-blue, with the Air Force emblem in gold in the centre. The flag of the Chief of General Staff is a square version of the National Flag with the Royal Crest in the same position as the Arms on the Prime Minister's flag.

Australia is a federation of six states, each of which was once a separate colony. Each has its own Arms and flag. The state flags are Blue Ensigns with the flag-badge inserted in the fly. The state Governors have Union Jacks with the flag-badge inserted in the centre within a garland, except for the Governor of New South Wales, who uses a plain Union Jack. The badges also form the quarterings representing the states in the Arms of Australia. The state flags all antedate the formation of the Commonwealth, and the badges usually also pre-date the Arms of the states, which they either inspired or of which they became parts.

New South Wales

Queensland

South Australia

Tasmania

Victoria

Western Australia

New South Wales   Dates from 15 February 1876.

Queensland   Adopted on 29 November 1876; the badge is now the crest in the Arms.

South Australia   The badge depicts a white-backed piping-shrike, the state bird; adopted on 13 January 1904.

Tasmania   The badge of this colony, once Van Diemen's Land, has always been a red lion passant. It now forms the crest of the Arms. The flag was officially adopted 25 September 1876.

Victoria   The oldest of the state flags in practice, although only adopted officially on 30 November 1877. A Blue Ensign with the Southern Cross was used by the one ship of Victoria's navy in 1865, and the badge was also that of the Anti-Transportation League.

Western Australia   Officially adopted on 27 November 1875, but with the black swan, the distinctive native bird, facing the sinister. This was corrected in 1953.

No badge or emblem exists as yet for the Northern Territory or any dependency of Australia.

An old Australian flag that is now being revived by those who would like to see the country become a republic is the 'Eureka Stockade' flag. This was a home-made flag used during the gold-field riots at Ballarat in 1854. It consisted of a blue field with a white plain couped cross, and an eight-pointed white star at each extremity of the cross, and another in the centre, evidently an attempt to represent the Southern Cross, and, it is said, it was an inspiration to the designers of the present National Flag. Frank Cayley, author of *Flag of Stars* was instrumental in resurrecting this flag in the 1960s.

'Eureka Stockade' Flag

Fiji became part of the British Empire on 10 October 1874, and an independent nation with dominion status within the Commonwealth on 10 October 1970. The National Flag adopted on independence is a modification of the former colonial Ensign, having a sky-blue field with the shield in the centre of the fly in place of the former ensign badge, which was a white disc with the whole Arms.

The Arms of Fiji were originally granted on 4 July 1908, and have not been altered. The shield is white with a red cross and a red chief. In the first quarter is a bunch of sugar cane, in the second a coconut palm, in the third a flying dove, in the fourth a bunch of bananas, and on the chief a British lion holding a coconut. The crest is an outrigger canoe, the supporters two natives with Fijian weapons, and the motto: *Rere vaka na Kalou ka koka na Tui* ('Fear God and Honour the King'). The dove in the Arms and also the motto and the coconuts appeared on the Arms of the last King of Fiji.

Fiji: National Flag

Fiji: Civil Air Ensign

The present range of flags is similar to the National Flag, but with fields of differing colours. A white field is used for the Naval Ensign, a red field for the Merchant Flag, and a blue field for government vessels, although since Fiji has no navy the Naval Ensign is as yet unused. The Civil Air Ensign is like that of Britain, except that it has the shield of Fiji placed on the arm of the cross. The flag of the Governor-General is unique in that it has the name Fiji on a *tupa* or whale's tooth instead of on the customary scroll.

Nauru is a small island lying just south of the equator, and is rich in phosphates. Before the First World War it belonged to Germany, but in 1920 it was made a mandate of Australia, and from 1947 was administered jointly by Australia, New Zealand and the UK. Complete independence as a republic having a special relationship with the Commonwealth was achieved on 31 January 1968.

The flag then adopted depicts Nauru's geographical position, the gold horizontal stripe representing the equator running across the blue ocean. The points of the large star stand for the twelve native tribes.

Fiji: Governor-General

Nauru: National Flag

New Zealand had several flags before the present design was adopted on 12 June 1902. The first flag was adopted before New Zealand became a British colony and was created because of the universal law that no ship can sail the seas without an internationally recognized flag. This flag was chosen by an assembly of Maori chiefs at Waitangi on 20 March 1834. It was very similar to that already in use by the Church Missionary Society, and was a white flag with a cross of St George throughout, and another cross bordered in black in the canton, and in each canton of this a blue field with a six-pointed star in white. This was approved by King William IV, although the black fimbriation was corrected to white. This flag lasted until the Treaty of Waitangi on 6 February 1840 when New Zealand was ceded to Britain. New Zealand ships in government service then began to fly the Blue Ensign, to which a pattern of four stars of the Southern Cross was ultimately added. In 1901 a special form of the Red Ensign was introduced which had the stars in white only. From that year they were depicted on the Blue Ensign in red with a white edging. This became the official National Flag in 1902 and was retained as such when the country became an independent dominion on 11 May 1907.

Although they may not appear to do so, in fact the stars vary slightly in size. According to the official specifications the star nearest the fly is five-sixtieths of the length of the flag in diameter, that nearest the bottom is seven-sixtieths, and the other two are six-sixtieths. This applies to the red part of the stars: the fimbriation on the blue flag accounts for a further one hundredth and twentieth part of the length.

The Naval Ensign, like that of Australia, was only recently adopted, New Zealand having previously used the British White Ensign, and the National Flag as a Jack. The new Ensign was established on 13 June 1968 and is the same as the Merchant Flag, but with the colours of the field and the stars reversed. The command flags of the navy are the same as those of the UK.

A Royal Banner for use in New Zealand was adopted on 25 August 1962. This has the proportions seventeen by nineteen, and the royal cypher on a blue disc within a chaplet placed over all in the centre. The Arms of New Zealand were originally granted on 26

New Zealand: National Flag and Jack

New Zealand: Merchant Flag

New Zealand: Naval Ensign

New Zealand: Queen's Personal Flag

New Zealand: Air Force Ensign

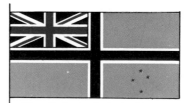

New Zealand: Civil Air Ensign

August 1911 and revised in 1956, although this did not include any alteration to the shield. The flag of the Governor-General follows the usual pattern.

As in Australia there is a distinctive flag for the Navy Board, based on the British Admiralty flag. In this case the field is divided vertically red and blue, with the yellow foul anchor horizontally over all. The Ministry of Transport has an Ensign established in 1968. This has a field of sky blue with the Naval Ensign forming the canton, and the Ministry's badge in the fly.

The Air Force Ensign is also like that of Britain, except that the target has the letters NZ in white in the central red disc. The Civil Air Ensign is the same as that of Britain except for the pattern of stars as in the Naval Ensign placed in the lower fly canton.

New Zealand has two territories in the South Pacific which are in the same relationship to her as the Associate States are to the UK. These are the Cook Islands and Niue.

New Zealand:
Ministry of Transport

Cook Islands

The **Cook Islands** achieved internal self-government on 4 August 1965 and adopted a distinctive flag on 23 July 1973. This is one by two with a green field bearing a ring of fifteen gold stars in the fly. It was designed by an inhabitant of Titikaveka and was the winning entry in a competition. The stars represent the islands of the group.

Niue, an island now detached from the Cook Islands, achieved internal self-government in October 1974 and has now adopted a distinctive flag for local use. This has the proportions of one by two, and a field in the unusual colour of dark yellow. In the canton is the British Union Jack, and on each arm of the St George's cross is a yellow star. A fifth yellow star appears on a blue disc in the centre of the cross. The Union Jack accounts for a quarter of the field.

Papua New Guinea is so called because it consists of two parts: the former German colony of New Guinea and the Solomon Islands, which became an Australian mandate in 1921, and the former Australian dependency of Papua. They were united under one

Niue

Papua New Guinea:
National Flag

government in 1949. Arms and a flag for the territory, as well as its official name, were adopted by the National Identity Ordinance of 24 June 1971. The arms reflect the widespread use of the bird of paradise as a local emblem. This also appears on the flag. A previous flag, which had no official standing, was green with a gold bird of paradise. In 1970 the Australian administration tried to introduce another, divided vertically: blue at the hoist with the stars of the Southern Cross as in the Australian flag, then white, then green with the yellow bird of paradise. This was never popular, and the matter was left to the House of Assembly. This voted on 12 March 1971 to accept a design proposed by Susan Karike, a local artist. Her concept used native colour combinations to bring together the Australian stars and the bird of paradise. This flag, and the Arms, were retained when the country became independent on 16 September 1975.

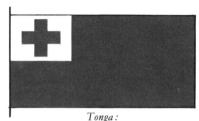

Tonga:
National and Merchant Flag

Tonga: Royal Standard

The Kingdom of **Tonga** has today exactly the same Arms and flags as it had before it became a British protectorate on 18 May 1900. The flag of Tonga dates from 1862 when the king called for a flag which would express the Christian faith. At first a plain white flag with the red couped cross was used, but this was subsequently found to be like that of the International Red Cross, adopted in 1863, and so the white flag was placed in the canton of a red one. Red and white were the colours used by nearly every Pacific state at this time. The Royal Standard is a banner of the Arms, which were adopted in 1862 and designed locally. The stars in the first quarter stand for the three main island groups; the crown in the second quarter symbolizes the monarchy; the dove in the third quarter the spirit of Christianity (see also **Fiji** p. 209); and the three swords the three dynasties of kings who have ruled over the islands. In the centre is a six-pointed star with the red couped cross from the National Flag. The National Flag has the proportions one by two, and the Royal Standard twenty-six by thirty-seven.

Western Samoa is that part of Samoa which was assigned to Germany in 1900, and which became a New Zealand mandate in 1920 (for the eastern part see **American Samoa**, above, p. 84). The kingdom had several flags before passing to Germany. After 1920 it had only an ensign badge showing a beach with three coconut palms. On 26 May 1948 a distinctive flag for use on land was adopted. This was like the present flag, but had only four stars, as in the flag of New Zealand. On 24 February 1949 the fifth smaller star was added, making the pattern representing the Southern Cross more like that of Australia. The flag was designed by the then joint heads of state on the basis of one used prior to 1900.

The flag became the National and Merchant Flag when the kingdom regained its independence on 1 January 1962, the first Pacific territory to do so. Although treated as a

Western Samoa:
National and Merchant Flag

member of the British Commonwealth, Western Samoa was not formally admitted until 1970, and still uses New Zealand as her only channel of diplomatic relations. The State Emblem of the country is based on that of the United Nations under whose auspices it became independent.

(11) International Organizations

The United Nations came into official existence on 24 October 1945, since recognized throughout the world as United Nations Day. A flag was adopted on 20 October 1947, and first hoisted the next day at UN Headquarters at Lake Success in New York. It has a field of a shade known officially as 'United Nations Blue', and the emblem of the UN in the centre in white. This is a conventional map of the world showing the continents centred around the North Pole, flanked by two olive branches.

Each of the various Branches of the UN has its own special emblem, but only those of the World Health Organization and of the World Meteorological Organization are flown as flags, having the same field as the UN flag. There is a special code for the display and protection of the UN flag, and its use has to be carefully supervised in areas of peace-keeping operations. Soldiers engaged in these wear helmets or berets of United Nations blue, and blue flashes on their sleeves.

There have been several previous attempts to establish international flags, but none was ever adopted for the League of Nations. During the First World War Allied shipping used a flag of horizontal stripes of white, sky blue and white, and several of the Commissions set up by the League adopted special flags, all now obsolete.

The first flag ever to establish itself internationally on a world-wide scale was that of the **International Red Cross**. This had its origin at a conference in Geneva in 1863 on ways of mitigating the horrors of war, which resolved that hospitals for the sick and wounded should have neutral status, as should officials engaged in relief work, and that there should be a distinctive sign for hospitals, ambulances, houses containing wounded men, and refugees and relief workers. This sign would be a red cross in the case of Christian armies, and the pattern chosen was that of Switzerland, with the colours reversed, in compliment to the host nation and in recognition of Switzerland's long record of neutrality. It was not expected that Moslems would agree to the use of the

United Nations Flag

Olympic Games Flag

Red Cross   *Red Crescent*   *Red Lion, Iran*

cross, and so a Red Crescent flag was also created. Countries which have adopted distinctive variations are Iran, where the flag is white with the national badge of the Lion and Sun; Israel, where it is a red Shield of David; and the Soviet Union, where the Crescent and Cross are combined on one flag. The flag flies over hospitals and medical stores, and doctors, nurses and stretcher-bearers wear a white armband with one of the recognized emblems. In Europe private cars used as ambulances fly a Red Cross flag when on duty.

The **Olympic Games** flag has also enjoyed international recognition for many years. The first modern Games were held in Athens in 1896 on the initiative of Baron Pierre de Coubertin. In 1906 the symbol of the five rings was introduced, representing the five continents joined on a field of harmony. In 1913 the flag design was adopted, and the first actual flag was created for the Games held at Antwerp in 1920. A flag was presented to the International Olympic Committee by the city corporation which has been passed on from Games to Games ever since, although replicas are of course also very widely used.

Europe has been the scene of many attempts at international organizations. There was a Congress of Europe at the Hague in 1948, which led to the formation of the **Council of Europe** on 5 May 1949. At the Hague Conference a flag known as the 'United Europe Flag' was hoisted. This had a green field with white inset making the letter 'E'. This is still the flag of the European Movement, a body which seeks to promote European unity. It was succeeded as the flag of the Council on 25 September 1953, when a flag of royal blue with a ring of fifteen gold stars was adopted. Each star stood for a member-state, but the same problem arose as in the United States, and so it was resolved on 25 October 1955 to have twelve stars only, not representing the member-states. The flag is two by three, and the ring of stars has a diameter equal to half of the length. This flag is awarded by the Council to bodies thought to have made a positive contribution to European unity, and is often seen in Europe used unofficially to represent the European idea.

Council of Europe Flag

European Movement

European Coal and
Steel Community

Benelux Flag

Danube Commission

The **European Economic Community**, or 'Common Market' still has no distinctive flag, although attempts are made to find one from time to time. The only flag it has ever had is that of the former Coal and Steel Community, which adopted a flag in 1958 of blue over black horizontally, with six gold stars representing the then membership.

The EEC was preceded by the **Benelux** organization, an economic and cultural union of Belgium, the Netherlands and Luxemburg. A flag was adopted in 1951 which expressed this, being a horizontal tricolour in the colours common to the Netherlands and Luxemburg, with a black panel in the centre of the white stripe, and over all a yellow rampant lion for Belgium.

Europe has two flags representing bodies controlling navigation on the 'internationalized' waters of the Rhine and the Danube. That of the **Central Commission for the Navigation of the Rhine** is sky blue with four dark blue stripes across the lower half, and in the centre of these a vertical yellow anchor; in the top half is a ring of six yellow stars.

The flag of the **Danube Commission**, a body originally sponsored by the League of Nations but revived in 1945, is royal blue with a red stripe equal to one third of the width running along the bottom, and fimbriated white. In the upper hoist are the initials CD in blue on a white disc framed by a gold wreath. On the obverse the initials are Cyrillic.

Outside Europe there are several other regional groupings of countries with distinctive international flags.

The **Arab League**, formed in 1945, includes all countries whose members are predominantly Arab. It has a flag of bright green with the seal in the centre. This consists of an upturned crescent with the name within its horns; around this is a gold chain, around this again a wreath of laurel, all in white.

The **Organization of African Unity**, open to all African countries except the

Arab League

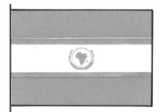

Organization of African Unity

'colonial' ones, was founded on 25 May 1963. It has a flag of three horizontal stripes, of green, white and green, the white fimbriated gold, and in the centre of the white stripe its seal. This shows a small map of Africa in gold on a disc bordered in green, and within a wreath of laurel which is also in gold. This superseded the flag of the now defunct *Union Africaine et Malgache* which linked the newly independent francophone states of Africa. Its flag, adopted in April 1962, was green with an outline map of Africa in red, within a ring of twelve gold stars, rather similar to the flag of the Council of Europe.

The **East African Community** was formed on 6 June 1967 to replace earlier organizations which had linked Kenya, Tanzania and Uganda. Its flag is also basically three horizontal stripes of green, white, blue, but the white stripe is overlaid by five narrower stripes of black, green, yellow, green and red. In the upper hoist are three red stars. This flag attempts to combine the colours of the flags of the three countries.

The **Organization of American States**, known popularly as the 'Pan-American Union', is one of the oldest international groupings, having been formed in 1890 and officially re-titled on 30 April 1948. It has a flag of medium blue, with a large white disc in the centre, containing a trophy of the flags of the member countries, which is presumably altered any time there is an alteration in these flags.

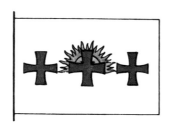

The Flag of the Race

South Pacific Commission

The **Flag of the Race** is a flag in widespread use in Latin America, and commemorates the discovery of the New World by Columbus, and is therefore widely flown on the Day of the (Hispanic) Race, 12 October. The flag is white with three purple crosses of Hispanic form, the central one slightly larger than the other two, and having a gold sun rising behind it. The crosses represent the ships of Columbus.

The **Organization of Central American States** has a flag of sky-blue with the seal in the centre. This is similar to the Arms of the Central American Federation of the 1830s, and bears a triangle containing five volcanoes within a circular band containing the name of the organization.

The **South Pacific Commission** links the independent countries of the South Pacific with the countries which still have dependencies there. Its flag is blue with a device resembling an atoll, with a reef made of eight six-pointed stars, and next to these a white palm tree. The six points of the stars represent the original six members, and the eight stars the current eight members. The Commission was formed on 6 February 1947.

As well as organizations for peace and progress there are also military alliances. The largest of these in the western world is the **North Atlantic Treaty Organization**, formed on 4 April 1949, linking Canada and the United States with their allies in Western

North Atlantic Treaty Organization

Central Treaty Organization

Europe. The NATO flag was adopted on 28 October 1953. It has a dark blue field representing the Atlantic Ocean and a compass rose in blue and white of four points with a narrow circle around, and four narrow white lines extending from the points towards the edges of the flag. The circle represents unity, and the compass rose the common direction towards peace taken by the member states. Ships of member countries on NATO service can fly a pennant of this flag, and there are command flags for its various zones.

The flag of the **Central Treaty Organization**, CENTO, is intermediate blue, in proportions forty-three by ninety-three, with the badge in the centre. This shows a green torch with red and yellow flames, flanked by white wings, within a green wreath.

The **South East Asia Treaty Organization**, SEATO, had a flag adopted on 19 February 1959. This was sky blue, with a white shield, the symbol of defence, charged with a globe outlined in the same colour as the field, and with the south-east quadrant having the colours reversed, i.e. solid blue with white lines. On the vertical axis of the globe was a gold olive branch, representing peace. The flag was two by three, and the shield was two thirds the width. The blue quadrants of the shield appeared on the observer's right on both sides of the flag. SEATO was disbanded in 1977.

The flags of voluntary organizations with an international significance are legion. They could perhaps be divided into three categories: recreational, idealistic and religious, and a few examples are given of each.

In the first category perhaps the best-known flag is that of the **Scouts**: purple with the well-known badge of a *fleur-de-lys* surrounded by a rope tied in a reef knot, all in white. The **World Guide** flag is similar but with the badge of a gold trefoil or clover leaf on a blue field.

South East Asia
Treaty Organization

World Guide Flag

An example of the second category is that of the **Co-operative Movement**, which recommends a new approach to commerce. Its flag recalls the sign of peace given by God to Noah, the rainbow, being of seven horizontal stripes of red, orange, yellow, green, blue, black and violet.

Another is that of the **Esperanto** movement, which 'hopes' to achieve peace by means of an international language. Its flag is green, the colour of hope, with a white canton charged with a green star.

There are several well-known religious flags. **Roman Catholics** in many parts of the world employ the flag of the Vatican (*see* p. 147), or the colours of yellow and white. There are also flags for various protestant churches with an international membership. The flag used by **Buddhists** throughout the world has vertical stripes of blue, yellow, red, white and orange, and the same colours repeated horizontally in the fly.

The flag of the **Salvation Army**, also an international church, has a field of red, bordered all round with blue, with a yellow star of eight points in the centre containing their motto: *Blood and Fire*.

Buddhist Flag

Salvation Army Flag

To vexillologists, or flag-students, the most interesting flag in any category is that of their own organization, the International Federation of Vexillological Associations. This was first flown at the second International Congress of Vexillology in 1967. It has a sky-blue field and a pattern of flag-halyards in gold running across the centre.

*International Federation of
Vexillological Associations*

[12]   Signal Flags; The International Code

One, if not the principle, function of flags has always been to convey a message. That message may have been no more than to proclaim the nationality or identity of the bearer of the flag. We have seen, in the first chapter, how Themistocles gave the signal to his fleet to attack the galleys of Xerxes by hoisting his red or purple cloak aloft on an oar. In this same battle there is also the old legend of how the wily Persian Queen Artemesia deceived the Greeks by hoisting the distinguishing sign of the Greeks. Whether she used a flag or not has never been established, for the Greek word *semeion* has at times been translated as 'flag' or 'banner', though its more usual meaning is 'device'.

However it was not until about the middle of the seventeenth century that the first flag signal codes, as we now know them, appeared. Up to that time ships were so small, and sailed so close to each other, that orders could be passed by word of mouth; but the increasing weight and range of the artillery they carried needed larger ships which could not sail so close to each other, and this in turn led to the introduction of naval signal codes.

In *Fighting Instructions 1530–1816*, so ably edited by Mr Julian Corbett for the Navy Records Society, we not only have a most interesting book, but are, for the first time, provided with the means of noting when the flags were introduced and the use that was made of them.

It is evident that up to the seventeenth century, flag signals were of an elementary character, and that from then onwards properly organized codes of naval signals were gradually evolved and adopted.

Various codes were tried out, and by the end of the eighteenth century the numerary method was well established. Lord Howe produced his first and second signal books in 1782 and 1790 respectively. From then onwards many alterations, improvements and additions were made; also Sir Home Popham drew up his *Telegraphic Signals*, or *Marine Vocabulary*—the word 'Telegraphic' being used in the literal sense of writing at a distance, for it was not until some thirty years later that the electric telegraph was invented. Popham's method was to use a short dictionary and interpret the words in it by numeral groups of flags.

This Vocabulary was used by the Fleet as a companion volume to Howe's 1799 *Signal Book for Ships of War*.

In order to make it perfectly clear that the signal hoisted was to be deciphered by the Vocabulary Code, Popham designed a special 'Telegraph or Preparative' flag. This had to be hoisted in a conspicuous position prior to making the signal. It could remain in this position throughout the period of the message, and then be hauled down to indicate that

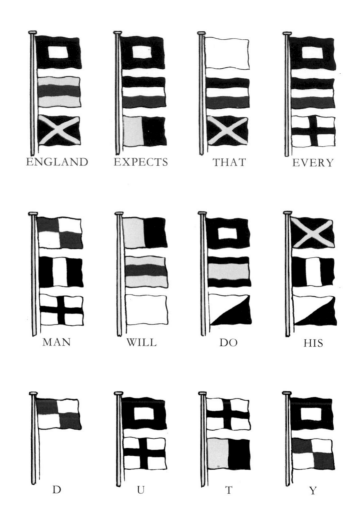

ENGLAND EXPECTS THAT EVERY

MAN WILL DO HIS

D U T Y

ENGAGE THE ENEMY  MORE CLOSELY

Nelson's famous signal

it had been completed or, alternatively, be hauled down before actually commencing to make the signal. In the latter case, provision was made for hoisting another special flag, called the 'Message finished' flag. However, as far as is known, the last mentioned was never used.

The field of these two flags was divided diagonally from the top of the fly to the bottom of the hoist. These flags are described in the text of Popham's Vocabulary thus:

Instructions for the Flags used with this Vocabulary only.

Preparative. Preparatory to any message a diagonal red and white flag.

Message finished. It is denoted by a diagonal blue and yellow flag, which may be hoisted or not according to circumstances, or the Telegraph flag hauled down.

Thus, Nelson used Howe's numeral flags in conjunction with Popham's Vocabulary at the battle of Trafalgar, 21 October 1805. His historic signal was made at approximately 11.56 a.m. in twelve hoists; the first words were to be found in the Vocabulary, each having a three-figured number, but the last word, 'duty', had not been included by Popham, and had therefore to be spelt out in full by the numerical alphabet, which was known by the numbers one to twenty-five. This alphabet had two peculiarities: (1) 'I' and 'J' were bracketed as one letter—thus only twenty-five flags were necessary; (2) 'V' preceded 'U', which accounts for the fact that many people have been puzzled at the spelling of the word 'duty'.

Nelson's famous message ran thus: *England* (253) *expects* (269) *that* (863) *every* (261) *man* (471) *will* (958) *do* (220) *his* (370) *d* (4) *u* (21) *t* (19) *y* (24).

Some twenty minutes after this signal was made, the general signal for close action was hoisted: it was Nelson's favourite, No. 16—'Engage the enemy more closely'.

When Nelson first dictated his message, to his signal officer, Lieutenant John Pasco, he used the words 'England confides that every man will do his duty'; however, the word 'confides' was not in the Vocabulary and, in order to save spelling out the word, he agreed to substitute the word 'expects'.

 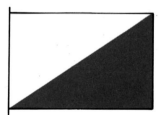

Telegraph Flag

There has always been some doubt as to the exact details of the Telegraph flag. Popham (see above) simply describes it as 'a diagonal red and white flag', and it is shown in the signal books of the day as being sometimes red over white and sometimes white over red. As the signal books of the day were illustrated in line only, leaving the colouring to the recipient, and as there were many manuscript copies, it is not unnatural that errors and variations crept in. But as there was no other red and white diagonally divided flag in the code there could be no mistaking the Telegraph flag for any other, whichever way the colours happened to be arranged.

Nelson's historic signal is flown annually in the *Victory* at Portsmouth on 21 October, and visitors will notice that the Telegraph flag is hoisted in accordance with the above official publications.

At the outbreak of the Second World War, the British Naval Code consisted of the following pieces: twenty-six Alphabetical Flags, ten Numeral Pendants, twenty-six Special Flags, ten Numbered Pendants and fourteen Special Pendants. In addition to these, the flags of the International Code were also used, making a grand total of 126 flags, some of which had definite meanings, but all of which could have their signification changed if and when it became necessary.

It will be readily appreciated that this state of affairs did not make for speedy inter-communication between units of the Royal Navy and those of the United States during the period of hostilities when the closest co-operation was of vital importance. Certain wartime arrangements were made, and worked reasonably well. Finally it was decided to revise our Naval Code and adopt a new one which closely resembled that of the United States, but with certain additions, resulting in a total of seventy-eight flags. This was brought into general use throughout the Service on 1 December 1948.

In the light of experience, and in order to ensure efficient intercommunication between all vessels taking part in combined exercises, a further revision was made in order to bring it into line with the signal books of members of NATO—the North Atlantic Treaty Organization—on 1 January 1952. It should be noted that there was a change in spelling—'pendants' became 'pennants'. Thus, at the time of writing, our Naval Code contains twenty-six Alphabetical Flags, ten Numbered Pennants, ten Numeral Flags, four Substitutes and twenty Special Flags and Pennants. Details of these are given on the 1952 Signal Card, No. B.R. 232 (2), which is obtainable from HM Stationery Office.

It is to be much regretted that one of our oldest signal flags, the well-known 'Preparative'—five horizontal stripes of equal width, three blue and two white—was superseded by the yellow over green over yellow pennant, which is extremely difficult to recognize in poor visibility.

Although Popham devised a code of signals for the East India Company in 1804, it was not until 1817 that Captain Frederick Marryat drew up what has been described as the forerunner of modern commercial codes. This was used as a basis in designing the 'Commercial Code of Signals for use of all nations', which the Board of Trade issued in 1857. It consisted of eighteen alphabetical flags and a 'Code & Answering Pendant'.

In the course of time this was translated into many languages, and by about 1880 its title had become the 'International Code'. This was revised and enlarged towards the end of the century to include a separate flag for every letter and came into use on 1 January 1901, as the 'First International Code of Signals'.

This code was in existence when the First World War broke out in 1914, and it was naturally subjected to a very severe test during the following four years. Speaking candidly, it failed that test. Experience showed that it was not really an International Code, for ships of different nationalities when making signals to one another often found that more messages were indecipherable than were clear.

It was thus realized that a revised code was necessary and advantage was taken of the International Radio Telegraph Conference which assembled in Washington in 1927, for Great Britain, in conjunction with France, Italy, Japan and the United States of America,

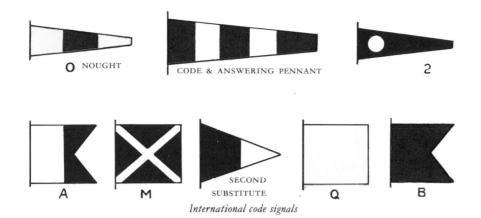

International code signals

to put forward revised rules for signalling, and a draft code in English, French and Italian.

The Conference then decided that Great Britain should be asked to undertake the work of revising the old code with the help of representatives from each of the Governments concerned. The Committee accordingly assembled in London in October 1928, and completed its labours in December 1930.

The new code came into use in January 1934. It had seven editions or copies, one each in English, French, German, Italian, Japanese, Spanish and Norwegian. The Scandinavian countries chose Norwegian as the Scandinavian language.

It was a great improvement on former codes and was divided into two volumes, Volume I for Visual Signalling, Volume II for Radio.

The chief improvements were that whereas formerly some of the alphabetical flags were rectangular in shape and some pennant-shaped, in the 1934 code all the alphabetical flags were rectangular. Also ten pennants were added to represent the numerals 0 to 9. In the 1901 code the alphabetical flags also represented numbers.

A further innovation was the institution of substitute flags; these were triangular in shape and made it possible to use any combination of four letters or figures.

As a result of international collaboration the international code of 1934 has been completely revised. The new code came into effect on 1 April 1969. Russian and Greek have been added to the previous seven languages, and whilst the colours and patterns of the former flags remain the same, the whole publication has been changed in principle, which is best explained by the following extract from the Preface:

'The revised code is intended to cater primarily for situations related essentially to safety of navigation and persons, especially when language difficulties arise. It is suitable for transmission by all means of communication including radiotelephony and radiotelegraphy, thus obviating the necessity for a separate radiotelephony code and dispensing with Volume II for radiotelegraphy. The revised code embodies the principle that each signal has a complete meaning. It thus leaves out the vocabulary method which was part of the old code. The Geographical Section, not being considered essential, was omitted. By these means it was possible to reduce considerably the volume of the code and achieve simplicity.'

It is sad to have to report that while signal flags are still used for a few specialized purposes they are becoming obsolete. superseded in this electronic age by the radiotelephone and radiotelegraph. There were few more lovely sights than that of a squadron of warships carrying out flag drill, with the strings of colourful flags being hoisted and lowered in rapid succession.

But, although signalling by flags may be on the decline, flags are still used on important festivals to dress ship, and all must enjoy the sight of ships dressed overall, or rainbow fashion as it is called. The flags used on the 'dressing lines' to dress ship should be the signal flags, and National, House and similar flags should not be used for this purpose. Ships should be dressed overall only while at anchor or moored in harbour; while under way only the extra masthead flags and jacks should be flown. Although this is the practice of warships, merchant ships frequently leave their dressing flags hoisted while moving.

[13]   Flags Worn by Merchant Ships

As mentioned in Chapter One, special National Flags, known as ensigns, have been adopted by many nations for their ships, both warships and merchant ships, and these are described in the chapter under the headings of the individual nations.

The ensigns of Great Britain were described on p. 32, where it was stated that the Red Ensign was established as the proper colours for British merchant ships by a proclamation dated 1674. The Merchant Shipping Act of 1894 brought up to date the law concerning the wearing of ensigns by British ships. Prior to this many ensigns of various designs were in use, perhaps the most interesting being those of the East India Company. There were various versions of these, one consisting of nine red and white horizontal stripes with the Union Flag in the upper canton, very like the 'Continental Colours' of the USA (*see* p. 66). Another version was similar, but consisted of thirteen red and white stripes, over which was superimposed a red St George's Cross—again with the Union Flag in the upper canton.

The relevant portions of the Merchant Shipping Act are as follows:

Section 73

(1) The Red Ensign usually worn by merchant ships, without any defacement or modification whatsoever, is hereby declared to be the proper national colours for all ships and boats belonging to any British subject, except in the case of Her Majesty's ships or boats, or in the case of any other ship or boat for the time being allowed to wear any other national colours in pursuance of a warrant from Her Majesty or from the Admiralty.

(2) If any distinctive national colours, except such Red Ensign or except the Union Jack with a white border, or if any colours usually worn by Her Majesty's ships or resembling those of Her Majesty, or if the pendant usually carried by Her Majesty's ships or any pendant resembling that pendant, are or is hoisted on board any ship or boat belonging to any British subject without warrant from Her Majesty or from the Admiralty, the master of the ship or boat of the owner thereof, if on board the same, and every other person hoisting the colours or pendant, shall for each offence incur a fine not exceeding £500.

(3) Any commissioned officer on full pay in the military or naval service of Her Majesty, or any officer of customs in Her Majesty's dominions, or any consular officer may board any ship or boat on which any colours or pendant are hoisted contrary to this Act, and seize and take away the colours or pendant, and the colours or pendant shall be forfeited to Her Majesty.

(4) A fine under this section may be recovered with costs in the High Court in England or Ireland, or in the Court of Session in Scotland, or in any Colonial Court of Admiralty or Vice-Admiralty Court within Her Majesty's dominions.

(5) Any offence in this section may also be prosecuted, and the fine for it recovered summarily, provided that: (*a*) where such offence is prosecuted summarily, the court imposing the fine shall not impose a higher fine than £100; and (*b*) nothing in this section shall authorize the imposition of more than one fine in respect of the same offence.

Section 74

(1) A ship belonging to a British subject shall hoist the proper national colours, (*a*) on a signal being made to her by one of Her Majesty's ships (including any vessel under the command of an officer of Her Majesty's navy on full pay), (*b*) on entering or leaving any foreign port, and (*c*) if of fifty tons gross tonnage or upwards, on entering or leaving any British port.

(2) If default is made on any such ship in complying with this section, the master of the ship shall for such offence be liable to fine not exceeding £100.

(3) This section shall not apply to a fishing boat duly entered in the fishing-boat register and lettered and numbered as required by the Fourth Part of this Act.

Section 75

The provisions of this Act with respect of colours worn by merchant ships shall not affect any other power of the Admiralty in relation thereto.

NOTE 1.   As there are now a large number of self-governing countries within the British Commonwealth of Nations, the term 'Her Majesty's dominions' has not the same significance that it bore in 1894 when the above Act came into force. The Act, therefore, no longer applies to these independent countries, unless it has specially been made to do so. NOTE 2.   In accordance with the Defence (Transfer of Functions) Act of 1964, the powers formerly vested in the Admiralty to grant warrants for the wearing of special privilege ensigns are now transferred to the Secretary of State for Defence (*see* p. 31).

The British Merchant Shipping Act has been quoted as an example; most other nations have similar laws covering the use of their National Flags and ensigns.

In addition to their ensigns most merchant ships wear a House Flag. This is usually flown at the main, but as so many modern ships have only one mast the flag has to be flown from the masthead.

The owners of most merchant ships are now large public companies and the House Flag is the 'marque' of the company; but this is a fairly modern innovation. The ownership of eighteenth-century ships was complex, and although there were exceptions, notably the East India Company and the Hudson Bay Company, the modern permanently established companies appeared after 1815. The earlier ships seem often to have worn the banner of their Master (who was sometimes a part-owner), and the expeditions of the merchant adventurers and explorers, such as Columbus (*see* p. 64), Magellan, Hudson and Cabot, usually sailed under the banner or flag of the leader.[1]

The modern version of the House Flag is said to have originated from the flags hoisted on Bidston Hill (overlooking the old entrance to the Mersey) to inform the owners in Liverpool of the comings and goings of their ships on the Mersey Estuary which was invisible from their office windows.

In the last few years there have been important changes in the merchant fleets of the world. Names which were household words have disappeared—these lines for the most part having merged with others, or like the Port Line (which was a subsidiary of the Cunard) having become a part of that company. Another development has been the formation of large 'consortia', or the grouping together of companies of different nations. In this case members of the consortium usually fly the same House Flag but wear their individual National Ensigns. The Dart Container Line is an example of one of these organizations. Its House Flag is a blue swallow tail with three red and white darts.

[1] *See* W. G. Perrin, *British Flags* (Cambridge University Press).

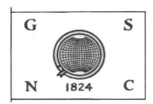

Peninsular and Oriental
(P & O) Line

General Steam Navigation
Company

Shaw Savill and Albion Line

One of the oldest and best-known flags of the British Mercantile Marine is that of the Peninsular and Oriental—known generally as the P and O. The P and O Company was originally Messrs. Wilcox and Anderson, who rendered great service to the Queen of Portugal in 1832–3; hence the four triangles of which the House Flag of the P and O is comprised are the blue and white, taken from the Portuguese Royal Standard, and the red and yellow of Spain.

The old East India Company does not appear to have had a House Flag, but had its own special ensigns (*see* p. 227).

Among the more interesting House Flags are those of the General Steam Navigation Company—perhaps the earliest steamship company, founded in 1824—and of Shaw Savill and Albion Line, which is said to have been originally designed as a National Flag for New Zealand and is still used, although the Line now operates as a subsidiary of the Furness Withy Group.

The former Canadian Pacific Railway Company has become C.P. Ships—Canadian Pacific. They have retained the House Flag of the 'C.P.R.', the unusual design of two shades of green and white which was adopted by the old company in the 1960s.

At the turn of the century the two principal British steamship lines operating in the North Atlantic were the Cunard Steam Ship Company and the White Star Company. These two lines were amalgamated and became the Cunard White Star Company, and for many years the ships of the amalgamation flew the House Flags of both the Cunard and the White Star. The Cunard flag, which used to be flown above that of the White Star, has a red field charged with a golden lion rampant guardant. The White Star flag is a red 'broad pennant' with two tails and charged with a white five-pointed star. In 1968 the flying of the White Star flag was discontinued and only the Cunard flag is flown by Cunard ships, except on one day of the year, 20 April, when the two flags are flown together as

Canadian Pacific

Cunard Line

The White Star

formerly in commemoration that this is the birthday of the last surviving officer of the old White Star Line.

In 1965 the old House Flag for the ships of British Railways, introduced in 1949, was replaced by a new flag. This has a field of blue, known as 'British Rail blue', with a device which can be described as symbolic double arrows, the latter in white. This flag is now flown by all the ships, and is the only flag in use by the Shipping Division of British Rail.

There is a similarly designed House Flag for use ashore by British Rail. This differs from the maritime flag by having a flame-red field.

The United States Lines fly a white flag charged with a representation of the American eagle in blue.

British Rail   *United States Lines*

The well-known Japanese Line, Nippon Yusen Kaisha, possesses a very simple flag, the same pattern appearing on its black funnels.

Messageries Maritimes, which once had an easily recognized flag of two black 'M's on a white field with red corners, have recently amalgamated with the Compagnie Générale Transatlantique to form the Compagnie Générale Maritime. The Compagnie Générale Transatlantique also had a well-known flag, with the name in red next to a red disc on a white field; this also used to fly over its chain of hotels in North Africa!

The Hamburg-America Line has merged with the Norddeutscher Lloyd, and the new company has adopted the title of Hapag-Lloyd A.G. They have also adopted the funnel markings of the former Hamburg-America Line and the House Flag of Norddeutscher Lloyd.

The two leading Italian Lines, Lloyd Triestino and Italia, fly flags of the same design; in the case of the former (which includes the Lloyd Triestino, Marittima Italiana and Sitmar Lines) the red cross is in the fly, while in the case of Italia, which covers the Cosulich, Lloyd Sabaudo and Navagazione Generale, the flag is reversed, and in this case the red cross appears in the hoist.

The Nigerian National Shipping Line was established and registered in Lagos early in 1959, and is a good example of the new lines which have taken to the seas from the newly-independent countries. For a House Flag it adopted one having an emerald-green field, two by three, bearing a large letter 'N', in white, in the centre thereof and occupying one half the depth of the hoist.

In addition to the Port Line, which has been mentioned above, British and Commonwealth Shipping Company, Devitt and Moore and Blue Funnel have ceased to exist and their flags have been replaced by the following: Dart Container (already mentioned),

Nippon Yusen Kaisha   *Italia Line*

Clan Line, F. T. Everard and Sons, Indo-China Steam Navigation Company and Farrell Lines Inc.

When a merchant ship is launched the shipbuilder's House Flag is generally displayed in company with that of the owners; the former is again flown during her trials. When these have been successfully completed it is replaced with that of the owners, thus indicating that she has been accepted.

The custom of displaying special flags in naval vessels during the launching and naming ceremony probably dates back some 450 years or more. It would appear, from the accounts recorded by contemporary chroniclers, that during the reign of Henry VIII this became a well established practice in the Royal Dockyard at Deptford (*Deptford Strond* as it was called in those days), on the River Thames, where subsequently Peter the Great studied the art of shipbuilding.

At that time, launching flags comprised banners and streamers bearing the Royal Arms and the Banner of St George. The Elizabethan striped ensigns were added towards the end of the Tudor period, and the first Union Flag in 1606. By the middle of the

Hapag-Lloyd A.G.

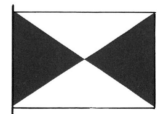

Dart Container Ships

Clan Line

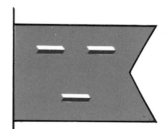

F. T. Everard & Sons

*Indo-China Steam
Navigation Company*

British Airways

eighteenth century the Royal Standard was displayed at the main, the Lord High
Admiral's or Admiralty Flag at the fore, and the Union Flag at the mizzen, also the Jack
and Ensign at their respective staves. Since 1906 the Royal Standard has ceased to figure
among a vessel's launching flags. Some two years later the Admiralty adapted and
regularized this very old custom to modern requirements, and issued an order in which it
was laid down that at her launching a vessel should wear her Ensign and Jack, and the
Admiralty Flag amidships. However, the flags to be worn on other masts erected
temporarily in intermediate positions were not specified. As a consequence, various flags
were used; these sometimes included the shipbuilder's House Flag. That of John Brown
was the last to be used in this way; the occasion was the launching of H.M.S. *Vanguard*
by Princess Elizabeth on 30 November 1944.

An addition to *King's Regulations and Admiralty Instructions* made on 4 October 1945,
restricted the number of launching flags displayed to three, namely, the Admiralty Flag,
Ensign and Jack.

Article No. 1242 of *Queen's Regulations and Admiralty Instructions 1956*, states:

> At all launches of ships built for the Royal Navy at which there is a naming ceremony, the
> White Ensign is to be hoisted at the ensign staff, the Union Flag at the Jackstaff and the
> Admiralty Flag at the main masthead or equivalent position. No other flag is to be worn.
> Exceptionally, in the case of launches with ceremony of Inshore Minesweepers, Seaward
> Defence Boats, Fast Patrol Boats (M.T.B.s, M.G.B.s) and other similar and small craft, only the
> White Ensign need be hoisted, unless it is desired to conform to the general practice stated in this
> clause.
>
> None of the aforesaid flags is to be hoisted again, whether or not the vessel is in commission,
> before her official acceptance from the shipbuilders, except dockyard-built ships temporarily
> commissioned for trials, which wear the White Ensign. Contract-built ships undergoing sea
> trials while still under the control of the contractor should wear the Red Ensign.

Although, as a result of the Defence (Transfer of Functions) Act of 1964, the
Admiralty Flag will in future be a Royal Flag, it is understood that it will still be worn by
ships built for the Royal Navy at their launching. At the successful conclusion of the
acceptance trial the ship is handed over to the Royal Naval crew at sea, when the Red
Ensign and the House Flag of the contractor are replaced by the White Ensign and the
Commissioning Pennant. A slightly different procedure is followed in the case of ships
built in one of the Royal dockyards.

In recent years it has become the custom to hold a commissioning ceremony just
before the ship proceeds on acceptance trials, and it is now usual to hoist the White

Ensign and Commissioning Pennant during this ceremony; but at the end of the
ceremony the Red Ensign and the builder's House Flag are rehoisted and worn until
finally hauled down after the acceptance trials.

Many countries have now adopted ensigns for their Civil Air Lines; details of these
flags will, like the maritime ensigns, be found in the sections dealing with the individual
countries. These ensigns do not have the same importance as the maritime ones,
because they can only be flown from the aircraft whilst it is at rest on the ground, or
over the offices etc. of the air companies. Like their shipping cousins airlines are also
adopting House Flags. These, of course, suffer from the same disabilities as do their
ensigns.

(14) Yacht Flags

Yachts usually fly the following flags: their national colours or ensigns, and the burgee or flag of the Yacht Club to which the owner belongs; yachts may also fly the owner's private or distinguishing flag. Owners of yachts who are officers of their club fly a special flag in place of the burgee. All these flags will be described later. The most important flag is the National Ensign. Quite a few countries, including Belgium, Denmark, Ireland, Italy, France, Netherlands, Poland, the United States of America and the United Kingdom, grant certain of their yachts the privilege of wearing a special ensign. The special Yacht Ensigns are described in the sections dealing with those nations which authorize the use of them.

This wearing of special Yacht Ensigns appears to have started in Great Britain, possibly because the first yacht owner was King Charles II. In more recent years it has been due to the desire to foster the sport of yachting, as yachtsmen provide a source of reserves for the Royal Navy. (In passing it can be said that the yachtsmen of the United Kingdom have served their country well in two World Wars.)

The rules permitting yachts to wear special or privilege ensigns differ in different countries. A number of countries have a principal or national club e.g. the Royal Norwegiar Yacht Club, the Yacht Club Italia, etc. These clubs are the bodies which control yachting in their countries, and only yachts owned by members of these clubs are privileged to wear the special ensign. In the USA all yachts may wear the special Yacht Ensign; there is also another special USA ensign for the 'US Power Squadron' (*see* p. 74). This is flown by members of this squadron, sometimes in place of the National Ensign and sometimes in addition. It is reported that the custom of wearing the US National Ensign in preference to the Yacht Ensign is growing.

The rules authorizing British yachts to wear a privilege ensign are very strict and the Secretary of State for Defence is the Authority which grants the privilege (*see* p. 31). There is an idea that the privilege of having a special ensign is connected with the title 'Royal', which many yacht clubs have, or that there is some difference between a yacht and a sailing club; this is not so. The prefix 'Royal' to the title is granted by the Sovereign, but in all matters concerning ensigns the Secretary of State for Defence is the sole arbiter. Briefly, the practice is that the yacht or sailing club is given a warrant permitting it to use a special or privilege ensign. This may be a plain Blue Ensign, or a Blue Ensign or Red Ensign defaced by a badge. This badge is almost invariably in the fly, but there are one or two cases where it is placed in the centre of the Union in the upper canton. The owner of a yacht, who is a member of a yacht or sailing club which holds a warrant, applies through his club to the Secretary of State for Defence for a warrant for his yacht to wear the privilege ensign; note that the warrant is granted to the yacht and

Royal Yacht
Squadron Burgee

Royal Cornwall
Yacht Club Burgee

Royal Thames
Yacht Club Burgee

Racing Flag: 'Bluebottle'

Royal Fowey
Yacht Club Burgee

Royal Lymington
Yacht Club Burgee

New York
Yacht Club Burgee

Yacht Club
Argentino Burgee

Royal Cornwall
Yacht Club Ensign

Royal Fowey
Yacht Club Ensign

not the owner. There are a number of other strict rules which it is impossible to go into in this book.

The history of our British National Flag and ensigns is a fascinating one. In the early years of the nineteenth century there were four British ensigns afloat, and not three, the fourth being a white one without a red cross; this one still remains with us as the flag of the Commissioners of Northern Lights, although this is defaced by a representation of a lighthouse, and uses the first Union Flag (pre-1801) in the upper canton (*see also* p. 45). Even as late as 19 February 1835, an Admiralty Warrant was granted to the Royal Thames Yacht Club, authorizing their vessels to carry a White Ensign without a red cross with the Union in the upper canton and bearing in the fly a crown over the letters RTYC in red. This Ensign, without any lettering, may have been flown unofficially by members of the Yacht Club, now the Royal Yacht Squadron, when it was founded in 1815, but it was replaced in 1821 (the year after we hear of the Royal Yacht Club) by the Red Ensign, which in its turn was replaced by the present White Ensign—known to many as the St George's Ensign—granted by the Admiralty Warrant of 1829.

The Royal Yacht Club, which by King William's wish in 1833 became the Royal Yacht Squadron, is the only yacht club now flying the Ensign of the Royal Navy, but the 1829 warrant did not grant an exclusive use, for in 1832 a similar warrant was issued to the Royal Western of Ireland. In 1842, at the request of Lord Yarborough, the Admiralty decided that the privilege should be restricted to the Squadron—of which he was then the commodore—and sent out copies of a minute to that effect to the Royal Thames, the Royal Southern, the Royal Western of England, the Royal Eastern, the Holyhead, the Wharncliffe and the Gibraltar clubs, which were all under the White Ensign, with or without the cross; but owing to there being two Royal Westerns, one of England and one of Ireland, the minute was sent by mistake to one and not to both, so that the Irish Club went on with the white flag, and in 1853 actually obtained permission to continue with it. In 1858, however, the Royal St George of Kingstown, and the Holyhead which had to haul down its White Ensign in 1842, applied for authority to enjoy the same privilege, thus bringing the matter officially before the Board, who promptly refused both applications, and at the time ordered the Irish Royal Western to strike its white colours, so that for the future they should be distinctive of the Squadron which has always been under the special patronage of the Royal Family.

It is not known when yacht clubs first obtained official recognition. The first Yacht Club in the British Isles was the Cork Water Club which was formed in 1720. This was also the first club to have its own distinctive flags; these were the Union Jack with in the centre a golden harp on a green escutcheon, and a Red Ensign with this Union in the canton. It does not appear that it had any official permission to use these special flags, which were eventually 'inherited' by the Royal Cork Yacht Club. It appears, however, that by the year 1788 there was some form of Admiralty Warrant or licence, for in the *Public Advertiser* of 7 June of that year there is an advertisement announcing a meeting of the members of the Cumberland Fleet (that is the Royal Thames in its early stage) at which 'the gentlemen who enter boats are to attend at the same time to draw lots for situation at starting, and are hereby informed that they are expected either to produce their licence from the Admiralty or other proofs of being owners of the vessels they intend to sail'.

It can therefore be seen that only those yachts whose owners are members of yacht

Royal Norwegian
Yacht Club (KNS) Burgee

Yacht Club de France Ensign

Yacht Club de France Burgee

Royal Cruising Club Burgee

Island Sailing Club Burgee

Royal Sydney Yacht
Club Squadron Burgee

United States Yacht Ensign

Royal Norwegian
Yacht Club (KNS) Ensign

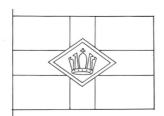

Royal Yachting Association

Belgian Yacht Ensign

clubs which hold Ministry of Defence Warrants are permitted to fly special ensigns, and all others whose owners belong to any club should wear the Red Ensign. It is interesting to note that the Island Sailing Club of Cowes, Isle of Wight, which has one of the largest memberships of any British club has no warrant and its members wear the Red Ensign.

In addition to the ensign nearly all yachts fly from their mainmast head a burgee. The burgee is the distinguishing flag of the yacht club to which the yacht belongs; it has been likened to the Commissioning Pennant flown by Her Majesty's ships. A burgee is a triangular flag, generally of dimensions two by three, and on it is the badge of the club. If the club has a warrant for a privileged ensign, the badge on the ensign is generally similar to the device on the burgee, but this is not always so; for instance, the badge on the Blue Ensign of the Royal Ocean Racing Club is a white 'Naval Crown', while the badge on the burgee is a white heraldic sea-horse, which is attractive and unusual.

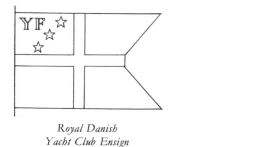

Royal Danish
Yacht Club Ensign

Royal Danish
Yacht Club Burgee

Although many of the designs of the burgees are pleasant and many have some local association, they are not particularly outstanding. Many of the clubs, of both foreign and British countries, which have the appellation 'Royal', incorporate a crown in the badge on their ensign and on their burgees, and of these one with a very neat design is that of the Royal Yacht Squadron; the white burgee with a golden crown and three red stars of the Royal Danish Yacht Club is very pretty.

It is worth noting that there are still a few Yacht Clubs in Southern Ireland that retain their old prefix 'Royal', and until quite recently they continued to use the British Blue Ensign. Now, with the exception of the Royal St George, they all use the blue yacht ensign of Southern Ireland. This has a blue field with the club badge in the fly and in the canton the National Flag, the green, white and orange tricolour. Among the latter is the Royal Cork, mentioned on p. 236, which has amalgamated with the Royal Munster Yacht Club.

As there are some 1200 yacht and sailing clubs in Great Britain alone, to say nothing of those in foreign countries, it is impossible to illustrate all of them—only a random selection can be illustrated here. Lloyd's Register of Shipping, however, publish a Flag Supplement of their Yacht Register, which illustrates a very large number of the yacht ensigns and burgees of all nations. This supplement also carries an extensive selection of the private distinguishing flags of yachtsmen. Many yachtsmen fly these private flags from their yachts while they are on board, and they are loosely called House Flags.

Formerly sailing yachts flew from the masthead a 'racing flag'. Like the coloured jacket of the jockey the racing flag displayed the colours of the owner of the yacht.

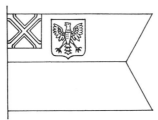

Polish Yacht Club Ensign

The individual colours of the racing flag were the means by which individual yachts were recognized. However in recent times practically every sailing yacht that races has some sort of insignia and number on her sails, and these provide a much simpler and better means of identification than the racing flag, especially as the numbers racing have increased so greatly. Thus it was that the International Yacht Racing Union, under whose rules nearly all yacht racing is now conducted, ruled that racing flags were no longer needed. Great Britain, who disagreed with this and ruled that racing flags were still to be flown, has now fallen into line and agreed that they are no longer obligatory. This of course permits an owner to fly such a flag should he so desire. It may only have been a conceit, but there were many who regarded their racing flags with affection and pride, and it is sad that they must be sacrificed on the altar of utility.

Over the years a comprehensive flag etiquette for yachts has grown up. Briefly, this lays down recommendations as to what flags to fly and when and where they should be flown. The official booklet on this subject is *Flag Etiquette for Yachts*, published by Iliffe.

Finally, the Royal Yachting Association—the British National Body which watches over the interests of all British yachtsmen, racers, cruisers, power and sail—has its own flag, a white rectangular flag with a blue cross superimposed and in the centre a badge consisting of a stylized Naval Crown.

Bibliography

GENERAL

The Bibliography of Flags of Foreign Nations, Whitney Smith, G. K. Hall & Co., Boston, Mass., USA, 1965

Flags of All Nations, Ministry of Defence (Navy), HMSO London, in 2 volumes 1955 and 1958, with supplements

The Book of Flags, I. O. Evans, Oxford University Press, 1974

Flags, I. O. Evans, Hamlyn, 1970

Flags Through the Ages and Across the World, Whitney Smith, McGraw-Hill, 1975

The Flag Book of the United States, Whitney Smith, William Morrow & Co, 1975

Flags of the States of the World, K. A. Ivanov, Moscow, 1971

Vlajky a Znaky Zemi Sveta, Ludvík Mucha, Prague, 1974

DTV-Lexikon Politischer Symbole, Arnold Rabbow, DTV, Munich, 1970

The International Flag Book in Colour, C. F. Pedersen, Blandford Press, 1970

Fahnen und Flaggen, Ottfried Neubecker, Leipzig, 1939

Recueils of the International Congress of Vexillology: Muiderberg, 1975; Zürich, 1967; Boston, 1969; Turin, 1971; Netherlands, 1975

FLAGS OF PARTICULAR COUNTRIES

The best source for this is the *Bibliography of Flags*. Particular use has been made of the following:

British Flags, W. G. Perrin, Cambridge University Press, 1922

Flags for Ship Modellers and Marine Artists, A. A. Purves, Percival Marshall, 1950

Flags and Signals, Royal Yachting Association, BP Yachting Books, 1969

National Flags, E. H. Baxter, Frederick Warne, 1934

Yacht Club Burgees, Colin Stewart, Adlard Coles, 1957

The Story of Canada's Flag, George F. Stanley, Ryerson Press, Toronto, 1967

Lions and Virgins, C. Pama, Human and Rousseau, Cape Town, 1965

Nederlands Vlaggenboek, Klaes Sierksma, Prisma Boeken, Utrecht, 1962

Choragwie i Flagi Polskie, Jan Miller, Warsaw, 1962

The Story of the Scottish Flag, W. McMilland and J. A. Stewart, Hugh Hopkins, Glasgow, 1925

Symbol, Nobarasha, Tokyo, n.d.

The New Zealand Ensign, W. A. Glue, Government Printer, Wellington, 1965

Flag of Stars, F. A. Cayley, Rigby, Adelaide, 1966

Brown's Flags and Funnels, J. S. Styring, Brown & Ferguson, Glasgow, 1971.

PERIODICALS

In addition to the *Recueils* of the Vexillological Congresses, frequent use has been made of the periodical journals of the various national flag research groups.
The Flag Bulletin, The Flag Research Center, Winchester, Massachusetts, USA
Flagmaster, The Flag Institute, Chester, England
NAVA News, The North American Vexillological Association, Oaks, Pennsylvania, USA
Vexilla Italica, Centro Italiano de Studi Vessillogici, Turin, Italy
Vexilla Nostra, Nederlandse Vereniging voor Vlaggenkunde, The Hague, Netherlands
Vexilologie, Vexillology Club of Czechoslovakia, Prague, Czechoslovakia
Vexillogia, Association Française des Études Internationales Vexillologiques
Vexilla Helvetica, Société Suisse de Vexillologie
Nordisk Flaggskrift, Nordic Flag Society, Copenhagen, Denmark
The Coat of Arms, The Heraldry Society, London, England
The National Geographic Magazine, Washington DC, USA, have published the following major articles on flags.
'Flags of the World', Vol. 32, No. 4, 1917
'Flags of the World', Vol. 46, No. 3, 1934
'Seals of our Nation, States, and Territories', Vol. 90, No. 1, 1946
'Flags of the Americas', May 1949
'Flags of the United Nations', Vol. 99, No. 2, February 1951
'New Stars for Old Glory', Vol. 116, No. 1, July 1959
'Flags of the United Nations', Vol. 120, No. 3, September 1961

FLAG INSTITUTE PUBLICATIONS

Flag Design
Have You Thought About a Flag?
The Historical Development of Flags

Index

Bold numerals indicate the principal entry and illustrations.